Covenant of Redemption in the Trinitarian Theology of Jonathan Edwards

Covenant of Redemption in the Trinitarian Theology of Jonathan Edwards

The Nexus between the Immanent Trinity and the Economic Trinity

REITA YAZAWA

Foreword by George Marsden

◥PICKWICK *Publications* · Eugene, Oregon

COVENANT OF REDEMPTION IN THE TRINITARIAN THEOLOGY OF JONATHAN EDWARDS
The Nexus between the Immanent Trinity and the Economic Trinity

Copyright © 2019 Reita Yazawa. All rights reserved. Except for brief quotations in critical publications or reviews, no part of this book may be reproduced in any manner without prior written permission from the publisher. Write: Permissions, Wipf and Stock Publishers, 199 W. 8th Ave., Suite 3, Eugene, OR 97401.

Pickwick Publications
An Imprint of Wipf and Stock Publishers
199 W. 8th Ave., Suite 3
Eugene, OR 97401

www.wipfandstock.com

PAPERBACK ISBN: 978-1-5326-4378-1
HARDCOVER ISBN: 978-1-5326-4379-8
EBOOK ISBN: 978-1-5326-4380-4

Cataloguing-in-Publication data:

Names: Yazawa, Reita, author. | Marsden, George M., 1939–, foreword.

Title: Covenant of redemption in the trinitarian theology of Jonathan Edwards : the nexus between the immanent trinity and the economic trinity / Reita Yazawa ; foreword by George Marsden.

Description: Eugene, OR : Pickwick Publications, 2019 | Includes bibliographical references and index.

Identifiers: ISBN 978-1-5326-4378-1 (paperback) | ISBN 978-1-5326-4379-8 (hardcover) | ISBN 978-1-5326-4380-4 (ebook)

Subjects: LCSH: Edwards, Jonathan,—1703–1758. | Trinity. | Trinity—History of doctrines—18th century.

Classification: BX7260.E3 Y39 2019 (paperback) | BX7260.E3 Y39 (ebook)

Manufactured in the U.S.A.   10/09/19

Scripture quotations from The Authorized (King James) Version. Rights in the Authorized Version in the United Kingdom are vested in the Crown. Reproduced by permission of the Crown's patentee, Cambridge University Press.

To the People of God at Calvin Theological Seminary,
my *alma mater* and a graceful community of learning

According as he hath chosen us in him before the foundation of the world, that we should be holy and without blame before him in love:

Having predestinated us unto the adoption of children by Jesus Christ to himself, according to the good pleasure of his will,

To the praise of the glory of his grace, wherein he hath made us accepted in the beloved. (Ephesians 1:4–6)

Contents

Foreword by George Marsden | **ix**
Preface | **xi**
Acknowledgments | **xiii**
Abbreviations | **xv**

1 Introduction: Criticism of the Immanent Trinity
in Contemporary Theology | **1**
    Present Status of the Problem
    Statement of the Problem
    Thesis Statement
    Present Status of Edwards Study
    Significance of the Study
    Proposed Method
    Outline

PART I

2 The Covenant of Redemption in Reformed Scholasticism | **25**
    Covenant in General
    Definition of the Covenant of Redemption
    Biblical Foundation of the Covenant of Redemption
    Doctrinal Formulation of the Covenant of Redemption
    Relation of the Covenant of Redemption to the Immanent and the Economic Trinity
    Implications of the Covenant of Redemption for Christian Practice

3 Trinity and the Covenant of Redemption in Edwards
and the Reformed Tradition | **51**
    Jonathan Edwards's Doctrine of the Trinity
    Definition of the Covenant of Redemption in Edwards
    Biblical Foundation of the Covenant of Redemption in Edwards
    Doctrinal Formulation of the Covenant of Redemption in Edwards
    The Unity of the Immanent and the Economic Trinity

PART II

4 Covenant of Redemption, Trinity, and Creation | 81
   Edwards's Idealism
   Edwards's Typology of Nature
   Issues of Panentheism and Dispositional Ontology
   Creation as a Trinitarian Work

5 Covenant of Redemption, Trinity, Justification,
and the Christian Life of Piety | 106
   Covenant of Redemption and Justification by Faith Alone
   Justification and Perseverance
   Christian Piety and Practice

6 Covenant of Redemption, Trinity, Church Covenant,
and National Covenant | 135
   The Communion between Christ and the Church
   The Communion Controversy in Light of the Covenant of Redemption
   Practical Significance of the Trinity for the Doctrine of the Church
   National Covenant
   The Practical Significance of the Doctrine of the Trinity for the View of a Nation

7 Covenant of Redemption, Trinity, History, and Eschaton | 162
   Covenant of Redemption and History
   Typology in History
   The Covenantal Dispensation in History
   Eschatological Communion as the Fulfillment of the Covenant of Redemption
   Practicality of the Trinity in History and Eschaton

PART III

8 Conclusion: The Significance of the Covenant of Redemption
for Trinitarian Theology Today | 199
   A Review of Contemporary Criticism of the Immanent Trinity
   Concluding Remarks: Edwards's Covenant of Redemption and Its Significance for
   Trinitarian Theology Today

Bibliography | 209
Name and Subject Index | 229

Foreword

GEORGE MARSDEN

DURING RECENT TIMES, THERE has been the widespread revival in Christian theology of emphasis on the doctrine of the Trinity. There has also been a resurgence of interest in Jonathan Edwards. Within just the past few decades, these two developments have converged with the recognition of the centrality of the Trinity in the formidable theological work of Edwards. That recognition has been expedited by the remarkable work of the Jonathan Edwards Center of Yale University. Until very recently, much of the Edwards's theological reflection was available only in unpublished notebooks written in his almost indecipherable hand. Today all of his work is available in searchable form on-line. That has led to a rich new literature commenting on and debating dimensions of his outlook in which his understanding of the Trinity plays an indispensable part. With this publication, Reita Yazawa's work takes its place as an essential contribution to the discussions. Others in the field will recognize Yazawa as a formidable peer whose impressive analysis will have to be taken into account of in future discussions of Edwards on the Trinity.

As Yazawa emphasizes, Edwards's understanding of the Trinity is intensely practical. What Edwards, following some of the categories of the time, calls "The Covenant of Redemption," is no mere abstraction. Rather, it is a way of emphasizing that at the very heart of reality is the intra-Trinitarian concord, flowing out of the love that is central to the God-head, that the purpose or end of creation is to share the depths of redemptive love with other beings. Nothing could be more practical than that, since it means that at the very center of reality and discernible in everything around us, if we have the eyes to see it, is the redemptive love flowing from the Trinity. Far from being an abstraction, it is the force that energizes reality at every moment.

Edwards often parallels love, beauty, and light in speaking of this ongoing energy radiating from God's being. The highest beauty is the most perfect love. And that perfect love is best manifested in redemptive love. That love is "The Divine and Supernatural Light," as Edwards puts it in one of his most famous sermons. When our eyes are opened to perceive beauty, the beauty of perfect sacrificial love of Christ for the undeserving, we cannot help but be drawn to it. Our own fundamental affections are changed, so that we are drawn away from love to self toward love to God and love to what God loves. Even in the natural world, fallen as it is, we can see that beauty, if our eyes are opened to see the beauties of creation as pointing ultimately to Christ's redemptive love. "The heavens declare the glory of God." They are part of the language of God. But it is the actual work of redemption revealed in Scripture that is the key to that language. That love, if we are open to it, has a transforming power that draws us to it. As Yazawa points out, one of Edwards's emphases is that God's end or purpose in creation "was to provide a spouse for his Son Jesus Christ that might enjoy him and on whom he might pour forth his love." History is to culminate in the everlasting "wedding feast" of the Lamb.[1] So our own only true end or purpose is to be drawn into that redemptive love that flows out of the very essence of the Trinity.

---

1. "Miscellany," no. 702 in Edwards, *WJE*, 18:298.

Preface

CONTEMPORARY TRINITARIAN THEOLOGIES TEND to hold that the doctrine of the Trinity, especially the immanent Trinity, became impractical, speculative, and abstruse over the years in the history of Christian theology. In response, the recent theologies of the Trinity explore various practical implications of the doctrine of the Trinity with emphasis on God's economic work of redemption in history. However, the Reformed idea of the covenant of redemption helps us to reconsider whether the doctrine of the Trinity, especially of the immanent Trinity, has been really so impractical.

In this study, I argue that the Reformed idea of the covenant of redemption in the theology of Jonathan Edwards (1703–1758) gives a light on the practical significance of the doctrine of the Trinity because the inner-trinitarian eternal pact between the Father and the Son has practical relevance for salvation in the Christian life. The doctrine of the covenant of redemption is the nexus between the immanent Trinity and the economic Trinity. If God's eternal plan of redemption is eternal and is therefore located already in the immanent Trinity, it is no longer valid to criticize the immanent Trinity as abstruse and impractical because salvation of the elect hinges on the eternal pact made within the immanent Trinity.

In chapter 1, I identify the criticism of the immanent Trinity as one of the major features of recent discussion. In chapter 2, I examine doctrinal and exegetical developments of the doctrine of the covenant of redemption by major Reformed thinkers who possibly influenced Edwards. In chapter 3, I constructively describe and examine Edwards's trinitarian theology of the covenant of redemption. It presents a counter example to contemporary discussion that stresses the impractical nature of the immanent Trinity.

Chapters 4 through 7 examine major manifestations of the practical implication of the covenant of redemption in various aspects of Edwards's theology, respectively: creation, justification and sanctification, church and national covenants, and history and eschaton. Finally, chapter 8 revisits the trend of the contemporary trinitarian theologies and reiterates the contribution that the retrieval of the doctrine of the covenant of redemption can possibly make to the trinitarian theologies today.

This study also emphasizes the methodological importance of paying attention to the historical context of the research object even if one conducts a study in systematic theology.

Acknowledgments

THIS BOOK WAS ORIGINALLY my doctoral dissertation submitted to Calvin Theological Seminary in 2013. I am thankful to many people who provided me with support and encouragement to complete this project. My doctoral mentor Dr. John Bolt shared with me interests in pneumatology and the theology of Jonathan Edwards. He supported me during my seven years of graduate work in the Master of Theology and Doctor of Philosophy Program at Calvin Theological Seminary and spent a lot of time with me to make sure that my dissertation project is meaningful and viable. I am grateful to my colleagues in the PhD program who participated in the PhD Dissertation Seminar in 2010–2011, 2011–2012, and 2012–2013. Every time I submitted the drafts of my dissertation for discussion, I received valuable input from them. Dr. Ronald J. Feenstra and Dr. Richard A. Muller led the seminars over these years and helped me with priceless feedback. My experience in the Dissertation Seminar helped me to learn the value of a community of learning and to appreciate the supportive accountability it provides.

I had the privilege of having Dr. George M. Marsden (Professor Emeritus, University of Notre Dame) and Dr. Steven M. Studebaker (McMaster Divinity College, Ontario, Canada) on the Dissertation Committee. It was great privilege to participate in doctoral seminars by Dr. Marsden, an eminent, distinguished scholar of Jonathan Edwards. I learned from Dr. Muller and Dr. Marsden the importance of carefully studying the historical context of my research object even when I conduct a study in systematic theology. This lesson has been confirmed as I read the writings of Dr. Studebaker.

Paul W. Fields and Lugene Schemper, theological librarians of the Hekman Library at Calvin College, helped me with conducting research and aligning the format and style of the dissertation. Kathleen Struck, the Interlibrary Loans (ILL) Program Coordinator of the Hekman Library kindly processed my numerous ILL requests to assist my research. Tom VanKeulen, the Systems Integration and Development Manager at Calvin

Seminary, helped me resolve some technical difficulties in formatting pagination. Sally Van Noord, Rhetoric Center at Calvin Seminary, provided valuable help with proofreading the entire draft of the dissertation. Ina De Moor and Barbara Blackmore, two Assistants to the Director of PhD program over the years during my doctoral studies, provided excellent administrative assistance and warm encouragement throughout my doctoral studies at Calvin Seminary.

Rev. Richard E. Sytsma, Dean of Students Emeritus, Calvin Seminary, and his wife Sandy Sytsma have been wonderful friends for my family, and, as former missionaries to my country Japan, know the challenges in cross-cultural experiences. Friends from John Knox Presbyterian Church gave valuable support during my study in the United States. They also helped me continue to grow as a pastor through various ministry opportunities. My parents Toshihiko and Kyoko Yazawa have been always constant supporters of my study and life decisions. They taught me, through their modeling, that parents are parents no matter what happens.

Finally, but not the least, I thank my family. Our son Towa Richard and daughter Konomi have been joyful challenges and comforts in my life. I am grateful for all the good things that helped them to grow in God's grace during our stay in the United States. I am thankful to my wife, Misako, who shared with me all the joys and challenges of this journey. I am grateful for this life partner God provided for me. May God ever sanctify and strengthen this "uncommon union."

Abbreviations

PRRD *Post-Reformation Reformed Dogmatics.* 4 vols. Grand Rapids: Baker, 2003.

WJE *The Works of Jonathan Edwards.* 26 vols. New Haven: Yale University Press, 1957–2008.

SCRIPTURE

Old Testament

Gen	Genesis
Exod	Exodus
2 Sam	Second Samuel
Job	Job
Ps	Psalm
Prov	Proverbs
Isa	Isaiah
Jer	Jeremiah
Zech	Zechariah

New Testament

Matt	Matthew
Luke	Luke
John	John
Acts	The Book of Acts
Rom	Romans
1 Cor	First Corinthians
2 Cor	Second Corinthians

Gal	Galatians
Eph	Ephesians
Phil	Philippians
1 Thess	First Thessalonians
1 Tim	First Timothy
2 Tim	Second Timothy
Heb	Hebrews
1 Pet	First Peter
Rev	Revelation

1

Introduction
Criticism of the Immanent Trinity in Contemporary Theology

PRESENT STATUS OF THE PROBLEM

KARL RAHNER ONCE REMARKED: "We must be willing to admit that, should the doctrine of the Trinity have to be dropped as false, the major part of religious literature could well remain virtually unchanged."[1] Rahner lamented by this statement that despite preceding studies of the history of trinitarian theology, "Christians are, in their practical life, almost mere 'monotheists.'"[2]

To be sure, the latter half of the twentieth century and the beginning of the twenty-first century have seen a remarkable resurgence of the doctrine of the Trinity. Already in 1946, H. Richard Niebuhr predicted that the doctrine of the Trinity would be of central theological interest in the coming years. After identifying major developments of contemporary theology: efforts to recover and renew theological heritage, reconsideration of human nature and destiny in light of cultural crises of the day, and ecumenical endeavors, Niebuhr remarked: "One Christian doctrine which has importance in all three respects and which may therefore be moved nearer the center of interest in coming years of theological discussion is the doctrine of the Trinity."[3]

---

1. Rahner, *Trinity*, 10–11.
2. Rahner, *Trinity*, 10.
3. Niebuhr, "Doctrine of the Trinity," 371.

As he predicted, varieties of studies on the doctrine of the Trinity ensued.[4] In this so called "Trinitarian Renaissance,"[5] one of the major characteristics of contemporary trinitarian theology is, as if in response to the Rahner's challenge, the exploration of practical implications of the doctrine of the Trinity.[6] For example, A. H. Mathias Zahniser sees trinitarian thinking as "a foundation for mission." Looking at the Trinity as "a model of how God carries out his mission in the world" helps believers to participate in God's mission effectively.[7] Michael Jinkins finds the triune God as the "theological ground of the church's unity."[8] The triune God as unity in diversity provides the foundation for ecclesiology. Daniel L. Migliore explores political and economic implications of the doctrine of the Trinity.

> The doctrine of the Trinity has the potential of playing a liberating role in the political and economic struggles of our time by exposing the idolatry of monarchical power and the control and consumption of the world's resources by a few at the expense of the many. Trinitarian faith in God tends in the direction of political and economic theory and practice based on mutuality, participation, and the distribution of power and wealth.[9]

In other words, the trinitarian faith patterns our social engagements. Miroslav Volf shares a similar point of view when he says: "A soteriology based on the indwelling of the Crucified by the Spirit (Gal 2:19–20) grounds a social practice modeled on God's passion for the salvation of the world."[10] Mary Ann Donovan sees the doctrine of the Trinity as a guide for pastoral care, which she defines as follows: "It is to enable people to relate to one

---

4. To name just a few: Boff, *Trinity and Society*; Coakley, "Why Three?," 29–56; *Re-thinking Gregory of Nyssa*; Grenz, *Named God*; *Rediscovering the Triune God*; Jenson, *Triune Identity*; McCormack, *Engaging the Doctrine of God*; Metzger, *Trinitarian Soundings in Systematic Theology*; Rahner, *Trinity*; Stirling, *Trinity*; Torrance, *Christian Doctrine of God*; Vickers, *Invocation and Assent*; Volf and Welker, *God's Life in Trinity*; Zizioulas, *Being as Communion*; *Communion and Otherness*.

5. Kärkkäinen, "Trajectories," 7. This article provides a succinct overview of this theological climate. See also Sanders, "State of the Doctrine," 153–75.

6. Cunningham, *These Three Are One*; Grenz, *Rediscovering the Triune God*, 223; Kärkkäinen, "Trajectories," 14–16; LaCugna, "Practical Trinity," 678–82; Mohler et al., "SBJT Forum," 86–101.

7. Zahniser, "Trinity," 70.

8. Jinkins, "Mutuality and Difference," 149.

9. Migliore, "Trinity and Human Liberty," 492–93.

10. Volf, "'Trinity Is Our Social Program,'" 418.

another as the Three Divine Persons do, and it is to assist people to give glory to God in public prayer and in their daily lives."[11]

In this way, scholars plumb the implication of the Trinity for theology of religions,[12] ecclesiology,[13] political theology,[14] feminist theology,[15] pastoral theology,[16] process theology,[17] or missiology.[18] Behind these diverse approaches to the doctrine of the Trinity there often seems to be an assumption that the traditional doctrine of the Trinity has been abstract and speculative, detached from God's economic work of redemption in history.

Traditional theology makes a distinction between the immanent Trinity and the economic Trinity. The immanent Trinity refers to God in himself, God's being, or the inner-relatedness of God, separate and independent from the existence of the world. The economic Trinity refers to God's relation to the world, God's work in history and the world, or God's being in relation to the world. Much of the recent discussions on the doctrine of the Trinity appears to assume that emphasizing the immanent Trinity results in a speculative formulation of the doctrine of the Trinity. Hence, the doctrine of the Trinity, many contemporary trinitarian theologians believe, became impractical, losing relevance for daily Christian life. They therefore attempt to reclaim the importance of the economic Trinity and reconsider the doctrine of the Trinity from God's concrete work of redemption in Christ through the Holy Spirit. Through this process, they make efforts to recover a doctrine of the Trinity that is relevant to Christian life and practice.

---

11. Donovan, "Trinity, Pastoral Theology," 356.

12. Heim, *Depth of the Riches*; Haight, "Trinity and Religious Pluralism," 525–40; Phelan, "Unity in Trinity," 37–50; Suchocki, *Divinity and Diversity*; D'Costa, *Meeting of Religions*; Panikkar, *Trinity and the Religious Experience*; Kärkkäinen, *Trinity and Religious Pluralism*.

13. Volf, *After Our Likeness*; Brown, "Speaking Again of the Trinity," 145–58; Jinkins, "Mutuality and Difference," 148–71.

14. Boff, *Trinity and Society*; Volf, *Exclusion and Embrace*; Volf, "Trinity Is Our Social Program," 403–23; Harrison, "Human Community," 347–64; Kevern, "Trinity and Social Justice," 45–54; Migliore, "Trinity and Human Liberty," 488–97; Chapman, "Social Doctrine of the Trinity," 239–54.

15. Johnson, *She Who Is*; Carr, *Transforming Grace*; Oxford-Carpenter, "Gender and the Trinity," 7–25; Coakley, "Living into the Mystery," 223–332; Bird and Shillaker, "Subordination in the Trinity," 267–83; Kimel, *This Is My Name Forever*.

16. Fiddes, *Participating in God*; Pembroke, "Trinity, Polyphony, and Pastoral Relationships," 351–61; McWilliams, "Only the Triune God," 345–59.

17. Bracken, *Triune Symbol*; Suchocki, "God, Trinity, Process," 169–74.

18. Newbigin, *Open Secret*; Zahniser, "Trinity," 69–82; Awart et al., "Toward a Missional Theology," 75–87.

For instance, Migliore stresses the economic Trinity as the starting point of theological appraisal.

> The doctrine of the Trinity, we have contended, must be approached not speculatively but evangelically. If we are to avoid arbitrary speculation, we must inquire first not about the immanent Trinity or the inner life of God but about the economic Trinity or God manifested to us in the work of salvation.[19]

By this, Migliore indicates that the immanent Trinity, if severed from God's economic work of salvation in the world, becomes increasingly abstract and arbitrary. In a similar vein, Thomas F. Torrance emphasizes the Incarnation as God's real self-communication by saying that "detached from God's economic condescension and self-revelation in history, a doctrine of the Trinity is nothing but a speculative projection"[20]

These modern trinitarian theologians therefore attempt to connect the doctrine of the Trinity with history, experience, practical life, or the economic trinitarian work of salvation. For example, Jürgen Moltmann sees the economic work of the triune God in this world as the history of God and articulates the doctrine of the Trinity inherently interwoven with the world.

> Because the "doctrine" of God originates in the experienced and proclaimed or recounted "history" of God, its duty is to lead into this history, while its danger is that this history may become lost in the abstract concept of God. If the trinitarian history of salvation is the point of departure for the doctrine of the Trinity, then the doctrine of the Trinity must be related to this history in such a way as to be verified by and to lead into this history. The concepts employed in the doctrine must be derived from, and remain applicable to, the trinitarian history of the Father, the Son and the Holy Spirit. This means, first of all, that the doctrine of the Trinity must begin with the three distinct subjects of this history.[21]

Henry P. Van Dusen claims that the doctrine of the Trinity stems from Christian experience.

> We tend to think of the doctrine of the Trinity as not only the most obscure and mystifying but also perhaps the most abstruse and speculative of all Christian beliefs. It is important to

---

19. Migliore, "Trinity and Human Liberty," 495.
20. Torrance, "Toward an Ecumenical Consensus," 339.
21. Moltmann, "Unity of the Triune God," 165.

recognize that the Trinity is, in the first instance, not a dogma of theology at all but a datum of experience.[22]

John Farrelly also notes the inseparable relation between the Trinity and salvation as follows: "One cannot understand Jesus' mediation of the kingdom or salvation without understanding his relationship with the Father and the Spirit. In this sense the mystery of Trinity is a salvific mystery."[23] Similarly, Wm. David Kirkpatrick argues:

> The critical nature of this revelation [revelation of God in the person of Jesus Christ through the presence and work of the Holy Spirit] for Christian theology is that God is not imprisoned in his eternity. While God 'cannot be moved from outside by an extraneous power,' he is 'capable of moving Himself' so that in the freedom of his self-disclosure there is an expression of the divine economy. In other words, as Father, Son, and Holy Spirit God has turned toward his creation, relationally providing a means for humanity's redemption. Trinitarian theology, therefore, is not some general assessment of ecclesiology that can be tacked on as an appendix after the constructive work of theology has been completed, nor is a mathematical conundrum to confuse the faithful. Rather, in its most profound and concrete way the church's Trinitarian faith is an affirmation that Jesus Christ is Lord; a confession made possible because of the active presence of the Spirit poured out upon the church.[24]

The doctrine of the Trinity is inherently related to the Christian experience of salvation in Jesus Christ through the Holy Spirit in this world. Thus by its nature, the doctrine of the Trinity has practical relevance for salvation in the Christian life. The doctrine of the Trinity is interwoven even with mundane daily life.

Certainly, it is possible to contest the claim that the Trinity has to be practical first of all. Why does the holy Trinity have to be practical? Is this perhaps another form of self-gratifying consumerism that tries to force even divine things to serve human interests? Yet one can also ask this question the other way around. What if the divine Trinity has nothing to do with daily life? What if the doctrine of the Trinity is totally irrelevant to the Christian life and practice? Would that not indicate that the very being and life of God is detached and severed from human beings and life? Would it not imply that God does not care about humanity? Miroslav Volf rightfully argues that

22. Van Dusen, "Trinity in Experience and Theology," 377.
23. Farrelly, "Trinity as Salvific Mystery," 103.
24. Kirkpatrick, "Trinity and Christian Spirituality," 62.

if a human being is created in the image of God, it is natural to infer that a human society is called to reflect a certain image of the divine personal communion.[25] Because there exists an inalienable relationship between the Creator and creation, human beings as God's image-bearers are called to reflect peace, harmony, diversity and unity of the trinitarian communion, however fragmentary and anticipatory it may be. Hence it is worthwhile and even necessary to explore various implications of the doctrine of the Trinity for practical Christian life. Exploration of practical implications of the Trinity in current discussions of trinitarian theologies is, therefore, helpful for Christians to recognize their own identity and to respond to their call and vocation in this world.

STATEMENT OF THE PROBLEM

However, an issue lies in a concomitant discussion often made with regard to the reason why some scholars believe that the doctrine of the Trinity has been detached from Christian life and practice. As noted before, scholars in this context tend to criticize particularly the immanent Trinity as irrelevant for Christian life and salvation. For instance, Catherine Mowry LaCugna concedes:

> As focus rested more and more on the 'inner life' of God—on the self-relatedness of Father, Son, and Spirit to each other—instead of on God's relation to us, eventually the doctrine of the Trinity could speak only of a Trinity locked up in itself, related to itself, contemplating itself perfectly and eternally, but essentially unrelated to us. It is no wonder that so many would find the theoretical explanations for this state of affairs uninteresting and irrelevant.[26]

Veli-Matti Kärkkäinen concurs with this observation as follows:

> One reason for the marginalization of the Trinity had to do with the theological method that began to change over the course of time. Unlike earlier theology, which discerned Trinity in the salvation history as unfolding in the biblical testimonies, later theology became more interested in the 'inner' life of God

---

25. Volf, "Trinity Is Our Social Program," 403–5.

26. LaCugna, "Practical Trinity," 681. See also, LaCugna, *God For Us*, 22–44; "Philosophers and Theologians," 169–81; Rahner, *Trinity*, 14–21.

instead of the 'economy' of salvation, making Trinity an abstract speculation rather than reading it from the works of God.[27]

Hence contemporary trinitarian theology tends to denounce the relevance of the immanent Trinity for salvation and Christian life.

For example, Maurice F. Wiles argues that "the immanent-economic Trinity distinction is a product of both Greek thought and post-exilic Jewish thought, and that the doctrine of the Trinity is 'an arbitrary analysis of the activity of God, which, though of value in Christian thought and devotion, is not of essential significance."[28] Likewise Cyril C. Richardson states that the doctrine of the Trinity is "an artificial construct." Traditional discourse on the immanent Trinity is full of "dark and mysterious statements, which are ultimately meaningless."[29] Gordon D. Kaufman thinks that human knowledge of God should be restricted to God's economic relation to the world and any attempt to speak about the intra-trinitiarian relations should be abandoned.[30]

However, the logic of the immanent Trinity is not necessarily an abstract, speculative discussion of threeness and oneness of divine persons and substance. What if God's plan of redemption is already located within the immanent Trinity? Indeed, what if the very foundation of God's economy of redemption is situated within the immanent Trinity? The Reformed teaching on the covenant of redemption provides an important clue to explore the connection between the immanent Trinity and God's redemptive work in history.

The eighteenth-century New England divine Jonathan Edwards (1703–1758) inherited the idea of the covenant of redemption from the Reformed tradition. He developed this doctrine in a way that the idea of the covenant of redemption plays a role of nexus between the immanent Trinity and the economic Trinity. By nexus I mean a connecting point between the immanent and the economic Trinity. The covenant of redemption stems from the immanent Trinity and at the same time founds and shapes God's economic work in relation to the world. For Edwards, the interrelatedness of divine persons in the immanent Trinity is an archetype to be replicated in God's work of redemption in the world. In this sense, the covenant of

---

27. Kärkkäinen, "Trajectories of 'Trinitarian Renaissance,'" 9. See also Wiles, "Some Reflections on the Origins," 104; Richardson, *Doctrine of the Trinity*, 148; Kaufman, *Systematic Theology*, 251, 102.

28. Wiles, "Some Reflections on the Origins," 104. See also Chung-Hyun Baik's survey of this theological trend in Baik, *Holy Trinity*, 179–89.

29. Richardson, *Doctrine of the Trinity*, 148.

30. Kaufman, *Systematic Theology*, 251n6, 102n9.

redemption in Edwards's theology indicates that reclaiming the Reformed idea of covenant for trinitarian theology today helps to shed a new light on the doctrine of the Trinity and its practical relevance of salvation for Christian life.

THESIS STATEMENT

Although many contemporary trinitarian theologies discuss various practical implications of the doctrine of the Trinity, practical implications of the covenant of redemption have not been explored fully in the trinitarian theology today. I will argue that Jonathan Edwards's theology of the covenant of redemption shows the practical nature of the immanent Trinity. The Reformed idea of the covenant of redemption in the theology of Jonathan Edwards sheds a new light on the practical significance of the doctrine of the Trinity because the inner-trinitarian eternal pact between the Father and the Son has practical relevance for salvation in the Christian life.

PRESENT STATUS OF EDWARDS STUDY

Although some recent studies on Jonathan Edwards indicate that the distinction between the immanent and the economic Trinity does not necessarily lead to the irrelevance of the doctrine of the Trinity for Christian practical life, they have their own interpretive issues. Sang Hyun Lee argues that Edwards's relational ontology interprets God as the eternal perfection and yet disposed to communicate himself to the world as reiteration and repetition of his perfect being.[31] In other words, Lee claims that Edwards developed God's relational ontology as highly relevant to the world and practical life without losing the distinction between God's inner life and God's relation to the world. However, his interpretation of Edwards's dispositional ontology has been challenged recently and calls for a careful examination.[32]

Amy Plantinga Pauw argues that Edwards falters between the Western psychological model and the Eastern social model of the Trinity, and that especially on divine simplicity Edwards ventured its redefinition, departing

---

31. Lee, *Philosophical Theology*; Lee, "Editor's Introduction," in *Works of Jonathan Edwards*, 21:32–38 (hereafter, abbreviated as *WJE* followed by volume and page numbers). Issues involved in Lee's dispositional ontological interpretation will be discussed in chapter 4.

32. Holmes, "Does Jonathan Edwards," 99–114; Crisp, *Edwards on God and Creation*, 14–36. See chapter 4 for further discussions.

from classical theism.³³ Yet her thesis has recently been challenged by scholars such as Steven M. Studebaker and Robert Caldwell. They argue that, rather than the undecided mixture of the Eastern and Western traditions, Edwards consistently uses what they call the "Augustinian mutual love model" in which the Holy Spirit functions as the bond of union between the Father and the Son.³⁴ One thing common to both positions, though, is that Edwards developed a consistent relationship between the immanent and the economic Trinity without losing the basic distinction between the two.

Relating to Edwards's doctrine of the Trinity, Edwards's idea of the covenant of redemption plays a key role as the nexus between the immanent and the economic Trinity. Despite the renaissance of Edwards's scholarship, attention specifically to his doctrine of covenant is quite limited. Perry Miller thinks that divine sovereignty and the covenant idea are incompatible with each other. He contends that Edwards rejected the idea of covenant and returned to the unmitigated determinism of Calvinism.³⁵

Conrad Cherry and Carl W. Bogue oppose this claim. Edwards is, Cherry argues, one of the faithful followers of this Puritan legacy of covenant theology.³⁶ In a similar context, Bogue argues that "Calvinism and the covenant of grace are clearly consistent and do not exclude one another."³⁷ Bogue's articulation of the covenant of grace and its inherent connection with the covenant of redemption as "a divine affair within the eternal counsel of the triune God"³⁸ indicates that God's economic work of salvation as the covenant of grace can be construed as the ectypal unpacking of the eternal, archetypal consent between the Father and the Son as the covenant of redemption.³⁹

---

33. Pauw, *"The Supreme Harmony of All,"* 57–89, 183–92. See also Pauw, "'One Alone Cannot be Excellent,'" 115–26. William J. Danaher Jr. basically follows Plantinga Pauw's interpretation in his analysis of Edwards's doctrine of the Trinity. See also Danaher, *Trinitarian Ethics of Jonathan Edwards*, 16–116.

34. Studebaker, *Jonathan Edwards's Social Augustinian Trinitarianism*; Studebaker, "Supreme Harmony or Supreme Disharmony?," 479–85; Studebaker, "Jonathan Edwards's Social Augustinian Trinitarianism," 268–85; Caldwell, *Communion in the Spirit*. Also, Studebaker and Caldwell, *Trinitarian Theology of Jonathan Edwards*.

35. Miller, *Jonathan Edwards*, 30; Miller, *New England Mind*, 485; Miller, *Errand into the Wilderness*, 65, 72.

36. Cherry, "Puritan Notion of the Covenant," 334. Richard M. Weber also claims: "despite modifications to the typical Reformed presentation, Edwards remained wholly orthodox in his Trinitarian theology" (Weber, "Trinitarian Theology of Jonathan Edwards," 298).

37. Bogue, *Jonathan Edwards and the Covenant*, 303.

38. Bogue, *Jonathan Edwards and the Covenant*, 303.

39. For the analysis of historical theological development of the idea of the covenant

The covenant of redemption and its relevance for practical Christian life receives little attention in contemporary theology. Subjects overlap and neat categorization is not easy; however, contemporary scholarly treatments of the theology of covenant can be classified into four major categories: biblical theology, historical theology, practical theology, and systematic theology. First, many scholars in biblical theology examine the biblical idea of covenant itself[40] or the relationship between the old covenant or covenants of the Old Testament and the new covenant of the New Testament.[41] The relationship between the old and new covenants has relevance for ecumenical dialogue between Judaism and Christianity.[42]

Second, several historical theologians have captured the historical manifestation of the idea of covenant in theological movements. John R. von Rohr identifies both the conditional and unconditional character of the covenant in the English Puritan thought in the early seventeenth century.[43] Lyle D. Bierma finds an incipient idea of covenant of redemption in the writings of Casper Olevianus.[44] Theodore Dwight Bozeman identifies in Elizabethan Presbyterians a notion of national covenant in which believers see the entire community in a covenantal relationship with God in the history of redemption.[45] Michael McGiffert plumbs the emergence of the covenant of works in the thought of Elizabethan Puritanism "as a means of preserving the perfect gratuity of God's salvific action."[46] William B. Evans sees that contemporary discussions among the Revisionists, the Represtinationists, and the biblical theology trajectory repeat in parallel the basic contours of American Reformed debates in the nineteenth century.[47] Richard Forrer claims that

---

of redemption, see Muller, "Toward the *Pactum Salutis*," 11–65. See also Muller, "God as Absolute and Relative," 56–73.

40. Alexander, "Genesis 22 and the Covenant," 17–22; Nicole, "Covenant, Universal Call," 403–11; Hubbard, "Hope in the Old Testament," 33–59; Wyrtzen, "Theological Center," 315–29; Levenson, "Theologies of Commandment," 17–33; Brueggemann, "Shape for Old Testament Theology," 28–46.

41. Janzen, "Metaphor and Reality in Hosea," 7–44; Karlberg, "Legitimate Discontinuities Between the Testaments," 9–20; Beckwith, "Unity and Diversity," 93–118.

42. Berger, "Jewish-Christian Relations," 5–32; Van Buren, "Theological Education for the Church's Relationship," 489–505; Eron, "You Who Revere the Lord," 63–73; Campbell, "Christianity and Judaism," 54–58.

43. Von Rohr, "Covenant and Assurance," 195–203.

44. Bierma, "Covenant or Covenants," 228–50.

45. Bozeman, "Federal Theology," 392–407.

46. McGiffert, "Grace and Works," 463–502.

47. Evans, "Déjà vu All Over Again?," 135–51.

the idea of covenant played a symbolic role in Puritan thought to make the ethical life and the religious life congruent to each other.[48]

Third, several scholars have explored the idea of covenant and its significance for pastoral practice. Suzanne Murphy Coyle points out that pastoral home visits may provide a context for a covenanting process to believers.[49] Walter Brueggemann sees the covenant as a helpful biblical metaphor for pastoral care.[50] Eric Mount Jr. points out that the idea of covenant lays out a foundation for intermediate social entities between individuals and states such as family and voluntary associations.[51]

Fourth, in contemporary systematic theology, several scholars often refer to covenant in conjunction with the debate between dispensationalism and covenant theology. While dispensationalism emphasizes a sequence of eschatological events and the restoration of Israel as a nation, covenantalism stresses the inclusion of gentiles into God's people and symbolic interpretation of the restoration of Israel. Walter C. Kaiser Jr. suggests that while covenantalism and dispensationalism provide different ways of reading the Scripture, a rapprochement between the two positions is possible by accommodating both positions.[52] This survey of the current scholarship on theology of covenant shows that the connection between the idea of covenant and practical Christian life is not necessarily traced back to the eternal pact between the Father and the Son. Contemporary theology tends to discuss the idea of covenant in the context of God's economic work in history.

What is missing in this contemporary scholarship is the connection between the covenant of redemption, practical Christian life, and the doctrine of the Trinity. Some scholars have paid attention to the connections of two of these three areas. As was reviewed above, some scholars have begun to pay attention to the doctrine of the Trinity and practical Christian life. Others investigate the connection between the idea of covenant and daily Christian life. A limited number of historical theological treatments on the seventeenth-century Reformed orthodoxy plumb the connection between the doctrine of the Trinity and the covenant of redemption. However, mutual relations between the doctrine of the Trinity, the covenant of redemption, and the practical life of Christian believers are not examined as a whole within an integrated scope.

---

48. Forrer, "Puritan Religious Dilemma," 613–28.
49. Coyle, "Covenanting Process," 96–109.
50. Brueggemann, "Covenanting as Human Vocation," 115–29.
51. Mount, "Homing in On Family Values," 77–89.
52. Kaiser, "Davidic Promise," 97–111.

SIGNIFICANCE OF THE STUDY

The legacy of Puritan covenant theology Edwards inherited sheds some light on the connection between this American theologian and a seventeenth-century continental Reformed tradition. Neither Plantinga Pauw nor Bogue fully examine Edwards's covenant of redemption in a broader context of the Reformed tradition. This study attempts to identify Edwards as a successor of the Reformed idea of covenant of redemption and aims to show that reclaiming the idea of the covenant of redemption for contemporary trinitarian theology helps to shed a new light on the practical relevance of the Trinity for salvation and Christian life.

While contemporary trinitarian theologies tend to emphasize God's economic work of redemption in history, they do so in a way that underrates and caricatures the immanent Trinity. This study defends the immanent Trinity and the importance of maintaining the unity and distinction between the immanent and the economic Trinity. If God's plan of redemption is already located in the eternal pact between the Father and the Son, thus within the immanent Trinity, it is no longer warranted to argue that the immanent Trinity is impractical and abstruse. Besides, if one plumbs into the historical context of the covenant of redemption in the Reformed tradition, a remarkable prevalence and continuity among the Puritan divines emerges. In fact, the doctrine of the Trinity had, in this sense, such highly practical implications among Puritans that one is prompted to wonder to what extent the charge to the immanent Trinity of its impracticality actually is accurate.

The charge from contemporary trinitarian theologies against the impracticality of the immanent Trinity needs to be reexamined in light of the Puritan covenant theology and the historical context of its development. A study in Jonathan Edwards's covenant of redemption in his trinitarian theology provides a viable point of departure for this endeavor. A substantive examination of Edwards in his relation to a broader context of the Reformed tradition, theology of covenant as the nexus between the immanent and the economic Trinity, its practical relevance for salvation, and its implication for contemporary systematic theology has been missing in scholarship and constitutes the rationale for this study.

PROPOSED METHOD

In this study, when I say that the doctrine of the covenant of redemption is "practical," I simply mean that the eternal pact within the immanent Trinity has relevance to and influence on the daily life of the elect. The immanent

Trinity is practical in the sense that salvation of the elect is already envisioned as the divine plan within the eternal communion of trinitarian persons. The eternal pact affects human life in time through a covenantal framework in a way that how we live our life daily matters. God's plan of redemption conceived in eternity echoes down into time. The covenant of redemption connects time and eternity. The covenant of redemption is the nexus of the immanent and economic Trinity. Far from being abstract and speculative, the doctrine of the Trinity is practical because salvation of the church elect is impossible without the Trinity. The goal of this study is to demonstrate this practical significance of the covenant of redemption for the doctrine of the Trinity in contemporary systematic theology. In order to demonstrate this thesis, I adopt a case-study method. As we have surveyed, contemporary trinitarian theology explores diverse practical implications of the doctrine of the Trinity. This study does not intend to argue the validity of each approach by engaging the details of the discussion. Rather, I hope to propose another possible practical implication found in the covenant of redemption in the immanent Trinity.

As a case of this practical implication of the immanent Trinity, I will expound the covenant of redemption in the trinitarian theology of Jonathan Edwards. In conducting this study, I am particularly mindful of Edwards's historical context and the continuity of his covenant theology within the broader Reformed tradition. Though this is a study in systematic theology, it pays attention to the historical context of the covenant theology in eighteenth-century New England. Sometimes past Edwards studies that were not sensitive enough to his historical contexts produced some defects or at least interpretive issues. A few examples are in order to show the case.

First, as mentioned earlier, Amy Plantinga Pauw sees in Edwards's trinitarian theology a resource for contemporary theology. She finds in Edwards's doctrine of the Trinity an ambivalent yet dexterous usage of a two-fold analogy: social model and psychological model.

> From these two streams of trinitarian reflection, he created an eclectic synthesis, one that informed his theology generally and served as the cornerstone of his intellectual constructions. The organizing centers of Edwards's theology—God, redemption, and the Christian life—were all deeply informed by his twofold trinitarian vision.[53]

In contrast, Steven M. Studebaker argues that "Edwards consistently utilized the mutual love model of the Trinity, which is a quintessential

---

53. Pauw, *Supreme Harmony of All*, 50.

Western Augustinian trinitarian model."[54] Given that the dichotomy of the social and psychological models itself is a modern invention by a French theologian Théodore De Régnon (1831–1893),[55] applying this category to Edwards's writings on Trinity is anachronistic. Thus, "Edwards's scholars should discard the paradigm as a hermeneutical tool for interpreting his trinitarianism."[56] The debate between Studebaker and Plantinga Pauw illumined the importance of interpreting Edwards first in his own historical and theological context.

Second, Carole Lynn Stewart in her study of American jeremiad shows another case in which imposing a modern paradigm onto Edwards's writings produces a misleading interpretation. Borrowing a paradigm from the social political science of Hannah Arendt, Lynn Stewart argues that Edwards's attempt to require public confession of faith in his church before admittance to the Lord's Supper led to the creation of public space and discourse, which in turn had a revolutionary impact in the New England society, tearing down the social hierarchical structure of the day and paving a way to social revolution for an egalitarian society that affirms plurality.[57] However, once the historical context of Edwards's time is examined, it is clear that Edwards attempted to introduce certain testimony of experiential faith in the church amidst the wide acceptance of the Half-Way Covenant since the middle of the seventeenth century in New England.[58] The purpose was not to subvert hierarchy but to defend the church membership of the converted. Lynn Stewart seems to impose her own framework on Edwards and fails to interpret Edwards in his own historical context. Edwards as an eighteenth-century New England pastor does not emerge from her account.

Third, Anri Morimoto and Gerald R. McDermott argue that the application of Edwards's dispositional ontology to his soteriology facilitates ecumenical dialogues between the Protestants and Catholic traditions. Edwards's conception of infused grace as a new disposition that waits to be activated by the Holy Spirit, Morimoto argues, indicates that Edwards's soteriology includes both the Protestant principle of *gratia increata* and the

---

54. Studebaker, *Jonathan Edwards's Social Augustinian Trinitarianism*, 106.

55. De Régnon, *Études de théologie positive*. See Studebaker, *Jonathan Edwards's Social Augustinian Trinitarianism*, 78. For an analysis of how this paradigm have influenced modern readings in systematic theologies, see Barnes, "De Régnon Reconsidered," 51–79; Barnes, "Augustine in Contemporary Trinitarian Theology," 237–50.

56. Studebaker, *Jonathan Edwards's Social Augustinian Trinitarianism*, 107. More on this will be discussed in chapter 3.

57. Stewart, *Strange Jeremiahs*, 14.

58. Marsden, *Jonathan Edwards*, 345–52. More on this will be discussed in chapter 6.

Catholic substance of *gratia creata*.⁵⁹ Furthermore, this dispositional soteriology opens the way towards a possibility of salvation of other religious faiths. Morimoto argues that the new disposition as abiding law indicates a potential for salvation of non-Christian believers. The new disposition may not be actualized yet, but as an abiding law that awaits actualization, it is virtually pointed towards salvation.⁶⁰ Morimoto concedes:

> There is no hard division between Christians and non-Christians in terms of the grounds on which they are saved. Those who do possess the disposition are all saved on account of that disposition, regardless of their explicit or conscious religious affiliation, or lack thereof. This is a paradigm of soteriology that is radically inclusive and yet theologically responsible.⁶¹

McDermott has developed this point and argues that Edwards's soteriology provides resources for inter-faith dialogue.⁶²

While these arguments attempt to illumine an unexpected resourcefulness of Edwards's theology for contemporary theological issues, it prompts one to wonder to what extent they are consistent with what Edwards actually thought and wrote in his own context. With regard to a possibility for using Edwards's theology for the Protestant-Catholic dialogue, it needs to be reminded that Edwards was an anti-Catholic typical of the Protestant of the age.⁶³

To be sure, Morimoto acknowledges that his comparative statements in his study should be taken as a contemporary attempt of appropriating Edwards's theology for today, as part of his effort "to better understand Edwards's soteriology on a broad scale."⁶⁴ Referring to previous studies that took Edwards's affinity with the Roman Catholic theology as problematic and tried to conceal or circumvent it,⁶⁵ Morimoto points out: "this defensive

---

59. Morimoto, *Jonathan Edwards and the Catholic Vision*, 162.

60. Morimoto, *Jonathan Edwards and the Catholic Vision*, 162.

61. Morimoto, *Jonathan Edwards and the Catholic Vision*, 162. See also Morimoto, "Salvation as Fulfillment of Being," 13–23.

62. McDermott, *Jonathan Edwards Confronts Gods*; "The Deist Connection," 39–51; "Jonathan Edwards, Deism, and the Mystery," 211–24; "Jonathan Edwards on Justification," 92–111; "Jonathan Edwards and the Salvation," 208–27; "Holy Pagans," 38–39; "Jonathan Edwards, John Henry Newman," 127–138. Most recently, McClymond and McDermott, *Theology of Jonathan Edwards*, 580–98, 695–708, 709–28.

63. Edwards, "God Does What He Pleases," 161. Stout, *New England Soul*, 48–49; Marsden, *Jonathan Edwards*, 12, 16–17, 88–90, 338, 415–416. See also Kidd, "From Puritan to Evangelical."

64. Morimoto, *Jonathan Edwards and the Catholic Vision*, 9.

65. For example, Tryon Edwards attempted to alter the text of *Charity and its Fruits*,

motivation has often placed undue pressure on the text to make it *look* 'Protestant,' resulting in misrepresentations of Edwards's true concerns."[66] However, if Edwards's theology is abstracted out of his own historical context and represented as a paragon for ecumenical and inter-faith dialogue beyond his own framework, does it not mean placing another kind of undue pressure on the text?

I do not categorically deny this way of theological appropriation that goes beyond a particular theological and historical context. Morimoto clearly sets the perspective of his study at the beginning.

> Learning from Edwards would be of little more than historical interest if Edwards were a mere representative—even the best representative—of a particular school of thought within a particular time and context. Naturally, his thought is somewhat defined by the context and the agenda of his own day. Yet, like Augustine, Thomas Aquinas, and John Calvin, Edwards offers us insights that are applicable beyond his own temporal, spatial, and confessional limitations. What is truly representative of a particular type always has a quality that transcends that particularity. With the present study I aim to establish Edwards as a theologian whose vision of salvation is significant not only to eighteenth-century Puritan America but to all people—whether Protestant or Roman Catholic, Puritan or Eastern Orthodox, American or Japanese—who share the basic premise of the Scripture that God's transformative power brings forth a new creation.[67]

Certainly, part of the task of systematic theology is to appropriate theological legacies, by using them as stepping stones to build on them, to critique, adjust, and modify them, and to constructively present theology that addresses issues and challenges the Christian church faces today.[68] Yet in order to wrestle with this task, it is important first to understand Edwards in his own historical context.

---

indicating his concern that the word "infusion" might sound too Roman Catholic. See Ramsey, "Editor's Introduction," 8:59–60n5. Also, Boardman, *History of New England Theology*, 155–56.

66. Morimoto, *Jonathan Edwards and the Catholic Vision*, 9–10.

67. Morimoto, *Jonathan Edwards and the Catholic Vision*, 2.

68. Even Studebaker, who criticizes Plantinga Pauw's interpretation of Edwards's doctrine of the Trinity from a historical analysis, has recently published his study that explores and endorses a possibility of using Edwards's trinitarian vision for constructing a renewed view of redemption and inclusive theology of religions. See Studebaker, *Trinitarian Vision of Jonathan Edwards*, 167–254. See also Studebaker, "Jonathan Edwards's Pneumatological Concept," 324–39; *From Pentecost to the Triune God*.

When one fails to grasp first Edwards's own historical context, sometimes a study in theology turns out to be anachronistic as a result of imposing the agenda of our day and of inferring conclusions of which Edwards himself never would have thought. Hence, for example, in his review of Robert Jenson's systematic theological study,[69] George M. Marsden notes: "Jenson, in his enthusiasm to make Edwards relevant to twentieth-century America, wants to create a new Edwards. To put it briefly, he wants to make Edwards into Karl Barth."[70] Consequently, "we often cannot tell where Edwards ends and where Barth or Jenson begins."[71] Even for a study in systematic theology, it is important to consider Edwards first in his own historical context.

When this historical examination is properly made, then based on it, it becomes possible to make a constructive theological contribution for today. When Marsden worked on a biography of Edwards, a part of his intention was to "help bridge the gap between the Edwards of the students of American culture and the Edwards of the theologians."[72] Marsden continues:

> Historians of American culture, thought, and literature are primarily concerned to understand Edwards in relation to his time or perhaps to understand his influence in relation to subsequent times. Theologians are concerned to appropriate aspects of Edwards's thought for their own times. As a biographer attempting to understand Edwards first as an eighteenth-century figure, I have been working most directly as a cultural historian. Yet I have been doing this always with an eye on the theological question, taking his thought seriously as part of the larger Christian tradition.[73]

Even when one conducts a study in theology, it is important to start first to understand "Edwards's own theological and spiritual concerns, including both his most profound insights and his peculiarities."[74]

> By attempting first to understand these in terms of his own eighteenth-century outlook, we can better see the assumptions and characteristic patterns of his thought. Once we have identified such assumptions and patterns and see how they differ from

---

69. Jenson, *America's Theologian*.
70. Marsden, "Edwardsean Vision," 24.
71. Marsden, "Edwardsean Vision," 24.
72. Marsden, *Jonathan Edwards*, 502.
73. Marsden, *Jonathan Edwards*, 502.
74. Marsden, *Jonathan Edwards*, 503.

our own, we are in a better position to respond to the particulars of his thought.[75]

A part of my intention in this study is to attempt to conduct a study in systematic theology with adequate sensitivity to Edwards's own historical context. While Marsden tried to bridge the gap between historians and theologians from a standpoint of a cultural historian, in this study I intend to do the same from a theologian's viewpoint.

The methodological question pursued in this study is whether it is possible to present a constructive proposal as a study in systematic theology in a way that is consistent with and faithful to Edwards's own historical context and theological framework. I am convinced that it is possible to be true to the limits and framework of Edwards's own theological and historical contexts and still to appropriate his theological richness for systematic theology today. In fact, when examining a theology in its own historical context is appropriately done, sometimes a systematic theological proposal for today naturally emerges. This study shows the case in presenting Edwards's covenant of redemption in his trinitarian theology in continuity with his own Reformed theological tradition. This will be an attempt to retrieve and recapture for today the strength and richness of tradition handed down and developed throughout history.

Relating to this methodological approach, I have in mind the issue of Edwards's modernity which scholars have been debating for many years. Many scholars have depicted Edwards as a remarkably modern figure in his theology and philosophy. For example, Perry Miller described Edwards as "intellectually the most modern man of his age."[76] Edwards was "so much ahead of his time that our own can hardly be said to have caught up with him."[77] Reacting to Miller, Peter Gay described Edwards as an anachronistic figure who tried to resist the modern development of the Enlightenment by hanging onto his outdated Calvinism. For Gay, Edwards was "Far from the first modern American," but rather "the last medieval American."[78] Years later, when Sang Hyun Lee published his study *The Philosophical Theology of Jonathan Edwards*, he wrote: "My contention in the present volume is that Edwards was actually more radically creative than Miller himself might

---

75. Marsden, *Jonathan Edwards*, 503.

76. Miller, *Jonathan Edwards*, 305.

77. Miller, *Jonathan Edwards*, xxxii.

78. Gay, *Loss of Mastery*, 116. Oliver Wendell Holmes made a similar assessment in 1880: "Edwards's system seems, in the light of to-day, to the last degree barbaric, mechanical, materialistic, pessimistic" (Holmes, "Jonathan Edwards," 24).

have realized."[79] The image of Edwards as a remarkably and unpredictably modern figure has been even more strengthened as Robert Jenson depicted Edwards as a precursor of Karl Barth in the twentieth century.[80] Now, as mentioned, some scholars conceive of Edwards as a pioneer in ecumenical and inter-faith dialogues.

In my assessment, in the wake of the renaissance of Edwards scholarship led by Perry Miller in the latter half of the twentieth century, sometimes scholars overemphasized the modernity of Edwards partly in order to rescue Edwards from an image of an archaic and outdated "Calvinist"[81] theologian in the hinterland. It seems that to save Edwards from his outmoded image the pendulum has swung to the other extreme: extraordinary modernity of Edwards. More recently, however, scholars are beginning to make more balanced and nuanced assessments by placing him in his own historical and theological contexts.[82] This study is conducted in line with this more recent attempt to redress overemphasis and assess Edwards's theology in his own historical context.

I also hope to show that even for a study in systematic theology it is important first to understand Edwards squarely in his own context and framework. In this sense, this is a study in systematic theology yet sensitive to Edwards's historical context. As we will see, specifically on the covenant of redemption, Edwards shares much with his preceding Reformed theologians. By locating Edwards in a broader Reformed tradition, I will describe Edwards in the eighteenth century as one of the faithful yet creative successors of the doctrine of the covenant of redemption from seventeenth-century Europe and New England.

---

79. Lee, *Philosophical Theology of Jonathan Edwards*, 3.

80. Jenson, *America's Theologian*, 42.

81. The use of the term "Calvinism" is problematic as it implies Calvin is the only central figure of the Reformed tradition and tends to overlook the diversity and unity of the Reformed tradition concomitant with its continuity and discontinuity between the Reformation magistrates and post-Reformation Reformed scholastics. McClenahan, *Jonathan Edwards and Justification*, 28–29; Asselt and Dekker, *Reformation and Scholasticism*, 14; Muller, "Calvin and the 'Calvinists,'" (1995) 345–75; "Calvin and the 'Calvinists,'" (1996) 125–60.

82. In response and as counter-arguments to Morimoto's study, recent studies on Edwards's doctrine of justification attempt to place Edwards more in his own historical context. See Moody, *Jonathan Edwards and Justification*; Cho, *Jonathan Edwards on Justification*; McClenahan, *Jonathan Edwards and Justification*.

OUTLINE

In this chapter 1, I have introduced the problem and the state of the question of this study. It provided an overview of diverse practical implications of the doctrine of the Trinity discussed in contemporary trinitarian theology. Particularly it identified the criticism of the immanent Trinity as one of the major features of today's discussion. The following study consists of three parts. Part 1 is a historical and systematic analysis of Edwards's theology of the covenant of redemption in the context of his broader Reformed tradition. This part is comprised of two chapters.

In the following chapter 2, I will situate Edwards in the context of the seventeenth and eighteenth-century Reformed orthodoxy. Through examining doctrinal and exegetical development of the covenant of redemption by major Reformed thinkers who possibly influenced Edwards, this chapter will describe Edwards as a successor of the Reformed idea of covenant of redemption. It will also point out that already in the tradition of the Reformed orthodoxy, the doctrine of the Trinity developed as archetypal and ectypal theology had an intimate connection with Christian life and piety.

Chapter 3 describes and examines Edwards's trinitarian theology of covenant. It attempts to show that for Edwards the immanent Trinity implies God's eternal pact of salvation between the Father and the Son, which will be unfolded in history. It thereby presents a counter example to contemporary discussion that stresses the impractical nature of the immanent Trinity. These first three chapters address the core of the argument.

Part 2, comprised of four chapters, articulates how the eternal covenant of redemption unfolds itself in history in a variety of dimensions: creation, justification and sanctification, issues of church membership and a view of a nation, and finally history itself which culminates in eschaton. Through these four significant examples, this part illustrates the various manifestations of the covenant of redemption in history and thereby underscores how the immanent Trinity actually has practical implications for Christian life.

Chapter 4 examines how the covenant of redemption unfolds itself in God's economic work of creation and thereby shows the practicality of the doctrine of the Trinity. Creation sets up the arena on which God's covenantal work of redemption unfolds its drama and story. Without the eternal pact in the immanent Trinity, even creation itself, not to mention Christian life, is not possible.

Chapter 5 will examine how the covenant of redemption unfolds itself in God's economic work of justification and sanctification and will thereby show the practicality of the doctrine of the Trinity. Given that justification and sanctification of sinners are an important part of God's work of redemption, and this redemptive work was eternally decreed within the immanent Trinity, the Trinity has an inherent relationship with salvation and the Christian life of piety.

Chapter 6 examines how the covenant of redemption influences the qualification of church membership and a view of a nation, thereby showing the practicality of the doctrine of the Trinity. At first glance it might be difficult to see how seemingly earthly issues such as qualification for church membership and one's view of a nation relate to the doctrine of the Trinity. Yet as the chapter will attempt to show, through the church covenant and the national covenant, the eternal covenant of redemption has at least an indirect connection with practical issues such as church membership and the shaping of corporate life as a nation or society.

Chapter 7 will examine how the covenant of redemption unfolds itself in God's economic work of history and eschaton, thereby showing the practicality of the doctrine of the Trinity. The entire course of history, as God's work of redemption, depends for its existence on the eternal pact between the Father and the Son in the immanent Trinity. If the entire history of redemption and the salvation of the elect hinge on the eternal pact in the immanent Trinity, it is groundless to say that the immanent Trinity is impractical and speculative.

Finally, chapter 8, as one chapter, constitutes part 3. This chapter, as a conclusion, will return to the contemporary discussion on the problem of the immanent Trinity introduced in chapter 1. By reviewing the main points of each chapter, this last chapter will reiterate that the Reformed doctrine of the covenant of redemption exemplified in Edwards's theology sheds new light on discussions in contemporary trinitarian theology. If God's eternal plan of redemption is located already in the immanent Trinity, it is no longer valid to criticize the immanent Trinity as abstruse and impractical because salvation of the elect hinges on the eternal pact made within the immanent Trinity.

PART I

2

The Covenant of Redemption in Reformed Scholasticism

IN THE PREVIOUS CHAPTER we identified a tendency in contemporary trinitarian theology to judge the immanent Trinity as speculative and impractical. Trinitarian theologians today instead attempt to reclaim the doctrine of the Trinity construed from the vantage point of God's economic work of redemption in the world and history. However, it is questionable whether this assumption of a dichotomy between the immanent and the economic Trinity itself is historically and theologically accurate. At least it is worth asking whether the alleged speculative retreat of the immanent Trinity into the inner-relatedness of divine life has always been the case in the history of trinitarian theology. In fact, the idea of the covenant of redemption, which is an act of the immanent Trinity, provides a definite counter example.

In this chapter, we survey the idea of the covenant of redemption in the Reformed tradition in its exegetical and doctrinal formation. I first overview the idea of covenant in the Reformed tradition more broadly. Then I examine the covenant of redemption in particular, its definition, its biblical foundation, its doctrinal formulation, and its relation to the immanent and the economic Trinity. Finally, I underscore the practical implication of the covenant of redemption for Christian life. The primary purpose of this chapter is to show that the idea of the covenant of redemption was current and widely known among the Reformed divines by the end of the seventeenth century. For the purpose of this study, it is sufficient to show that the doctrine of the covenant of redemption was prevalent and widely held by the time preceding the life and work of Jonathan Edwards.[1]

COVENANT IN GENERAL

As William Wakefield McKee declares, "it was Reformed church circles that the idea of covenant developed as a particular interpretation of Christian theology."[2] Reformed theology developed the idea of covenant from the time of the Reformation in the sixteenth century through Protestant scholasticism in the seventeenth century.[3] While nuances of the idea of covenant can vary, it "denotes properly a pact and agreement entered into between God and man, consisting partly in a stipulation of duty (or of the thing to be done) and partly in the promise of a reward."[4] Sometimes covenant has a certain range of meanings such as law or testament. A law is an order bestowed upon by a sovereign lawgiver and must be obeyed whether one agrees to it or not. A testament is a unilateral endowment of promised legacies that does not require any action from the part of the recipient.[5] Yet properly a covenant is "a mutual agreement and commitment, in which the consent of each of the participants is essential."[6] A covenant presupposes two agents who come into agreement on a certain condition: God and a human being.

> This covenant consists of two parts: Gods promise to man, Mans promise to God. Gods promise to man, is that, whereby he bindeth himselfe to man to be his God, if he performe the condition. Mans promise to God, is that, whereby he voweth his allegiance unto his Lord, and to performe the condition between them.[7]

Puritan divines regarded the covenant as God's gracious way of engaging with his people. Because God uses covenant as a means to communicate with his people, the creature can know what to expect from the Creator

---

1. For a study that reaches back to the origin of the covenant thought in the Reformed tradition, see, for example, Woolsey, *Unity and Continuity*; Von Rohr, *Covenant of Grace*, 193–96; Bierma, *German Calvinism*.
2. See also McKee, "Idea of Covenant," 1.
3. See Heppe, *Reformed Dogmatics*, 281–319, 371–447
4. Turretin, *Institutes of Elenctic Theology*, 172).
5. Von Rohr, *Covenant of Grace*, 35.
6. Von Rohr, *Covenant of Grace*, 35.
7. Perkins, *Golden Chaine*, 32.

and what to repel in order to walk faithfully in covenantal relationship.[8] Furthermore, the covenant framework was the most suitable approach to human beings as rational beings. As John Ball points out, "Such manner of dealing suites best with the nature of the reasonable creature, and his subordination to the Almighty." Indeed, "It hath pleased God to deale with the reasonable creature, by way of Promise and restipulation, that is, by way of Covenant."[9] The covenantal relationship between God and human beings has thus inherently an ethical implication of faithful commitment and integrity about how one conducts oneself.

As Michael McGiffert points out, Reformed thought on covenant "began with the single covenant of grace by which God ruled the great sweep of the *Heilsgeschichte*, from the first promise to fallen Adam forward through the age of the law to the Incarnation and beyond to the end of the world."[10] In this sense, covenant theology was from the very beginning "a theology of history—the history of the chosen people, first Jews, then Christians, to whom God bound himself by promise, oath, and sacramental seal."[11] Hence the idea of covenant underscored God's consistent commitment with his people as the penetrating principle throughout history. The covenantal thought "formed part of the broad common foundation of Reformed divinity."[12] Bruce M. Stephens writes: "Perhaps no single concept was used more in Puritan theology to bring the glory of an inscrutable God into relationship with sinful man than that of the covenant."[13] In this way, continental Reformed thought delineated God's gracious engagement with his chosen people through history within the covenantal framework.

Ursinus, Olevianus, and Junius developed this idea of covenant, which was handed on through the Herborn school of Martinus, Crocius, and Alsted to Cocceius and Burman. It became "a central issue in the structuring of system" by the time of seventeenth-century Reformed scholastics such as Witsius, Heidegger, Turretin, and Mastricht.[14] While some of the Lutherans shared a notion of covenant as a unifying theme that penetrates from creation through consummation as a series of historical development, it was in the Reformed tradition that this covenantal idea took its central and crucial

8. Ball, *Covenant of Grace*, 6.
9. Ball, *Covenant of Grace*, 6.
10. McGiffert, "Grace and Works," 469.
11. McGiffert, "Grace and Works," 470.
12. McGiffert, "Grace and Works," 469.
13. Stephens, *God's Last Metaphor*, 5.
14. Muller, *Post-Reformation Reformed Dogmatics*, 206–7. Hereafter abbreviated as *PRRD*.

place in a theological system.[15] As William K. B. Stoever notes, though varieties of application existed, "The 'federal' or 'covenant' theology, which sought to comprehend God's salvific relationship to mankind in covenantal terms, took shape among Reformed orthodox divines in the later sixteenth century, and became widespread in the seventeenth."[16]

DEFINITION OF THE COVENANT OF REDEMPTION

During the sixteenth to seventeenth century, covenantal theology developed as covenant of works and covenant of grace.[17] The covenant of works signifies the agreement between God and human beings that on the condition of human perfect obedience God pours blessings of eternal life upon them. Its archetype can be found in the covenant between God and Adam.

> God agreed with Adam to reward perfect obedience with eternal bliss and to punish the contrary appropriately, in a transaction suited to Adam's capacity as created—suited, that is, to Adam as a perceptive, reflective, consenting being, with the moral law 'written in his heart.' The moral law is God's perfect and universal rule for human behavior, and in the covenant of works mankind acquired an unalterable obligation to fulfill it.[18]

The covenant of works "presumes humanity's ability to carry it out, a prerequisite obligated by God's rectitude and satisfied by Adam's pristine integrity."[19] An assumption was that Adam, in his originally created condition, was able to obey and observe all divine law and commandments perfectly.

The covenant of grace points to God's redemptive work through Christ in history after the breach of the covenant of works on the part of Adam. In Adam's fall, sin "vitiated the Image of God and rendered man incapable of complying."[20] God the Father sent his only Son as truly God and truly human in order to fulfill the perfect obedience that human beings failed to practice.

> The covenant of works, however, does not prohibit God from accepting satisfaction from someone other than the proper

---

15. Muller, PRRD, 1:206–7; Von Rohr, Covenant of Grace, 8.

16. Stoever, 'Faire and Easie Way,' 81. For a detailed discussion on the development of the covenant idea on the continent, see McKee, "Idea of Covenant," 6–37.

17. Beeke and Jones, Puritan Theology, 217–36, 259–78.

18. Stoever, 'Faire and Easie Way,' 90.

19. Cohen, God's Caress, 57.

20. Cohen, God's Caress, 60.

debtors, provided the payment is sufficient to cover the debt owed. Accordingly, it is Christ's office, as 'surety' for the elect, to suffer the punishment due mankind for breach of the law and to render the perfect obedience required by the law for eternal reward.[21]

As Charles Lloyd Cohen summarizes, "By successfully performing the Law and by sacrificing himself under the curse, Christ wholly discharged the Covenant of Works, and because he did so for the Elect's sake, Christ redeems them from the Law and its penalty."[22] The elect can participate in merits of this work of Christ through faith.[23] This time the extent of this new covenant is "limited to the elect" and its foundation is "Christ alone."[24] The covenant of grace "promises not only life but also righteousness and, most significantly, all the *means* of restoring to life."[25] This new covenant "not only shows what righteousness is, but actually bestows it, and with it assurance of salvation."[26]

Even after the covenant of works is broken by the fall of humankind, it is to be noted that the covenant of works "was not abrogated."[27] As Stoever writes, "Satisfaction of the covenant of works remains the condition of man's salvation."[28] Yet this time the required perfect obedience to the law has been fulfilled by Christ and the law now begins to have a renewed role in Christian life.

> The same law written in Adam's heart, delivered by Moses, and preached and fulfilled by Christ becomes incarnate in the sanctified lives of believers, who incur under the covenant of grace an obligation of thankful obedience to God's will as the standard of human action.[29]

In other words, the goal of the covenant of works and the covenant of grace is the same. Yet this goal is now fulfilled by a different means. As William J. Van Asselt explains:

---

21. Stoever, 'Faire and Easie Way,' 94.
22. Cohen, *God's Caress*, 64.
23. Stoever, 'Faire and Easie Way,' 93.
24. Stoever, 'Faire and Easie Way,' 86.
25. Stoever, 'Faire and Easie Way,' 86.
26. Stoever, 'Faire and Easie Way,' 86.
27. Stoever, 'Faire and Easie Way,' 93.
28. Stoever, 'Faire and Easie Way,' 93.
29. Stoever, 'Faire and Easie Way,' 93.

> The fundamental difference, however, is that the end or goal of the covenant of grace, namely, the fulfillment of the commandment established in creation, is now fulfilled not by humanity, but by Christ. The goal of the covenant of works and the covenant of grace is the same—fellowship and friendship with God—only the means are different. The right that is formulated in the covenant of works is now restored and maintained on the cross. The roots of the doctrine of justification, therefore, can already be detected in the covenant of works; only now it is not humanity, but Christ who, on the basis of his obedience, acquires the right to eternal life.[30]

The law remains to lead believers in the Christian life as a guide for their thankful obedience and response to God's grace.

The Puritan theologians, out of these doctrinal formulations and in line with the continental Reformed scholastics, developed the doctrine of the *pactum salutis*, or covenant of redemption.[31] This doctrine traces the historical economy of redemption back into God's eternal communion of divine persons and conceives the eternal pact between the Father and the Son as the foundation of God's economic work of redemption in the world. It is "a pact between the will of the Father, who designates his Son as the Head and Redeemer of his foreknown people, and the will of the Son, who offers himself in order to procure salvation."[32] As Beeke and Jones put it, "the covenant of redemption between the Father and the Son provides the eternal, inviolable foundation of the temporal covenant of grace."[33] The covenant of grace in history stems from the eternal transaction between God the Father and God the Son. In this way, Reformed divines employed this teaching "as an argument for the *ad intra* trinitarian grounding for the *ad extra* work of salvation."[34]

In this covenantal arrangement, the Holy Spirit does not play a direct role as a covenant partner.[35] Nevertheless, the Holy Spirit plays a crucial

---

30. Asselt, *Federal Theology of Johannes Cocceius*, 266–67.

31. Beeke and Jones, *Puritan Theology*, 237–58. See also Lee, "Biblical Exegesis, Federal Theology"; Ballor, *Covenant, Causality, and Law*.

32. Asselt, *Federal Theology of Johannes Cocceius*, 229.

33. Beeke and Jones, *Puritan Theology*, 237.

34. Beeke and Jones, *Puritan Theology*, 237.

35. Traditionally reformed thinkers articulated the covenant of redemption as a pact between the two persons: the Father and the Son. John Gill's description of the covenant of redemption as the pact between three persons is a later development. See Gill, *Complete Body*, 318.

role as "the one who actualizes the result of the pact."[36] The Holy Spirit participates in this covenant not as "a legal partner" or "a negotiating subject,"[37] but as "an implementing subject" who "implements, safeguards, and administers" this covenantal agreement throughout the history.[38] Salvation was "never construed in Reformed circles as purely the work of the second person of the Trinity become flesh," but "the work of the Triune God."[39]

With the doctrine of the covenant of redemption, "the whole work of redemption was grounded in the eternal and immutable divine counsel."[40] What this doctrine teaches is that the covenant ultimately "finds its theological resting point in the eternal pact" and that the covenant is "by no means rooted in the creature, but in God's own essence."[41] Accordingly, this doctrine "provides the starting point of any discussion of God's soteric purposes in the history of redemption."[42] In order to illustrate this eternal plan of redemption within the immanent Trinity, several examples are in order.

The Westminster Confession of Faith (1647), though it did not use the term itself, articulated the idea of an eternal pact in which the Father gives the church elect from eternity to be redeemed on account of the Son's work as mediator.

> It pleased God, in his eternal purpose, to choose and ordain the Lord Jesus, his only begotten Son, to be the Mediator between God and man, the Prophet, Priest, and King, the Head and Saviour of his Church, the Heir of all things, and Judge of the world: unto whom He did, from all eternity, give a people to be his seed, and to be by him in time redeemed, called, justified, sanctified, and glorified.[43]

In order to clarify the covenantal nature of this agreement, the Savoy Declaration of Faith inserted eight words to the passage here in the Westminster—"according to a Covenant made between them both."[44] Furthermore, David Dickson and James Durham's *The Sum of Saving Knowledge*, sometimes called "the unofficial fourth Westminster standard" because it

---

36. Asselt, *Federal Theology of Johannes Cocceius*, 234.
37. Asselt, *Federal Theology of Johannes Cocceius*, 235.
38. Asselt, *Federal Theology of Johannes Cocceius*, 234.
39. De Jong, *Covenant Idea in New England Theology*, 53.
40. De Jong, *Covenant Idea in New England Theology*, 54.
41. Asselt, *Federal Theology of Johannes Cocceius*, 232.
42. Beeke and Jones, *Puritan Theology*, 237.
43. Schaff, *Evangelical Protestant Creeds*, 619.
44. Congregational Churches in England, *Declaration of the Faith*, 22; Beeke and Jones, *Puritan Theology*, 238.

was often printed together with the Westminster standards in Scotland and America for many years,[45] declares: "For the accomplishment of this Covenant of Redemption, and making the Elect partakers of the benefits thereof in the Covenant of Grace, Christ Jesus was clad with the threefold Office of Prophet, Priest, and King."[46]

An English Puritan, Thomas Goodwin (1600–1680), developed a lengthy account of the covenant of redemption. He sees the eternal transaction between the Father and the Son that dates back to before the foundation of the world. It is "God the Father's eternal counsel and transaction with Christ, to undertake the work of redemption for man, considered as fallen."[47] According to Goodwin, the "great design of the gospel" is "those eternal transactions between God the Father and God the Son for the salvation of man."[48] Before the economic unfolding in temporality, the divine plan of redemption was already established as God's eternal pact between the Father and the Son within God's internal communion. Here, the immanent Trinity is not detached from the economic work of redemption. Rather, the eternal transaction between the Father and the Son underpins the execution of God's plan of redemption in temporality.

David Dickson (1583–1662) also defines the covenant of redemption as a "pact between God, and Christ God appointed Mediatour, before the world was, in the council of the Trinity."[49]

> Whereby the Son is both the party offended as God, one essentially with the Father and holy Spirit; and the party contracter also, as God designed Mediatour personally for redeeming man, who with consent of the Father and holy Spirit, from all eternity willed and purposed in the fulnesse of time, to assume the humane nature in personall union with Himself, and for the elects sake to become man, and to take the cause of the elect in hand, to bring them back to the friendship of God, and full enjoyment of felicity for everyone.[50]

> It is a bargain, agreed upon between the father and the Son designed Mediatour, concerning the elect (lying with the rest of mankind in the state of sin and death, produced by their own merit) wisely and powerfully to be converted, sanctified and

---

45. Beeke and Jones, *Puritan Theology*, 238.
46. Dickson and Durham, *Summe of Saving Knowledge*, 202.
47. Goodwin, *Of Christ the Mediator*, 3.
48. Goodwin, *Of Christ the Mediator*, 3.
49. Dickson, *Therapeutica sacra*, 22–23. See also Williams, "Decree of Redemption."
50. Dickson, *Therapeutica sacra*, 24.

> saved, for the Son of Gods satisfaction and obedience (in our nature to be assumed by Him) to be given in due time to the Father, even unto the death of the crosse.[51]

Clearly, Dickson sees God's will for the salvation of the elect already echoed in the covenant of redemption. The incarnation of the Son and ensuing development of God's work of redemption were all conceived in the mind of God. The blueprint of God's plan of redemption already existed in the immanent Trinity.

Samuel Willard (1640–1707), a New England predecessor of Edwards, also concurs with this basic definition as follows:

> Hence, to the firm and immutable constituting of the Son of God a Redeemer in the *Decree*, there past an Eternal *Transaction* between the Father and him, which is best shadowed to us, by the notion of a *Covenant*: and because it had a proper respect to the Ransoming of his Chosen from sin and misery, it may therefore well be called the *Covenant of Redemption*. If the Son of God became a Redeemer by his own Consent freely, and was determined unto it before the World began, it infers, according to our Capacity, that there was something propounded to him, and that he did accordingly accept it.[52]

Willard notes that the effect of the incarnation presupposes the cause that should be located within the eternal communion of the Father and the Son.

> Hereupon the *Undertaking* of the Son of God to be man, is in order before the *futurition* of his *Incarnation*. It hath a Causal Antecedence; to the futurity of this Assumption, because that which made it future from Eternity, was the Compact which past between his Father and him about it in the Days of Eternity.[53]

As von Rohr puts it, the covenant of redemption is, so to speak, "a metahistory located solely in the life of God." He continues:

> It is interesting, however, that though human history plays so important a role in the outworking of the covenant of grace, the actual origin of the covenant itself was, in this Puritan understanding, not within that historical process. Rather, its beginning was in what might be called 'divine history,' a kind of meta-history located solely in the life of God. The source of the covenant of grace was a still prior covenant between

---

51. Dickson, *Therapeutica sacra*, 25.
52. Willard, *Doctrine of the Covenant*, 18.
53. Willard, *Doctrine of the Covenant*, 30.

God and Christ, designated theologically as the covenant of redemption.[54]

The covenant of redemption is the eternal foundation for the work of redemption in time.

BIBLICAL FOUNDATION OF THE COVENANT OF REDEMPTION

Modern scholars such as O. Palmer Robertson, Roger T. Beckwith, and others argue that the doctrine of the covenant of redemption is biblically unwarranted, artificial, and a speculative construction.[55] However, this doctrine actually took its shape based on the accumulation of biblical exegesis since the early era of the Reformation.[56]

What is striking about Dickson is that he provides a lengthy exposition of scriptural evidences of the covenant of redemption. According to him, the Scripture underscores the covenant of redemption by expressions that denote covenantal parties (Eph 1:7, 1:14; Acts 20:28; 1 Cor 6:20; 1 Pet 1:18, 19, 29, 21; Matt 26:28), by diverse titles given to Christ the Redeemer ("Mediatour" 1 Tim 2:5, 6; "Redeemer" Job 19:24; "Surety" Heb 7:22; "reconciliation" Rom 5:11; "propitiation" 1 John 2:2; and Rom 3:25), by expressions that relate to the execution of an eternal decree (Acts 15:18; Eph 1:9; Luke 22:22; Acts 2:23; Ps 2:7; John 1:14, 1:2, 3; Prov 8:22–32; 2 Tim 1:9; Eph 1:3–5; 1 Pet 1:18–20), by representation of the covenant of redemption in the Levitical types (Pss 84:11, 73:24), by incarnation as ratification of the covenant (Luke 2:49; Matt 3:13; John 5:39, 8:26, 10:15; Luke 24:25) and by presenting articles that articulate the essence of the covenant of redemption.[57] For example, commenting on Eph 1:3–5, Dickson states: "For, as before the beginning of the World, the elect were given to the Son designed Mediatour to be incarnat, and the price agreed upon; so also grace to be given in time to the redeemed by compact, was given from eternity unto Christ, their designed Advocat."[58] Dickson's exposition indicates that the

---

54. Von Rohr, *Covenant of Grace*, 43.

55. Robertson, *Christ of the Covenants*, 54; Beckwith, "Unity and Diversity of Covenants," 99. See also Weir, *Origins of the Federal Theology*, 158.

56. For a fuller treatment of the exegetical background of the covenant of redemption, see Muller, "Toward the *Pactum Salutis*," 25–48.

57. Dickson, *Therapeutica sacra*, 25–32.

58. Dickson, *Therapeutica sacra*, 30.

doctrine of this covenant emerged not as an unbiblical, speculative construction, but as the result of collations of biblical exegesis.[59]

In a similar way, Willard sees the eternal election of a certain number of people as the source of salvation (Eph 1:3–5; 1 Thess 1:4), the foundation of effectual calling (Acts 13:46; Rom 11:7) and conversion (Jer 31:3). The Son is called "Chosen One" (Ps 89:3) or God's "Elect" (Isa 42:1) because the Son of God "was not only an *actual* Redeemer in time, but a *chosen* Redeemer from Eternity."[60] Thus this redeemer is called "A Lamb slain from the Foundation of the World" (Rev 13:8).[61] The "counsel of peace" is identified as the covenant between the Father and the Son (Zech 6:13).[62]

By way of another example, expounding the passage of 2 Cor 5:18–19, Goodwin makes a distinction between "*in* Christ" and "*by* Christ." On the one hand, when it is said that "God was in Christ, reconciling the world unto himself" (v. 19 KJV),[63] it denotes the immanent transaction between the Father and the Son.

> It implies and notes out those immanent acts of God in Christ; the preparation of all mercies and benefits we have by Christ, from him, and laying them up in him really for us in Christ, as in our head, in whom God looked upon us when we had no subsistence but *in him;* when God and he were alone plotting of all, framing of all that was after to be done by Christ for us, and applied unto us.[64]

On the other hand, when God is said to have "reconciled us to himself by Jesus Christ," this "imports the actual performance of all this by Christ, and application of it to us."[65] Prior to the execution of the divine plan of re-

---

59. "Arguably the doctrine of the *pactum salutis* arose out of a concerted examination of a series of biblical texts, collated with one another, according to the typical methods of the era, in concert with a series of theological issues, both positive and polemical" (Muller, "Toward *Pactum Salutis*," 64).

60. Willard, *Doctrine of the Covenant*, 15.

61. Willard, *Doctrine of the Covenant*, 15.

62. Willard, *Doctrine of the Covenant*, 18. Even if some contemporary biblical scholars may argue that reading Zechariah 6:13 as the counsel of peace between the Father and the Son is exegetically unwarranted, Muller's study shows that this passage came into scope much later in the late seventeenth century after the preceding accumulation of other texts such as Isa 11; 42:1–6, 52:13, 53:10–12; Pss 2:7–8; 40; 110. See Muller, "Toward *Pactum Salutis*," 37.

63. The entire Bible translation used for citation in this study will be from the King James Version as it was the translation Jonathan Edwards actually used.

64. Goodwin, *Of Christ the Mediator*, 11.

65. Goodwin, *Of Christ the Mediator*, 11.

demption *by* Christ in history, for God the Father, "the main of his work was transacted secretly from everlasting."[66] Goodwin adds: "But yet lest they should think that this was a business begun of late to be done by him, then when Christ died, and they were converted, he [God the Father] further says, that he hath made it his main business from all eternity."[67]

Based on his biblical exegesis of Luke 22:29; Isaiah 42, 49, 53, and 61; Pss 110:4, 2:8; Hebrews 10; Gal 4:4, John 10, 15, and 17, Francis Turretin concludes:

> For thus the Scriptures represent to us the Father in the economy of salvation as stipulating the obedience of his Son even unto death, and for it promising in return a name above every name that he might be the head of the elect in glory; the Son as offering himself to do the Father's will, promising a faithful and constant performance of the duty required of him and restipulating the kingdom and glory promised to him. All these things are plainly gathered from the Scriptures.[68]

When scholars claim that the idea of the covenant of redemption is biblically unwarranted, they fail to take into account the rich tradition of biblical exegeses used by Reformed theologians.

DOCTRINAL FORMULATION OF THE COVENANT OF REDEMPTION

Many of the biblical exegetes not only consider God's purpose in redemption as part of his eternal decree, but also define the decree of redemption as a covenant. For example, Dickson developed the doctrine of the covenant of redemption in relation to divine decree. He says:

> This covenant of *redemption*, is in effect one with the eternall decree of redemption, wherein the salvation of the elect, and the way how it shall be brought about is fixed, in the purpose of God, who worketh all things according to the counsell of His own Will.[69]

> And the decree of redemption is in effect a covenant, one God in three persons agreeing in the decree, that the second Person, God the Son, should be incarnat, and give obedience and

---

66. Goodwin, *Of Christ the Mediator*, 11.
67. Goodwin, *Of Christ the Mediator*, 11.
68. Turretin, *Institutes of Elenctic Theology*, 2:177.
69. Dickson, *Therapeutica sacra*, 24. Dickson cites Eph 1:15.

satisfaction to divine justice for the elect: unto which piece of service the Son willingly submitting Himself, the decree becometh a reall covenant indeed.[70]

The covenant of redemption, in effect, means God's eternal decree of redemption. Because the redemption of the elect is predetermined in the eternal decree, its economic unfolding in time is firmly guaranteed. As Witsius puts it, "God had, by an eternal and irrevocable decree, appointed, *promised*, and *confirmed by oath*, the inheritance of all blessings in Christ."[71] Willard makes the same point:

> It is certain that the whole concern of Mans Redemption and Salvation, had it consideration and determination in Gods eternal Decree. It is a sure rule, *That whatsoever God doth in time, be purposed to do it before time: for he worketh all things according to the counsel of his will.*[72]

> Among the means, that which shines forth most illustriously, is mans deliverance from Sin and Wrath by the *Obedience of Christ*, who is the Eternal Son of God, and in fullness of Time was made man, in order to his Redeeming of us. This way of mans *Redemption*, had a room in Gods Eternal Purpose: Our *Election* therefore was *in him*, and that before the Creation Eph. 1.4.[73]

In other words, "Christ was not sent in haste into the World: it was not a rash and indeliberate Undertaking of his, but it was all determined in the Counsel of God."[74] Because of this understanding, the doctrine of the covenant of redemption largely has an affinity with a supralapsarian framework rather than an infralapsarian. God's plan of redemption was conceived from before the foundation of the world, even preceding the fall.

In this way, the covenant of redemption was doctrinally formulated in close association with God's eternal decree of redemption, or the doctrine of election. It means that ultimately the ground of the covenant of redemption is God's sheer love for the elect. The salvation of the elect was eternally designed because it was simply in accord with God's pleasure and manifestation of his glory.

---

70. Dickson, *Therapeutica sacra*, 24.
71. Witsius, *Oeconomy of the Covenants*, 250.
72. Willard, *Doctrine of the Covenant*, 6. Willard cites Eph 1:11.
73. Willard, *Doctrine of the Covenant*, 7.
74. Willard, *Doctrine of the Covenant*, 15.

> In the Decree we find such a thing as *Election*, wherein God hath appointed men unto Salvation, and also contrived the way in which he will accomplish it; and to this way doth the *Covenant of Redemption* appertain: and therefore the rise of it was the *meer good Pleasure of God, to advance the glory of the Riches of his Grace, by the Redemption of his Chosen, and bringing of them to Enjoy Eternal Life*, for which end, he appointed his own Son to be the Redeemer, and Indented about it in a free Covenant.[75]
>
> The ultimate end of Gods design in this Covenant, was the Illustration of the Glory of his Rich Grace in them that are saved, so we are told. *Eph.* 1.6. God is his own last end in all his works of Efficiency, and therefore had that . . . respect in his Decrees.[76]
>
> And why did he so? it was because he loved them. The reason of this love is his good pleasure. The first act wherein this love was exprest, was in Chosing us in Christ, and Covenanting with him to Redeem us; in which he laid a sure and firm foundation for our Salvation: Gods sending of Christ is for the reason ascribed to his unparallel'd love.[77]

God's eternal decree of redemption rooted in pure love and pleasure in God is the ground of the covenant of redemption. Given that glorification of God means advancement or manifestation of what God takes delight in, it is also pertinent to say that God and his glory is the ultimate ground of the covenant of redemption.

However, the covenant of redemption seems to incur a potential doctrinal problem of subordinationism. While the summary of God's economic plan of redemption already located within the immanent Trinity refutes the accusation that the immanent Trinity is impractical and speculative, the introduction of economic order into the internal communion of God seems to imply the subordination of the Son. Reformed scholastics were well aware of this potential problem and addressed it in their defense of this doctrine. For instance, Willard argues that the subordination of the Son took place only in the economic administration of his office whereas the Son remains coessential with the Father in his nature.

> Christ, not only as he is Man, but also as he is Son, is in the *Oeconomical* Dispensation of things, *Subordinated* to his Father. Though in the Divine Essence he is Equal as he is God, (for, where there is a compleat sameness, there must needs be a

---

75. Willard, *Doctrine of the Covenant*, 31.
76. Willard, *Doctrine of the Covenant*, 33.
77. Willard, *Doctrine of the Covenant*, 34.

perfect equality) yet in the *Oeconomy* of the Administration of the Affairs of his Kingdom, he is Subordinate.[78]

By his nature, the Son of God, "who was thus constituted Redeemer in the Decree, is a Person in the God-head, infinitely free and uncompellable."[79] Hence when the Son agreed to subject himself to humiliation according to the will of the Father, it was out of the Son's free and willing decision.

> He is thereupon incapable of Compulsion. So that, upon an impossible supposition, that the Son had not complied with his Fathers Will in this matter, he could not have been Decreed to be a Redeemer; and from this very Argument the Apostle proves, that what Christ did upon this account was his own voluntary act, *Phil.* 2. 5, 6, 7. The Father no sooner proposed it to him, than he readily complied with it.[80]

Therefore, the subordination of the Son in his economic operation does not mean that the Son is subordinate to the Father by nature or essence.

This argument also has relevance for vindicating the covenant of redemption against a charge of tritheism. While each of the three persons has a distinct subsistence, all three persons share the same divine essence. Given that the divine will belongs to this one and the same divine essence, each of the three persons has this same divine will.

> The Son of God, who was thus constituted Redeemer in the Decree, is a Person in the God-head, infinitely free and uncompellable. Though the Doctrine of a Trinity of Persons in the Unity of the Divine Essence, be a Mystery beyond the capacity of our short Understandings to fathom; yet in as much as these are exhibited to us under the notion of three Persons, each one having a distinct Subsistence, (though all have but one and the same Essence) we must therefore allow to each of them all that is essential to the God-head: and thus we are to conceive of each of them to have a Divine Will; though it be one and the same in all.[81]

> The Decrees is an act of Divine Counsel, exerted by the Divine Will, which is undivided, and common to the three persons; and

---

78. Willard, *Doctrine of the Covenant*, 27
79. Willard, *Doctrine of the Covenant*, 17.
80. Willard, *Doctrine of the Covenant*, 17.
81. Willard, *Doctrine of the Covenant*, 17. Also cited is Phil 2:6; Zech 13:7.

> thus the Deity is the one party Covenanting, because the Essential acts of the Trinity are undivided, Job. 5. 17, 19.[82]

This may explain why there was no contradiction or disagreement among the three persons in the eternal transaction of the covenant of redemption. While each divine person has a will, ultimately there are not three different wills but one and the same will. Hence perfect accord and harmony exist in this eternal pact.

In other words, Reformed scholastics made a distinction between the language regarding "God's *essential being* (considering God's being from the standpoint of the divine attributes)" and the language regarding "God's relative being (considering God from the standpoint of the three persons)."[83] For example, when Francis Turretin discusses the doctrine of divine simplicity and its compatibility with three divine persons, he notes this distinction: "simplicity in respect to essence, but Trinity in respect to persons. In this sense, nothing hinders God (who is one in essence) from being three persons."[84] In the present context, from a standpoint of three persons, each person has its own will, whereas from the standpoint of the divine essence, each will is ultimately one and the same divine will. Therefore it was possible to describe the remarkably trinitarian diverse works of God appropriated to each person without undermining divine simplicity and without succumbing to tritheism.

> That in these Essential Works, the Scripture frequently observes a personal propriety, and an order of working according to the order of their Subsistence and manner of working: so that in whatever work, any one persons order of Subsistence, and manner of working doth principally appear, it is, by way of specialty, ascribed to that person; not because that person is alone in it, but because God doth herein manifest himself to us most clearly in such a manner of being or Subsistence. The Father is the first Person, hence beginning Works are Attributed to him, as Election and Creation. The Son is the Second Person, and therefore secondary works are ascribed to him, such as Redemption. The Holy Ghost is the Third and Last Person, and therefore finishing works are given to him, such as Application. The Father works of himself, by the Son and Spirit. The Son works from the Father by the Spirit. The Holy Ghost works from them both; Job. 5.19.16.13. and this Order is to shew the Oeconomy of the

---

82. Willard, *Doctrine of the Covenant*, 21.
83. Studebaker and Caldwell, *Trinitarian Theology of Jonathan Edwards*, 131.
84. Turretin, *Institutes of Elenctic Theology*, 1:193.

Divine Persons. Now in this regard, Essential Works may have a peculiar Appropriation to a person not exclusive, but inclusive of the other.[85]

In his *essential being*, God has one and the same will and is involved in all of his works. In his *relative being*, each divine person has a distinct will and specific works ascribed to each. "Trinity and simplicity thus do not directly contradict for they describe God from two different vantage points."[86] Having articulated the covenant of redemption in the Reformed tradition, we are now ready to examine its relation to the immanent and the economic Trinities.

RELATION OF THE COVENANT OF REDEMPTION TO THE IMMANENT AND THE ECONOMIC TRINITY

The significance of the covenant of redemption in the Reformed tradition, specifically for the purpose of this study, lies in the reality that the economic work of redemption is already located within the immanent Trinity in its core or as an idea. Here, the immanent Trinity is not detached from the economic work of redemption. Rather, the eternal transaction between the Father and the Son underpins the execution of the plan of redemption in temporality.

Reformed scholastics developed the basic distinction between the *ad-intra* and *ad-extra* work of the Godhead, operations of the Trinity which stands somewhat oblique relationship to the immanent Trinity and the economic Trinity. This distinction constituted a "fundamental architectonic device in the older Reformed theology" and a "device that offers considerable insight into the nature and character of the older Reformed approach to the questions of divine absoluteness and divine relationality."[87] In accord with the former distinction, the Reformed orthodox introduced specific terminologies: *archetypal* theology and *ectypal* theology. Archetypal theology refers to "the *ad intra* absolute and necessary knowledge concerning creation, providence, and salvation that God alone can know," whereas ectypal theology refers to "the relative and accommodated *ad extra* knowledge of those divine works that is accessible to creatures."[88] Muller summarizes the

---

85. Willard, *Doctrine of the Covenant*, 21–22.
86. Studebaker and Caldwell, *Trinitarian Theology of Jonathan Edwards*, 131
87. Muller, "God as Absolute and Relative," 57. See also Asselt, "Fundamental Meaning of Theology," 319–35.
88. Muller, "God as Absolute and Relative," 57.

point of this fine distinction as follows: "for our theology (*theologia nostra*) to be true theology, it must be ectypal, specifically, a finite reflection of the divine archetypal theology, grounded by God's own working in the archetype itself."[89] In other words, human knowledge of God can be formulated only according to what God reveals to humans about himself and to the extent which our theology reflects in human finite language what God is in himself. Put differently, human knowledge of God can truly be reliable only in so far as it rests in and is grounded by the reality of God in himself. "It is therefore God himself who is the source, origin and efficient cause of what we know in this life as true theology."[90]

Now when our theology (human knowledge about God) delineates the distinction between the immanent Trinity and the economic Trinity, an assumption behind this formulation is that, though in a finite and limited way, humans can trace back to God in himself insofar as God revealed himself to creation, particularly to humans.

> That in all his Works of Efficiency, he aims at the Declaration of the Glory of his own Perfections. What else is the Declarative Glory of God, but a display of his Essential Glory to the Creature, so far as he sees meet? He had all in himself before there was a World; but he would have a World to be a Mirror of his Perfections; and those to be in it who should be able to read them, and acknowledge him therein; and therefore these are to declare it, Psal. 19. and he is said to be known by them.[91]

> The things which are done in time for the actual Accomplishment of it. They that would Search the Love of God to the Original, and follow it up to the Wellhead of it, must ascend beyond the Creation of the Word, and look for it in that Eternity which had no Beginning. Not only the things that he hath done for us, but the thoughts also which he had of us.[92]

Thus, in the context of the covenant of redemption and in line with the distinction between God in himself and God in relation to the world, God's economic transaction in relation to the world has its source and origin in the eternal communion and agreement of divine persons. In other words, the covenant of redemption is "a doctrinal argument for the *ad intra* trinitarian

---

89. Muller, "God as Absolute and Relative," 58.
90. Muller, *PRRD*, 1:232.
91. Willard, *Doctrine of the Covenant*, 70.
92. Willard, *Doctrine of the Covenant*, 2.

grounding of the *ad extra* work of salvation as it terminates on individual persons of the Trinity."[93]

> It manifests God's redemptive plan as eternal and as something far more than a reaction to the problem of sin. For all that this doctrine of eternal covenanting between Father and Son appears as the most speculative element in the covenant theology, it represents that most basic issues in the Reformed system—the eternal, divine, and consistently gracious ground of the plan of salvation, the resolution of the seemingly unbridgeable gap between the eternal and the temporal, the infinite and the finite, undertaken redemptively and by grace alone from the divine side.[94]

Indeed, the unity between the *ad-intra* reality of the divine willing and the *ad-extra* execution of the divine plan of salvation appears to answer the modern demand for the nexus between the immanent and the economic Trinity.

What, then, is the exact difference between the covenant of redemption and the other two covenants: covenant of works and covenant of grace? While the covenant of works or the covenant of grace is the covenant between God and humans made in temporality, the covenant of redemption signifies the mutual agreement between the Father and the Son consented from eternity.

> *An Everlasting Compact clearly made, and firmly Ratified, between God the Father, and God the Son, about the Redemption and Salvation of a number of the Children of Men*; and this is a Covenant distinct from that which we call the *Covenant of Works*, which past between God and Man at the first in Adam; as also from the *New Covenant*, or that of Grace, which is Indented between God and Man, in Christ as the *Mediator* of it.[95]

In the covenant of redemption, on the one hand, the Father demands "*the obedience of the Son* even unto death, and for it promising him that name, which is above every name, even that he should be the head of the elect in glory." On the other hand, the Son is, "as *presenting himself* to do *the will* of the Father, *acqiescing* in that *promise*, and in fine, requiring *the kingdom* and *glory promised* to him."[96]

---

93. Muller, "Toward *Pactum Salutis*," 15.
94. Muller, "Toward *Pactum Salutis*," 15.
95. Willard, *Doctrine of the Covenant*, 8–9.
96. Witsius, *Oeconomy of the Covenants*, 222.

This pre-temporal transaction between the Father and the Son in the immanent Trinity, so to speak, sets a stage for its economic unfolding in the covenant of grace. After the fall, human beings depraved by sin are unable to attain the eternal blessings within the framework of the covenant of works. Only God himself can fulfill the requirement of the covenant of works.

> He bids his ambassadors declare, that as to that point men need not trouble themselves, nor take care about it; for he himself hath further been so zealously affected in this business, that he himself hath made full provision, and took order for that aforehand, and done it to their hand.[97]

> In him, and by him, as a mediator, and umpire, and surety between them and him, this great matter hath been taken up and accorded. For he and Jesus Christ his only Son have from all eternity laid their counsels together (as I may so speak with reverence), to end this great difference; and they both contrived and agreed, that Christ should undertake to satisfy his Father, for all the wrong was done to him, all which he should take upon himself, as if he were guilty of it.[98]

As only God himself can fulfill perfect obedience to the divine law by Christ the Son of God, the covenant of redemption between the Father and the Son comprises the foundation for the covenantal communion between God and the elect in the covenant of grace. The covenant of redemption is the foundation of the covenant of grace.

> The sum of all is: his Father promiseth to him to give all spiritual blessings in him, and then makes a deed of gift to him for our good and use; even as goods may be given to and by a feoffee in trust for one that is yet not born. And so our life is said to be "hid with Christ in God"; and so it was from everlasting there laid up by God with Christ.[99]

> But whence is it that there are such liberal offers made to the children of man? why it flows from the *Covenant of Redemption*, and had it not been for this, there had never any such news been heard of in the World. Here was the Foundation laid for all, the

---

97. Goodwin, *Of Christ the Mediator*, 4.
98. Goodwin, *Of Christ the Mediator*, 4.
99. Goodwin, *Of Christ the Mediator*, 30. Goodwin also cites Eph 1:3; 3:10–11; 2 Tim 1:9; 1:1.

Saving Grace which is Dispensed in time to any of the children of men; and so it must needs be a *Covenant of Grace*.[100]

The salvation of the elect was already purposed in the eternal transaction between the Father and the Son within the immanent Trinity.

Herman Witsius (1636–1708) also builds up his discussion on the covenant of redemption through exploring the implication of the covenant of grace.

> THAT the nature of *the covenant of grace* may be the more thoroughly understood, two things are above all to be distinctly considered. 1. The COMPACT which intervenes *between* GOD THE FATHER, and CHRIST THE MEDIATOR. 2. That TESTAMENTARY DISPOSITION, by which GOD BESTOWS, by an immutable covenant, ETERNAL SALVATION, and every thing relative thereto, upon THE ELECT. The former agreement is between GOD and THE MEDIATOR; the latter between GOD and THE ELECT. This last presupposes the first, and is founded upon it.[101]

The covenant of redemption, the eternal pact between the Father and the Son, for the purpose of the redemption of the elect constitutes the foundation and presupposition of the covenant of grace: the actual unfolding of God's work of redemption in history. The eternal pact between the Father and the Son entails the will of the Father, "giving *the Son*, to be the *Head* and *Redeemer* of the elect" and the will of the Son "presenting himself as a *Sponsor* or Surety for them."[102]

Furthermore, Witsius sees three phases in this covenantal transaction. The first period of the covenant of redemption is the eternal constitution of Christ as the head of the elect.

> Christ himself *was constituted from everlasting, the Head* of those that were to be saved, and *they were given unto him,* for whom he was to merit salvation, and in whom he was to be glorified and admired. From this constitution, the Son from everlasting bore a peculiar relation to those that were to be saved.[103]

---

100. Willard, *Doctrine of the Covenant*, 46–47.

101. Witsius, *Oeconomy of the Covenants*, 222. For a study of the covenant of redemption in the covenant theology of Herman Witsius, see Beach, "Doctrine of the *Pactum Salutis*," 101–42. See also Beeke, *Analysis of Herman Witsius*.

102. Witsius, *Oeconomy of the Covenants*, 222.

103. Witsius, *Oeconomy of the Covenants*, 239.

The second period of the covenant of redemption starts once the human falls into sin and the eternal plan of redemption is now put into actualization. The Son, as mediator, starts his intercession between the Father and the elect.

> Immediately upon the fall of man, he offered himself to God, now offended by sin, actually to perform those things, to which he had engaged himself from eternity; saying, Thou hast given them to me, I will make satisfaction for them: and so making way for the word of grace to be declared to, and the covenant of grace to be made with them. Thus Christ *was actually constituted Mediator*, and declared as such immediately after the fall; and *having undertaken the suretiship*, he began to act many things belonging to the offices of a Mediator.[104]

The third period of the covenant of redemption is when the Son took on human flesh and "engaged himself as a voluntary servant to God, from love to his Lord the Father, and to his spouse the church, and his spiritual children."[105] While the first period of intra-trinitarian agreement, precisely speaking, is the covenant of redemption and the latter two periods belong to the covenant of grace, here Witsius views the latter two periods as so naturally an outworking of the first period of the covenant of redemption that he seems to recognize all three periods within a framework of the covenant of redemption in a broader sense.

The covenant of grace is the organic outworking of the covenant of redemption. The covenant of grace in the economic Trinity is grounded by the covenant of redemption in the immanent Trinity. This covenant of redemption as a bridge between the immanent Trinity and the economic Trinity certainly has positive repercussions to the practical Christian life of piety.

IMPLICATIONS OF THE COVENANT OF REDEMPTION FOR CHRISTIAN PRACTICE

While contemporary theology criticizes the immanent Trinity for being speculative and impractical, it is worth noting that the Reformed scholastics conceived the term "theoretical" and "practical" in a different way from contemporary use. While contemporary usage tends to mean that "theoretical" pertains to "metaphysical rationalization" or "a statement of abstract principle" and "practical" pertains to "pragmatic enterprise" or a statement "of

---

104. Witsius, *Oeconomy of the Covenants*, 239.
105. Witsius, *Oeconomy of the Covenants*, 240.

application," the Reformed scholastics traditionally meant by *theoria* simply something beheld and by *praxis* something done with a teleological goal in perspective.[106]

On one hand, theory (*theoria*) pertains to a pure beholding of the object in and of itself with no other end in view, and is thus "understood in terms of the *visio Dei* and the ultimate enjoyment of God (*fruitio Dei*) by man." On the other hand, practice (*praxis*) refers to a certain act that leads to a specific goal beyond itself, "namely salvation, and is designed therefore to conduce to a righteous life and the love of God."[107] The majority of the Reformed orthodox conceived of theology as both theoretical and practical, both intellectual and voluntary, with a primary emphasis on practical character.[108]

Since God's work of salvation is already located in its seminal form within the immanent Trinity, far from being purely speculative (in a modern sense of "impractical"), the covenant of redemption in God *ad intra* apparently has practical implications for the Christian life. First, the covenant of redemption has direct relevance for salvation of the elect. When the Son makes a covenant with the Father in the eternal communion, "the only reward he seeks for, is the salvation and justification of his elect, and of those whom God hath given him."[109] Citing John 6:38–39, Goodwin argues for the salvation of the elect as the people whom God the Father has given to Christ the Son: "And as he gave them to be his, so also with a special charge to bring them to salvation, to lose not one of his tale and number."[110] Salvation already exists as the divine plan and intention in the immanent Trinity.

Second, the covenant of redemption lays the foundation for the Christian life of piety. It teaches the elect that "our sanctification and salvation is ascribed as much to God's will and covenant with Christ . . . as to Christ's offering himself."[111] Since salvation of the elect ultimately stems from the will of God the Father before the foundation of the world, the certainty of salvation is firmly established. The covenant of redemption "undergirds with this strengthened certainty the covenant of grace."[112]

---

106. Muller, *PRRD*, 1:340.
107. Muller, *PRRD*, 1:341.
108. Muller, *PRRD*, 1:354.
109. Goodwin, *Of Christ the Mediator*, 28.
110. Goodwin, *Of Christ the Mediator*, 28.
111. Goodwin, *Of Christ the Mediator*, 28. Cited biblical references are Heb 10:10; Rom 3:24; 8:33.
112. Von Rohr, *Covenant of Grace*, 45.

> And by all this you see that our salvation was in sure hands, even afore the world was; for God and Christ had engaged themselves by covenant each to other for us, the one to die, the other to accept it for us.
>
> And though Christ was yet to come and die, yea, and though there were not one word of promise written that was made to us expressing God's mind, yet this everlasting obligation made all sure it should be done.[113]

> It is agreed between God and Christ, that the elect shall be converted invincibly and infallibly, and that saving faith shall be bestowed on them, and that they shall persevere in the obedience of faith so, as they shall not totally and finally fall away from Gods grace.[114]

Dickson contends that the covenant of redemption makes "the mater fast concerning the elect, founding their conversion, faith, repentance, perseverance, and salvation, upon the unchangeable covenant of Redemption, fixed upon the setled agreement between God, and God the Son Mediatour and Redeemer."[115] Precisely because "the decree of redemption is in effect a covenant,"[116] the covenant of redemption in God *ad intra* has an intimate connection with salvation as God's economic work of redemption in history.

Knowing that salvation does not depend on human performance but on the sheer grace of God's willingness and intention gives the elect comfort and consolation and prompts the life of joy and happiness.

> Hence also it is manifest, how fit a high Priest is appointed over us, who is touched with our infirmities and temptations; by whom we may have so solid consolation in all the pangs of our tormented consciences, and in whom we have a solid foundation laid down to all that flee to him, for setling our faith and hope in the Son of God, who hath of set purpose, with the Fathers consent, suffered so many and great evils that he might redeem us.[117]
>
> This covenant therefore which God made with Christ, to bestow all the merits of his obedience on us, which he called him unto,

---

113. Goodwin, *Of Christ the Mediator*, 33.

114. Dickson, *Therapeutica sacra*, 57. Cited are Ps 110:3; Titus 1:1; Acts 13:48; John 6:37, 39, 44; 10:26, 28; Isa 59:21; Jer 32:40.

115. Dickson, *Therapeutica sacra*, 59.

116. Dickson, *Therapeutica sacra*, 25.

117. Dickson, *Therapeutica sacra*, 55.

> is the main foundation of all our happiness. As it obliged and
> engaged God firmly to us in Christ, so it makes all that Christ
> purchased to be of grace."[118]

The covenant of redemption, as "the source of the covenant of grace," provides "an additional foundation for comfort."[119] God's eternal decree of redemption provides the elect with the source of comfort and a solid foundation of peace and security for faith.

Third, while the covenant of redemption signifies God's sovereign grace of salvation for the elect, at the same time it is also requires human responsibility and participation for its fulfillment in the covenant of grace. As Von Rohr clarifies, the Puritan idea of covenant is both conditional and absolute.

> Puritan theology was not a rational whole, but was drawn by
> its own inner impulses into two directions, those generated by
> the experiential and voluntaristic concerns of Gospel piety and
> those precipitated by the inherited dogmatic demanded for the
> doctrine of predestination. Evangel and election bequeathed to
> Puritan theology a double agenda, and the idea of the covenant
> became, at least in some measure, the point of connection, if
> not also of reconciliation. So the one covenant has two qualities: it is, on the one hand, the instrument of the mutuality of
> divine-human commitment and, on the other hand, the instrument of God's sovereign rule in all that pertains to salvation. In
> the terminology of the Puritans the covenant of grace is both
> conditional and absolute.[120]

Human daily actions and practices do matter in relation to salvation and eternal destiny. Puritan covenant theology constantly affirms both the sovereign grace of God and human responsibility in fulfilling covenantal promise.

> The doctrine of predestination, they would affirm, can be
> thoroughly integrated into the idea of covenant. For one thing,
> predestination does not abolish human action, but enhances it,
> for the divine and the human must go together in fulfillment
> of covenantal conditions. But further, the covenant, in the last
> analysis, is also more than a conditional matters. Its fulfillment

---

118. Goodwin, *Of Christ the Mediator*, 31. Goodwin cites Rom 5:17.
119. Von Rohr, *Covenant of Grace*, 45.
120. Von Rohr, *Covenant of Grace*, 53.

> rests in a still prior sense upon election by God, for the covenant likewise is absolute.[121]

For example, Richard Sibbes says that in covenant "wee enter into tearmes of friendship with God, in the Covenant of Grace."[122] Then Sibbes continues: "Now friends must have the same mind, there must be an answering."[123] The conditional character of covenant still remains here. Particularly the answering act is faith and following obedient life of sanctification.

> Now this answer is especially faith, when we believe, and from Faith, sanctified obedience, that is called the restipulation, or engagement of a good conscience to God, when the promise is made, wee engage our selves to believe, and to live as Christians.[124]

Hence Von Rohr maintains: "Puritans, in affirming contingency but in denying meritoriousness, avoided all charges of work-righteousness and yet saved the conditionality of the covenant."[125]

In this way, the covenant of redemption has practical relevance for salvation, a Christian life of piety, and daily life as a response to God's grace. As the following chapters will show, the covenant of redemption in the trinitarian theology of Jonathan Edwards presents instantiations of some of these practical implications. Before getting into the manifestations of the practical relevance of the covenant of redemption in Edwards's theology, in the next chapter, we shall first examine Edwards's own articulation of the covenant of redemption. It will show that Edwards's theology of the covenant of redemption generally resonates with the articulation of the Protestant scholasticism surveyed above.

---

121. Von Rohr, *Covenant of Grace*, 114–15.
122. Sibbes, *Evangelicall Sacrifices*, 180.
123. Sibbes, *Evangelicall Sacrifices*, 181.
124. Sibbes, *Evangelicall Sacrifices*, 181.
125. Von Rohr, *Covenant of Grace*, 54.

3

Trinity and the Covenant of Redemption in Edwards and the Reformed Tradition

As was surveyed in the previous chapter, by the late seventeenth century, the doctrine of the covenant of redemption was widely shared among the Reformed circles. As will be seen in this chapter, Jonathan Edwards formulated his doctrine of the covenant of redemption with this Reformed background in mind. The purpose of this chapter is to exposit Edwards's doctrine of the covenant of redemption and to show the basic continuity and consistency between Edwards's idea of the covenant of redemption and that of his Reformed predecessors. The idea of the eternal pact between the Father and the Son shows that God's plan of redemption was already conceived in the eternal and internal communion of the trinitarian persons. This eternal agreement of persons in the Trinity indicates that God's economic work of redemption is already implied in the eternal communion of the immanent Trinity. The contention in modern readings that the doctrine of the immanent Trinity is abstruse, speculative, and dissociated from God's economy in the world does not necessarily hold in this doctrinal scope. Since Edwards articulated his doctrine of the covenant of redemption in the context of his doctrine of the Trinity, it is pertinent to start with his exposition of the Trinity.

JONATHAN EDWARDS'S DOCTRINE OF THE TRINITY

Edwards starts his *Discourse on the Trinity* with an affirmation of the perfection and self-sufficiency of God's *ad intra* communion. For Edwards, this contentment and happiness in God's own self entails the co-essential but distinct three divine persons.

> When we speak of God's happiness, the account that we are wont to give of it is that God is infinitely happy in the enjoyment of himself, in perfectly beholding and infinitely loving, and rejoicing in, his own essence and perfections. And accordingly it must be supposed that God perpetually and eternally has a most perfect idea of himself, as it were an exact image and representation of himself ever before him and in actual view. And from hence arises a most pure and perfect energy in the Godhead, which is the divine love, complacence and joy.[1]

Enjoyment of oneself indicates having one's own image and representation within oneself. This idea of the self, according to Edwards, is the Son.[2] Furthermore, the energy in the Godhead as love, complacence, and joy between the Father and the Son proceeds as the Holy Spirit.[3] Edwards's articulation of each divine person is in order.

When God reflects on himself in enjoyment, "The knowledge or view which God has of himself must necessarily be conceived to be something distinct from his mere direct existence."[4]

> If God beholds himself so as thence to have delight and joy in himself, he must become his own object: there must be a duplicity. There is God and the idea of God, if it be proper to call a conception of that that is purely spiritual an idea.
>
> And I do suppose the Deity to be truly and properly repeated by God's thus having an idea of himself; and that this idea of God is a substantial idea and has the very essence of God, is truly God, to all intents and purposes, and that by this means the Godhead is really generated and repeated.[5]

---

1. Edwards, "Discourse on the Trinity," *WJE* 21:113. Steven M. Studebaker examines how the particular interests of the contemporary theology affected the interpretation of Jonathan Edwards's trinitarianism. Studebaker, *Jonathan Edwards's Social Augustinian Trinitarianism*, 11–65. See Pierce, "Suppressed Edwards Manuscript," 68–76; Bushnell, *Christ in Theology*, vi; Park, "Remarks of Jonathan Edwards," 147–87, 333–69; Richardson, "Glory of God"; Sairsingh, "Jonathan Edwards." See also Weber, "Trinitarian Theology of Jonathan Edwards," 297–318.
2. Studebaker, *Jonathan Edwards's Social Augustinian Trinitarianism*, 172–90.
3. Studebaker, *Jonathan Edwards's Social Augustinian Trinitarianism*, 190–99.
4. Edwards, "Discourse on the Trinity," *WJE* 21:114.
5. Edwards, "Discourse on the Trinity," *WJE* 21:114.

God's having an idea of himself amounts to the self-repetition of the divine essence. "This representation of the divine nature and essence is the divine nature and essence again."[6] In this self-repetition and representation begets the second person of the Trinity.

> Hereby there is another person begotten; there is another infinite, eternal, almighty, and most holy and the same God, the very same divine nature.
>
> And this person is the second person in the Trinity, the only begotten and dearly beloved Son of God. He is the eternal, necessary, perfect, substantial and personal idea which God hath of himself.[7]

God's beholding of himself and enjoyment of the self entail the second person of the Trinity.

While this account of the second person of the Trinity might sound speculative for modern trinitarian theologians, it is notable to recognize here that Edwards confirms this view based on ample examples from his biblical exegesis.[8] For example, citing John 12:45, 14:7-9, and 15:22-24, Edwards argues:

> Seeing the perfect idea of a thing is to all intents and purposes the same as seeing the thing; it is not only equivalent to the seeing of it, but it *is* the seeing it: for there is no other seeing but having the idea. Now by seeing a perfect idea, so far as we see it we have it; but it can't be said of anything else, that in seeing of it we see another, strictly speaking, except it be the very idea of the other.[9]

This proposition is corroborated by biblical representation of the Son as the "image of God that is the object of God's eternal and infinite love" (Prov 8:30),[10] as "the face of God" (Exod 33:14),[11] as "the brightness, effulgence or shining forth of God's glory,"[12] as "the wisdom of God" (1 Cor 1:24; Luke 11:49; Prov 8:22-31),[13] as "the logos of God," or as "the AMEN" (truth).[14]

---

6. Edwards, "Discourse on the Trinity," *WJE* 21:116.
7. Edwards, "Discourse on the Trinity," *WJE* 21:116-17.
8. Caldwell, *Communion in the Spirit*, 28-32.
9. Edwards, "Discourse on the Trinity," *WJE* 21:118.
10. Edwards, "Discourse on the Trinity," *WJE* 21:118.
11. Edwards, "Discourse on the Trinity," *WJE* 21:118.
12. Edwards, "Discourse on the Trinity," *WJE* 21:119.
13. Edwards, "Discourse on the Trinity," *WJE* 21:119.
14. Edwards, "Discourse on the Trinity," *WJE* 21:120.

> I think we may be bold to say that which is the form, face, and express and perfect image of God, in beholding which God has eternal delight, and is also the wisdom, knowledge, logos and truth of God, is God's idea of himself. What other knowledge of God is there that is the form, appearance, and perfect image and representation of God, but God's idea of himself?[15]

Edwards's articulation of the inner trinitarian communion between the Father and the Son is based on the divine revelation in Jesus Christ testified in the Scripture.

In other words, Edwards's account of the second person in the immanent Trinity is based on God's economic work in the world. In this regard, Edwards makes a significant remark here:

> The inward word is the pattern or original of which the outward word, by which God has revealed himself, is the copy. Now that which is the original, from whence the revelation which God hath made of himself is taken and the pattern to which it is conformed, is God's idea of himself. When God declares himself, it is doubtless from and according to the idea he hath of himself.[16]

This statement indicates that Edwards explicates the second person of the Trinity in the immanent Trinity based on biblical revelation in God's economic work. Using the terms of Reformed scholastics, the ectypal manifestation of God's trinitarian work in the world is based on and consistent with the archetypal inner-relatedness of God's *ad intra* communion. Because the Scripture testifies that God has revealed himself through his Son, Jesus Christ, as his own image and representation, it is safely assumed that the second person of the Trinity is the image and representation of God's self in the immanent Trinity also.

The same reasoning takes place when Edwards gives an account of the Holy Spirit.[17] For Edwards, the Holy Spirit is the deity in act, love and joy itself between the Father and the Son.

> The Godhead being thus begotten by God's having an idea of himself and standing forth in a distinct subsistence or person in that idea, there proceeds a most pure act, and an infinitely holy and sweet energy arises between the Father and Son: for their love and joy is mutual, in mutually loving and delighting in each other. Proverbs 8:30, "I was daily his delight, rejoicing

---

15. Edwards, "Discourse on the Trinity," *WJE* 21:120.
16. Edwards, "Discourse on the Trinity," *WJE* 21:120.
17. Caldwell, *Communion in the Spirit*, 32–33.

always before [him]." This is the eternal and most perfect and essential act of the divine nature, wherein the Godhead acts to an infinite degree and in the most perfect manner possible. The Deity becomes all act; the divine essence itself flows out and is as it were breathed forth in love and joy. So that the Godhead therein stands forth in yet another manner of subsistence, and there proceeds the third person in the Trinity, the Holy Spirit, viz. the Deity in act: for there is no other act but the act of the will.[18]

Edwards provides scriptural foundations for the proposition that the Holy Spirit is the deity in act, the perfect love and joy flowing forth between the Father and the Son. First, the Word of God tells that "the Godhead or the divine nature and essence does subsist in love" (1 John 4:8).[19] Second, the name of the third person of the Trinity, the Holy Spirit, "expresses the divine nature as subsisting in pure act and perfect energy, and as flowing out and breathing forth in infinitely sweet and vigorous affection."[20] Third, this character resonates with the work of the Holy Spirit with respect to creatures: "to quicken, enliven and beautify all things; to sanctify intelligent [creatures]; and to comfort and delight them" (Gen 1:2; 1 John 4:12–13; 1 Thess 1:6).[21] Fourth, the emblem of the Holy Spirit as love and diffusiveness resonates with types and metaphors used for the Holy Spirit in Scripture such as "water, fire, breath, wind, oil, wine, a spring, a river, a being poured out and shed forth, a being breathed forth" (Titus 3:5–6; Matt 3:17; Ps 133:1–2; John 7:38–39; Ps 36:8).[22] Fifth, the idea that the Holy Spirit is the love and delight can be confirmed by Scripture which testifies that "the saints' communion with God consists in their partaking of the Holy Ghost."[23]

> Communion is a common partaking of goods, either of excellency or happiness. So that when it is said the saints have communion or fellowship with the Father and with the Son, the meaning of it is that they partake with the Father and the Son of their good.[24]

---

18. Edwards, "Discourse on the Trinity," *WJE* 21:121.
19. Edwards, "Discourse on the Trinity," *WJE* 21:121.
20. Edwards, "Discourse on the Trinity," *WJE* 21:122.
21. Edwards, "Discourse on the Trinity," *WJE* 21:123.
22. Edwards, "Discourse on the Trinity," *WJE* 21:129.
23. Edwards, "Discourse on the Trinity," *WJE* 21:129.
24. Edwards, "Discourse on the Trinity," *WJE* 21:129.

For Edwards, the Holy Spirit as love and happiness is amply demonstrated through predicates attributed to the works of the Holy Spirit attested in Scripture.

While the New Testament frequently suggests that the Father loves the Son and the Son loves the Father, deity and personhood of the Holy Spirit is not much articulated. Edwards raises this question in his treatise on grace: "though we often read in Scripture of the Father loving the Son, and the Son loving the Father, yet we never once read either of the Father or the Son loving the Holy Spirit, and the Spirit loving either of them."[25] Edwards's answer to this question is simply that the Holy Spirit *is* the love itself between the Father and the Son.

> It is because the Holy Spirit is the divine love itself, the love of the Father and the Son. Hence also it is to be accounted for, that we very often read of the love both of the Father and the Son to men, and particularly their love to the saints; but we never read of the Holy Ghost loving them, for the Holy Ghost is that love of God and Christ that is breathed forth primarily towards each other, and flows out secondarily towards the creature. This also will well account for it, that the apostle Paul so often wishes grace, mercy and peace from God the Father, and from the Lord Jesus Christ, in the beginning of his epistles, without even mentioning the Holy Ghost, because the Holy Ghost is himself the love and grace of God the Father and the Lord Jesus Christ.[26]

This implicit character of the Holy Spirit is the reason why the description of the divine persons in the New Testament is seemingly "binitarian."[27] This "hiddenness" of the Holy Spirit is due to the fact that the Holy Spirit is the bond of union itself between the Father and the Son.[28] The holiness of God consists in "his love, especially in the perfect and intimate union and love there is between the Father and the Son."[29] In fact, "the Spirit that proceeds from the Father and the Son is the bond of this union."[30] As Roland A. Delattre points out, "God's holiness is not simply an idea or quality of God but is something of the substantial reality of God's very being"[31] because

---

25. Edwards, "Treatise on Grace," *WJE* 21:186.
26. Edwards, "Treatise on Grace," *WJE* 21:186.
27. Caldwell, *Communion in the Spirit*, 48.
28. Caldwell, *Communion in the Spirit*, 47.
29. Edwards, "Treatise on Grace," *WJE* 21:186.
30. Edwards, "Treatise on Grace," *WJE* 21:186. See also Studebaker, *Jonathan Edwards's Social Augustinian Trinitarianism*, 196–99.
31. Delattre, *Beauty and Sensibility*, 152.

this mutual love between the Father and the Son *is* the Holy Spirit. This portrayal of the Holy Spirit as the bond of union between the Father and the Son is, as Studebaker points out, "a key datum for locating Edwards within the Augustinian trinitarian tradition."[32]

It is true that Edwards wrote at one point that reason can sufficiently tell that there must be three distinctions within the deity. He says:

> Reason is sufficient to tell us that there must be these distinctions in the Deity, viz. of God (absolutely considered), and the idea of God, and love and delight; and there are no other real distinctions in God that can be thought [of].[33]

Yet as has been shown above, it is also to be noted that Edwards was convinced that what reason can plumb is consistent with and can be confirmed by revelation in God's economic work attested in Scripture. Even this seemingly speculative account of the ontological contours of the immanent Trinity is actually developed within the scope of the economic work of the Trinity *ad extra*. As Sang Hyun Lee points out, the intimate connection between the immanent and the economic Trinity is crucial to unpack Edwards's trinitarian theology.

> The continuity of the immanent and economic Trinity is a hallmark of Edwards's theology. For Edwards, God's inner life is not a puzzle subject to theologians speculations but rather a living truth about God that emerges from the believers' heartfelt experiences of God's self-communication of himself in Jesus Christ and in all history and space. What believers have experienced from God's redemptive activities in their own lives is a reflection of the way God himself is in his own life *ad intra*. In this way, Edwards restores the Trinity doctrine's original connection with the lived faith of the Christian community.[34]

The economic Trinity is the *ad extra* ectypal unfolding of the immanent Trinity: God *ad intra* as the archetype. With this exposition of the crux of Edwards's ontological Trinity, it is pertinent to move into his discourse on the covenant of redemption.

---

32. Studebaker, *Jonathan Edwards's Social Augustinian Trinitarianism*, 199.

33. Edwards, "Discourse on the Trinity," *WJE* 21:131. "I think that it is within the reach of naked reason to perceive certainly that there are three distinct in God, each of which is the same [God], three that must be distinct" (Edwards, *WJE* 13:257)

34. Lee, "Editor's Introduction," *WJE* 21:31.

DEFINITION OF THE COVENANT OF REDEMPTION IN EDWARDS

Edwards provides a definition of the covenant of redemption that is broadly consistent with that of the Reformed tradition explored in the previous chapter. According to Edwards, the covenant of redemption is "the eternal Covenant that there was between the F & the Son which X undertook to stand as mediator for fallen men."[35] The definition of the covenant of redemption as the eternal agreement between the Father and the Son for the purpose of redeeming the elect is consistent between Edwards and the preceding Reformed tradition.

Edwards's most developed articulation of the covenant of redemption can be found in his miscellany 1062. This miscellany was first published by Egbert C. Smyth in 1880 with the tile: *Observations concerning the Scripture Oeconomy of the Trinity and Covenant of Redemption*.[36] On this miscellany, Sang Lee notes: "Edwards strongly affirmed the equal divinity of each of the persons of the Trinity, but at the same time he talked about an order of being and of acting among them upon which God's activities are based."[37] With this observation in mind, Lee discerns five interrelated levels in Edwards's doctrine of the Trinity.

First, according to Lee, Edwards affirms "the ontological equality of the three persons."[38] Edwards states:

> Tis very manifest that the persons of the Trinity are not inferior one to another in glory and excellency of nature. The Son, for instance, is not inferior to the Father in glory; for he is the brightness of his glory, the very image of the Father and the express and perfect image of his person. And therefore the Father's infinite happiness is in him, and the way that the Father enjoys the glory of the Deity is in enjoying him.[39]

Because the Son is the repetition and image of the Father and the Holy Spirit is himself love and joy between the Father and the Son, all three persons are ontologically equal.

Lee says that the second level is "the order of subsisting among the three persons, and is a matter of their origin and relation."[40] Because "with

---

35. Edwards, "Sermon on 1 Cor 13:1–10," *WJE* 53:L.6v.
36. Edwards, *Observations*. See also Helm, *Treatise on Grace*, 1–23.
37. Lee, "Editor's Introduction," *WJE* 21:27.
38. Lee, "Editor's Introduction," *WJE* 21:28.
39. Edwards, *WJE* 20:430.
40. Lee, "Editor's Introduction," *WJE* 21:28.

respect to his subsistence he is wholly from the Father and begotten by him," the Father has "a priority of subsistence" though it is not "superiority." Hence, there is "a kind of dependence of the Son, in his subsistence, on the Father."[41] In the same way, because the Holy Spirit proceeds from the Father and the Son, the Holy Spirit is "in some respect dependent" on them.[42] These priority and dependence derive from "the natural order of the eternal and necessary subsistence of the persons of the Trinity."[43]

Third, Lee sees the correspondence between the order of subsisting and the order of acting in Edwards's doctrine of the Trinity. There is an "order of their acting that is agreeable to the order of their subsisting."[44] Edwards explains:

> That as the Father is first in the order of subsisting, so he should be first in the order of acting; that as the other two persons are from the Father in their subsistence, and as to their subsistence naturally originated from him and dependent on him, so that, in all that they act, they should originate from him, act from him and in a dependence on him; that as the Father, with respect to the subsistences, is the fountain of the Deity, wholly and entirely so, so he should be the fountain in all the acts of the Deity.[45]

Because three persons have specific order and manner of subsistence, whenever divine persons move forth to economic transactions, it is fitting that they act in accordance with this order of subsistence. As Lee notes, these three prior levels constitute the background for the covenant of redemption.[46] While it is God's disposition to communicate his glory, the concrete decision to choose a particular method and scheme for channeling out this disposition should logically follow the order of procession and acting among the divine persons. The covenant of redemption, which is "an establishment of wisdom wonderfully contriving a particular method for the most conveniently obtaining a great end," and "that establishment that is founded in fitness and decency and the natural order of the eternal and necessary subsistence of the persons of the Trinity" need to be distinguished.[47] The latter (the necessary subsistence) constitutes the background and foundation for the former (the covenant of redemption).

 41. Edwards, *WJE* 20:430.
 42. Edwards, *WJE* 20:431.
 43. Edwards, *WJE* 20:432.
 44. Edwards, *WJE* 20:433.
 45. Edwards, *WJE* 20:431.
 46. Lee, "Editor's Introduction," *WJE* 21:29.
 47. Edwards, *WJE* 20:432.

Thus Lee lists the fourth level, namely, the covenant of redemption: "the agreement that the Father and the Son primarily make in their plans to redeem the fallen creation."[48] This is a new determination added to the prior natural constitution and necessary subsistence.

> It is evident by the Scripture that there is an eternal covenant between some of the persons of the Trinity about that particular affair of man's redemption; and therefore that some things that appertain to the particular office of each person, and their particular order and manner of acting in this affair, does result from a particular, new agreement, and not merely from the order already fixed in a preceding establishment founded in the nature of things, together with the new determination of redeeming mankind. There is something else new besides a new, particular determination of a work to be done for God's glorifying and communicating himself: there is a particular covenant entered into about that very affair, settling something new concerning the part that some, at least, of the persons are to act in that affair.[49]

This covenantal transaction is initiated by the Father, which is very much in line with the account of the Protestant orthodoxy surveyed in the previous chapter.[50] The Father makes a proposal regarding the redemption of a portion of the fallen humanity.

> It is the Father that begins that great transaction of the eternal covenant of redemption, is the first mover in it, and acts in every respect as Head in that affair. He determines to allow a redemption, and for whom it shall be. He pitches upon a person for a Redeemer. He proposes the matter unto him, offers him authority for the office, proposes precisely what he should do as the terms of man's redemption, and all the work that he should perform in this affair, and the reward he should receive, and the success he should have.[51]

In response to the Father's proposal, the Son agrees and consents to this plan of redemption freely, without compulsion or obligation. This pact is "a free covenant entered into between him and his Son," and by entering this covenant, "the Son (though he acts on the proposal of the Father) yet

---

48. Lee, "Editor's Introduction," *WJE* 21:29.

49. Edwards, *WJE* 20:432–433.

50. See for example Goodwin, *Works*, 1:7–11; Witsius, *Oeconomy of the Covenants*, 222.

51. Edwards, *WJE* 20:435–36.

acts as one wholly in his own right, as much as the Father, being not under subjection or prescription in his consenting to what is proposed to him, but acting as of himself."[52]

The fifth level in Edwards's doctrine of the Trinity, according to Lee, derives from this new arrangement called the covenant of redemption.[53] It entails "a new kind of subordination and mutual obligation between two of the persons, arising from this new establishment."[54] As a consequence of the mutual covenant between the Father and the Son, mutually agreed subordination takes place. This mutually agreed subordination involves more than the natural order of subsistence of persons of the Trinity. Given that the Father is, as "supreme rector, legislator and judge," the person who is "especially injured by sin, and who is therefore the person whose wrath is enkindled, and whose justice and vengeance is to be executed and must be satisfied," it seems natural that the Father is the first mover who initiates this covenantal proposal to the Son.[55] However, Edwards also hastily adds that the covenant of redemption is, though based on the prior natural order of subsistence and consistent with it, an agreement that includes something more and new. That is to say, in the covenant of redemption, the Father prescribes to the Son humiliation and subjection far beyond what the natural order of subsistence would entail.

> The whole tenor of the gospel holds this forth: that the Son acts altogether freely, and as in his own right, in undertaking the great and difficult and self-abasing work of our redemption, and that he becomes obliged to the Father with respect to it by voluntary covenant engagements, and not by any establishment prior thereto; so that he merits infinitely of the Father in entering into and fulfilling these engagements. The Father, merely by his economical prerogative, can direct and prescribe to the other persons of the Trinity in all things not below their economical character. But all those things that imply something below the infinite majesty and glory of divine persons, and which they can't do without as it were laying aside the divine glory, and stooping infinitely below the height of that glory, those things are below their oeconomical divine character, and therefore the Father can't prescribe to other persons anything of this nature, without a new establishment by free covenant empowering him so to do. But what is agreed for with the Son concerning his

---

52. Edwards, *WJE* 20:436.
53. Lee, "Editor's Introduction," *WJE* 21:29.
54. Edwards, *WJE* 20:437.
55. Edwards, *WJE* 20:433.

> coming into the world in such a state of humiliation, and what he should do and suffer in that state, is his descending to a state infinitely below his divine dignity; and therefore the Father has no right to prescribe to him with regard to those things, unless as invested with a right by free covenant engagements of his Son.[56]

Because this transaction for the redemption of the elect requires "stooping infinitely below the height" of the divine glory of the Son, it necessitates a new establishment in which both the Father and the Son voluntarily come into an agreement.

In this agreement, the Son takes on human flesh and comes down into the world by humbling himself, and the Father empowers the Son to carry out this plan of redemption by bestowing the Father's authority. On the part of the Son, under this newly established pact, he undertakes "to put himself into a new kind of subjection to the Father, far below that of his oeconomical station, even the subjection of a proper servant to the Father and one under his law," "engaging to become a creature, and so to put himself in the proper circumstances of a servant."[57] On the part of the Father, he "acquires a new right of headship and authority over the Son, to command him and prescribe to him and rule over him as his proper lawgiver and judge." At the same time, the Father also "comes under new obligation to the Son, to give him such success, rewards, etc."[58] Furthermore, the Father commissions the Son as his "vicegerent." The Father appoints the Son as the "head of authority and rule to the universe, as Lord and Judge of all."[59] Though this authority belongs to the Father according to the natural order of subsistence, according to the covenant of redemption, the Son is by the Father "advanced into his throne, by having the Father's authority committed unto him, to rule in his name and as his vicegerent."[60] This is the reward and special arrangement that obtains until the end of the world when God's plan of redemption is completed.

> This the Father promised him in the covenant of redemption, as a reward for the forementioned subjection and obedience that he engaged in that covenant. And to put him under greater advantages to obtain the success of his labors and sufferings in the work of redemption, this vicarious dominion of the Son is to

---

56. Edwards, *WJE* 20:436.
57. Edwards, *WJE* 20:437.
58. Edwards, *WJE* 20:437.
59. Edwards, *WJE* 20:439.
60. Edwards, *WJE* 20:439.

continue to the end of the world, when the work of redemption will be finished, and the ends of the covenant of redemption obtained, when things will return to be administered by the Trinity only according to their economical order.[61]

In this way, based on the internal glory and excellency equally shared among the persons of the Trinity and still inherent natural order of personal subsistence, the Father and the Son set out into a mutual agreement that goes beyond the natural order of God's internal being in order to put into practice God's plan of redemption for the elect. This is Edwards's covenant of redemption.

As noted in chapter 1, Amy Plantinga Pauw finds in Edwards's doctrine of the Trinity two strands: the social vein and the psychological vein.[62] According to this paradigm, the articulation of the Trinity in *Discourse on the Trinity* indicates the psychological vein, whereas the discussion of the covenant of redemption signifies the social model of the Trinity. Thus, Plantinga Pauw concludes about Edwards's doctrine of the covenant of redemption that an "unnuanced social model of the Trinity risks succumbing to tritheism."[63]

However, this is an anachronistic application of the threeness-oneness paradigm to a trinitarian theology of the eighteenth century.[64] While Edwards does use words such as "family" and "society" when he articulates the doctrine of the Trinity,[65] this usage does not imply the social trinitarian sense in a modern sense today as Plantinga Pauw takes it.[66] If she charges the Edwards's doctrine of the covenant of redemption as tritheism, then, given that Edwards follows his Reformed predecessors in the rendition of this doctrine, her charge has to be applied also to other Reformed scholastics such as David Dickson, Herman Witsius, Petrus van Mastricht, and Francis Turretin.

In an initial observation, it seems that the picture of two divine persons consulting with each other making an agreement looks closer to a social trinitarian model where each person has his own consciousness and will. This is why Plantinga Pauw charges the doctrine of the covenant of redemption as "anthropomorphism"[67] and contends that "the notion of *pactum*

61. Edwards, *WJE* 20:439.
62. Pauw, *Supreme Harmony of All*, 30–55.
63. Pauw, *Supreme Harmony of All*, 114.
64. Studebaaker, *Jonathan Edwards's Social Augustinian Trinitarianism*, 64, 88–107
65. Edwards, *WJE* 18:367; *WJE* 18:110
66. Pauw, *Supreme Harmony of All*, 30–41.
67. Pauw, *Supreme Harmony of All*, 114–15.

salutis, the eternal covenant of redemption made between the Father and the Son on behalf of human sinners, lent itself to a variety of explicitly social metaphors for the Godhead."[68] However, as Studebaker and Caldwell point out, it is to be noted that "the entire discussion assumes a logically prior decision by the Godhead to reflect economically the order of the immanent subsistent relations."[69] Thus even a covenantal transaction between the Father and the Son assumes subsistence of divine persons in one substance,[70] the Son as the divine understanding and the Holy Spirit as divine will. Even in the transaction of the covenant of redemption made by distinct trinitarian persons, "the ontological and scholastic definition of person was most fundamental to his trinitarian thinking."[71]

Plantinga Pauw's charge of tritheism is based on her interpretation of Edwards's doctrine of divine simplicity. The Reformed doctrine of divine simplicity maintains that the divine being and action are one and divine attributes are identical with the divine being.[72] In other words, the being of God is non-composite.[73] Plantinga Pauw seems to think that this doctrine is incompatible with Edwards's articulation of the Trinity based on the idea of excellency.[74] In his miscellany 117, Edwards writes: "We have shown that one alone cannot be excellent, inasmuch as, in such case, there can be no consent. Therefore, if God is excellent, there must be a plurality in God; otherwise, there can be no consent in him."[75] Hence, Plantinga Pauw thinks that "Excellency largely supplanted simplicity as a marker of divine perfection in Edwards's thought" and hence Edwards departed from his Reformed tradition of divine simplicity.[76] Thus she concludes: "While not entirely absent, his use of the simplicity tradition was infrequent and idiosyncratic."[77]

However, despite the charge of Edwards's departure from the Reformed tradition of the divine simplicity, Edwards actually maintained the doctrine of divine simplicity as one of his basic assumptions in the doctrine of the Trinity. In his miscellany 308, Edwards argues:

---

68. Pauw, *Supreme Harmony of All*, 31.
69. Studebaker and Caldwell, *Trinitarian Theology of Jonathan Edwards*, 143.
70. Edwards, *WJE* 20:431.
71. Studebaker and Caldwell, *Trinitarian Theology of Jonathan Edwards*, 143.
72. Studebaker, *Jonathan Edwards's Social Augustinian Trinitarianism*, 94.
73. Muller, *PRRD*, 3:276.
74. Pauw, "One Alone Cannot be Excellent," 115–23. See also Oliver Crisp's treatment of this issue in Crisp, *Jonathan Edwards on God*, 94–116.
75. Edwards, *WJE* 13:284.
76. Pauw, "One Alone Cannot be Excellent," 115.
77. Pauw, *Supreme Harmony of All*, 70.

> In the first place, we don't suppose that the Father, the Son, and the Holy Ghost are three distinct beings that have three distinct understandings. It is the divine essence understands, and it is the divine essence is understood; 'tis the divine being that loves, and it is the divine being that is loved. The Father understands, the Son understands, and the Holy Ghost understands, because *every one is the same understanding divine essence*; and not that each of them have a distinct understanding of their own.[78]

As Studebaker notes, this means that "each divine person understands because each is identical with the one understanding essence."[79] This is consistent with the traditional Reformed understanding of divine simplicity. Edwards is able to talk about the generation of the Son from the Father, the procession of the Holy Spirit from the Father and the Son, and the identity of all these three persons in one essence, precisely because of the doctrine of divine simplicity. "Divine simplicity is the ground," Studebaker argues, for the "identification of the divine persons with the divine essence."[80] Hence, "far from a marginalized doctrine, simplicity was a central presupposition for Edwards's understanding of the trinitarian God."[81]

While Plantinga Pauw appears to think that divine simplicity and divine excellency are not compatible with each other, traditionally the Reformed theology conceived divine simplicity as the foundation for the doctrine of the Trinity. Plantinga Pauw thinks that "the existence of distinct personal agency within the Trinity" would "disturb the uncompundedness of the Deity"[82] Yet "from the time of the fathers onward, divine simplicity was understood as a support of the doctrine of the Trinity and necessarily defined in such a manner as to argue the 'manifold' as well as the non-composite character of God."[83] The "simplicity-Excellency dilemma" simply does not exist in Edwards.[84] In short, the doctrine of divine simplicity and relational excellency of three divine persons do not contradict with

---

78. Edwards, *WJE* 13:392 (emphasis mine). See also Edwards, "Discourse on the Trinity," *WJE* 21:113; "Freedom of the Will," *WJE* 1:377; *WJE* 13:295.

79. Studebaker, *Jonathan Edwards's Social Augustinian Trinitarianism*, 95.

80. Studebaker, *Jonathan Edwards's Social Augustinian Trinitarianism*, 94.

81. Studebaker, *Jonathan Edwards's Social Augustinian Trinitarianism*, 94.

82. Pauw, "One Alone Cannot be Excellent," 120.

83. Muller, *PRRD*, 3:276. Muller also notes that "The correlation of simplicity with Trinity in the theology of the Cappadocians is an element of patristic trinitarianism carefully neglected by modern so-called social Trinitarianism" (Muller, *PRRD*, 3:276n263). See, for example, the work of Prestige that fills this gap in Prestige, *God in Patristic Thought*.

84. Crisp, *Jonathan Edwards on God*, 100–7.

each other in Edwards and this is consistent with his preceding Reformed tradition.

Certainly Edwards does not simply repeat the traditional discourse on the doctrine of the Trinity. At least he finds two areas to be reconceived in his Reformed theological tradition. First, Edwards attempts to reevaluate the place of the Holy Spirit in relation to other divine persons. He thinks that the traditional interpretation of the Holy Spirit as the agent of applying the benefits of salvation to the elect is not enough. The Spirit "does not merely apply the benefits of redemption procured by Christ," but rather the Spirit "is the benefit of redemption."[85]

> Merely to apply to us or immediately to give or hand to us the blessing purchased after it was purchased (as subservient to the other two persons), is but a little thing to the purchasing of it by the paying an infinite price by Christ's offering up himself in sacrifice to procure; and 'tis but a little thing to God the Father's giving his infinitely dear Son to be a sacrifice for us, and upon his purchase to afford to us all the blessings of his purchase.[86]

Accordingly, Edwards thinks that the Holy Spirit is equal in glory to the Son because the Holy Spirit himself *is* the thing purchased. Edwards says: "to be [the] thing purchased was as much as to be the price: the price, and the thing bought with that price, are equal."[87]

Second, he had a difficulty in interpreting the relation between divine attributes and the divine essence. Edwards says:

> It is a maxim amongst divines that everything that is in God is God, which must be understood of real attributes and not of mere modalities. If a man should tell me that the immutability of God is God, or that the omnipresence of God and authority of God [is God], I should not be able to think of any rational meaning of what he said.[88]

While Plantinga Pauw concedes based on this passage that "Edwards self-consciously departed from the scholastic and Puritan consensus regarding the identity of all of God's attributes with God,"[89] it seems that the better

---

85. Studebaker, *Jonathan Edwards's Social Augustinian Trinitarianism*, 98.

86. Edwards, "Discourse on the Trinity," *WJE* 21:137.

87. Edwards, "Discourse on the Trinity," *WJE* 21:137–138. See also Edwards, "Treatise on Grace," *WJE* 21:189–191; Studebaker, *Jonathan Edwards's Social Augustinian Trinitarianism*, 95–98; Studebaker and Caldwell, *Trinitarian Theology of Jonathan Edwards*, 79–81.

88. Edwards, "Discourse on the Trinity," *WJE* 21:132.

89. Pauw, *Supreme Harmony of All*, 72.

assessment is that he simply misunderstood this scholastic maxim.[90] The maxim certainly does not mean that the immutability of God is God. Rather, the "modification of the syntax to 'God is immutable' captures the meaning of the doctrine."[91] Given that Edwards maintained the doctrine of divine simplicity as was seen above, rather than hastily concluding that Edwards departed from the Reformed tradition, it is more plausible to say that for "whatever reason, this explanation eluded Edwards."[92] Hence Studebaker and Caldwell conclude: "His misunderstanding of the scholastic maxim, then, is the anomaly in his doctrine of simplicity that is otherwise consistent with the Reformed scholastic notion of the doctrine."[93] Both the modification of the status of the Holy Spirit and the irregular misunderstanding of the simplicity, then, are within the scope of the broader Reformed tradition Edwards inherited.

BIBLICAL FOUNDATION OF THE COVENANT OF REDEMPTION IN EDWARDS

As overviewed in the previous chapter, the doctrine of the covenant of redemption came into being through exegetical works in collation and comparison of several texts in the Old and the New Testaments. With numerous preceding biblical exegesis and collated comparisons, perhaps Edwards did not have to establish the biblical foundation of the doctrine of the covenant of redemption. Nevertheless, it is possible to identify some of the key texts used to formulate the doctrine in the era of the Reformed orthodoxy such as Ps 40, Isa 53, 1 Pet 1, Luke 22, and Eph 1 also appear as Edwards refers to the covenant of redemption in preaching these texts.[94]

For example, when Edwards preached Ps 40:6–8 on true sacrifice, he saw the execution of the covenant of redemption in Christ's sacrifice and obedience to the will of the Father.

> Christ was under no obligation to offer it till he became mediator, not till he had undertaken to be our surety; indeed, consider him as having already undertaken and having become mediator. And so he became the Father's servant: he was subject to

90. Studebaker, *Jonathan Edwards's Social Augustinian Trinitarianism*, 98–100.

91. Studebaker, *Jonathan Edwards's Social Augustinian Trinitarianism*, 99.

92. Studebaker, *Jonathan Edwards's Social Augustinian Trinitarianism*, 99. See also Studebaker and Caldwell, *Trinitarian Theology of Jonathan Edwards*, 144–152.

93. Studebaker and Caldwell, *Trinitarian Theology of Jonathan Edwards*, 149.

94. Muller, "Toward the *Pactum Salutis*," 25–48; Gerstner, *Rational Biblical Theology*, 2:79–141, esp. 90–94.

> his command, and it was in obedience to his command that he laid down his life. But he was under no obligation to become mediator: that was what he freely consented to in the covenant of redemption.[95]

Christ the mediator's sacrifice as obedience to the Father was the eternal covenant of redemption put into practice.

Also, with regard to Isa 53:10–12, "there were virtually no exegetes in the precritical tradition who did not identify this, together with the other Servant Songs, as teaching of Christ and his work."[96] Reformed scholastics such as Witsius, Coccejus, Burgess, Dickson and Bulkeley cited this text as they formulated this doctrine as a part of their collated exegetical work.[97] Aligned with these theologians of Reformed orthodoxy, Edwards sees in the suffering servant the life and work of redemption of Jesus Christ.

> Christ's success in his work of redemption, in bringing home souls to himself, applying his saving benefits by his spirit, and the advancement of the kingdom of grace in the world, is the reward especially promised to him by his Father in the covenant of redemption, for the hard and difficult service he performed while in the form of a servant; as is manifest by Isaiah 53:10–12.[98]

Edwards sees in the life and work of Jesus Christ the execution of the eternal covenant of redemption.

Another frequently cited passage that contributed to the formulation of the doctrine is 1 Pet 1:20. Herman Witsius, Gulielmus Bucanus, and William Perkins all refer to this passage as they discuss either the covenant of redemption or its trinitarian background.[99] When Edwards expounds the covenant of redemption, he also cites 1 Pet 1:20 ("Who verily was ordained before the foundation of the world, but was manifest in these last times for you"). Then he continues:

> And Christ from all eternity, from his great love to them, undertook to stand for their security, and to die for them. Christ became engaged to the Father to become incarnate, to go through such great labors and extreme sufferings in these conditions;

---

95. Edwards, "Sacrifice of Christ Acceptable," *WJE* 14:451.

96. Muller, "Toward *Pactum Salutis*," 36.

97. Witsius, *Oeconomia foederum*, 224–29; Coccejus, *De leer van het verbond*, 88; Burgess, *True Doctrine of Justification*, 376; Dickson, *Therapeutica sacra*, 36–40; Bulkeley, *Gospel-Covenant*, 29–31.

98. Edwards, "True Saints," *WJE* 25:238.

99. Witsius, *Oeconomia foederum*, 5; Bucanus, *Institutions of Christian Religion*, 28; Perkins, *Works*, 1:24.

that such and such particular persons might be redeemed, might have all their sins pardoned, and might have eternal life, who were the objects of his eternal love. And God the Father did in that covenant of redemption, give such and such persons by name to Jesus Christ from his eternal love to them.[100]

Texts that pertain to God's eternal appointment of the redeemer and the election of his people that date back to before the foundation of the world contributed to the formation of this doctrine.

Furthermore, Luke 22:29 is also often cited as Reformed scholastics discuss the covenant of redemption.[101] Edwards sees in Luke 22:29 ("I do by covenant dispose unto you a kingdom, as my father by covenant disposed unto me") a correlation between the covenant of redemption and the covenant of grace. As the Greek word "διατίθεμαι" is also used in Acts 3:25 ("Ye are the children of the prophets and of the covenant which God made [διαθήσομαι] with our fathers") and Hebrews 8:10 ("This is the covenant I will make [διαθήσομαι] with the house of Israel"), Edwards concludes that the noun "διαθήκη" that comes from this verb signifies "covenant, which is the word translated 'covenant' in the New Testament."[102] Edwards says: "That the parties contracting in the covenant of redemption are the Father and the Son, but the parties contracting in the covenant of grace, Christ and believers, is what seems to be taught in that Luke 22:29."[103] Because the Son inherited the kingdom from his Father, the Son can confer the kingdom to the elect.[104]

Ephesians 1:1-15 is another text often cited when Reformed scholastics develop the doctrine of the covenant of redemption.[105] Edwards also refers to this passage when he articulates that all divine decrees are in some way or another related to the covenant of redemption. "Hence all the decrees of God are spoken of in Scripture as one purpose which God purposed in Christ Jesus (Eph 1:9–11)."[106] Moreover, when Edwards expounds that all eternal decrees and counsels are subordinate to one "grand affair" of

---

100. Edwards, "Everlasting Love of God," *WJE* 19:480.

101. For Luke 22:29, see Witsius, *Oeconomy of the Covenants*, 2–5; Turretin, *Institution of Elenctic Theology*, 177; Piscator, *Analysis*, 380–82; Diodati, *Pious and Learned Annotations*.

102. Edwards, *WJE* 20:445.

103. Edwards, *WJE* 20:445.

104. Muller, "Toward the *Pactum Salutis*," 24–25.

105. Dickson, *Therapeutica sacra*, 25; Witsius, *Oeconomia foederum*, 6; Wollebius, *Compendium theologiae christiana*, 25. See also Williams, "Decree of Redemption," 195–96, 210–11.

106. Edwards, "Approaching the End," *WJE* 25:119.

redemption, the covenant of redemption, and the purpose is to magnify God's infinitely rich mercy, he cites Eph 1:5–7 together with Rom 9:23 and Eph 2:4–7.

> But God's declared design in this grand affair is to magnify the infinite riches of his grace. Romans 9:23, "That he might make known the riches of his glory on the vessels of mercy." Ephesians 1:5–7, "Having predestinated us unto the adoption of children by Jesus Christ to himself, according to the good pleasure of his will, to the praise of the glory of his grace, wherein he hath made us accepted in the beloved. In whom we have redemption through his blood, the forgiveness of sins, according to the riches of his grace." And Ephesians 2, Ephesians 2:4–7, "But God, who is rich in mercy, for his great love wherewith he loved us, even when we were dead in sins, hath quickened us together with Christ, (by grace ye are saved); and hath raised us up together, and made us sit together in heavenly places in Christ Jesus: that in the ages to come he might show the exceeding riches of his grace in his kindness toward us through Christ Jesus."[107]

Because these texts support that the elect have been predestined to be saved as God's adopted children from before the foundation of the world, together with other collated texts, it was plausible that the doctrine of the covenant of redemption came into being.

In sum, many of the key Bible texts that collectively formulated the doctrine of the covenant of redemption in the preceding era also appear in Edwards's own articulation of this doctrine. Edwards owned several books that address the covenant of redemption written by major Reformed scholastics such as *Oeconomia foederum* by Herman Witsius, William Perkins's (1558–1602) *Works* that includes *The Golden Chaine*,[108] Samuel Willard's (1640–1707) *The Doctrine of the Covenant of Redemption*,[109] Petrus van Mastricht's (1630–1706) *Theoretico-practica theologia*,[110] or Francis Turretin's (1623–1687) *Institutio theologiae elencticae*.[111] Contrary to Loonstra

---

107. Edwards, "Terms of Prayer," *WJE* 19:776.
108. Perkins, *Golden Chaine*.
109. Willard, *Doctrine of the Covenant*.
110. Mastricht, *Theoretico-practica theologia*. For more on Petrus van Mastricht, see Neele, *Petrus van Mastricht*; Neele, *Art of Living to God*; Goudriaan, *Reformed Orthodoxy and Philosophy*.
111. Turretin, *Institutio theologiae elencticae*. Edwards probably owned a 1688–89, 1696, or 1701 set. See Edwards, *WJE* 13:384n5; "Catalogues of Books," *WJE* 28:341–42, 152–53, 199, 339, 349–50. For more on Edwards's intellectual context and background of readings, see Fiering, *Jonathan Edwards's Moral Thought*, 13–47; Morris, *Young Jonathan Edwards*, 219–86.

and Beckwith who argue that the doctrine of *pactum salutis* is not supported by plausible exegetical groundwork, this doctrine actually came into being "out of a concerted examination of a series of biblical texts, collated with one another, according to the typical methods of the era, in concert with a series of theological issues, both positive and polemical."[112] Based on the biblical texts Edwards uses to infer the doctrine of the covenant of redemption, it seems plausible to say that Edwards formulates this doctrine in line with the preceding exegetical works of Reformed scholastics.

DOCTRINAL FORMULATION OF THE COVENANT OF REDEMPTION IN EDWARDS

Perry Miller argues that Edwards "threw over the whole covenant scheme" and "declared God unfettered by any agreement or obligation."[113] Furthermore, Miller maintains that "The Federal Theology is conspicuous in his sermon by its utter absence."[114] However, the preceding examination amply shows that the opposite is actually the case. That is to say, Jonathan Edwards inherited a continental and English Puritan Reformed tradition of covenant theology.[115] As Bruce Stephens summarizes, "The idea of the covenant is grounded in the doctrine of the trinity, and rather than abandoning covenant theology, Edwards sought to restore its trinitarian base."[116] In this section, I lay out contours of the doctrine of the covenant of redemption in Edwards in relation to the doctrine of divine decree, covenant of works, and covenant of grace.

As was seen in the previous chapter, the divine decree of redemption logically precedes the establishment of covenant. Even the eternal covenant of redemption is logically preceded by divine decree of redeeming the sinners. "The covenant itself," Kevin Woongsan Kang writes, "is established in the first place for the purpose of redemption as a way/method/means to execute the decree of salvation."[117] God's covenant arrangement is to establish a framework through which God's decree of the redemption of the elect is carried into practice. This precedence of the divine decree over the covenant of redemption is true also in Edwards.

---

112. Muller, "Toward the *Pactum Salutis*," 64.
113. Miller, *Errand into the Wilderness*, 98.
114. Miller, *Jonathan Edwards*, 30.
115. See also Cherry, "Puritan Notion of the Covenant," 328–41.
116. Stephens, *God's Last Metaphor*, 6.
117. Kang, "Justified by Faith in Christ," 37.

> God could not decree before the foundation of the world, to save all that should believe in, and obey Christ, unless he had absolutely decreed that salvation should be provided, and effectually wrought out by Christ.[118]

Edwards makes a distinction between the covenant of redemption and the covenant of grace. On the one hand, the covenant of redemption is "The covenant of God the Father with the Son, and with all the elect in him, whereby things are said to be given in Christ before the world began, and to be promised before the world began."[119] On the other hand, referring to the covenant of grace as the marriage covenant, Edwards explains: "There is another covenant that is the marriage covenant between Christ and the soul, the covenant of union, or whereby the soul becomes united to Christ."[120] These two covenants are "by no means to be confounded one with another."[121]

Yet as Kang notes, "it is often found to be the case in Edwards that neither the covenant of redemption nor the covenant of grace are conceived apart from one another."[122] Ultimately Edwards perceives these two covenants within a unified perspective of God's overarching work of redemption.[123]

> The due consideration of these things may perhaps reconcile the difference between those divines that think [the covenant of redemption] and the covenant of grace the same, and those that think 'em different. The covenant that God the Father makes with believers is indeed the very same with the covenant of redemption made with Christ before the foundation of the world, or at least is entirely included in it.[124]

For Edwards, the covenant of grace is included in the covenant of redemption in the sense that the covenant of grace stems from the eternal covenant in the immanent Trinity. The covenant of grace is a part of the movement that originates from the covenant of redemption and reaches out to the world. In his sermon on Heb 13:8, Edwards maintains: "And the covenant of grace is not essentially different from the covenant of redemption: it is but an expression of it: it is only that covenant of redemption partly revealed to

---

118. Edwards, "Freedom of the Will," *WJE* 1:286.
119. Edwards, *WJE* 18:536.
120. Edwards, *WJE* 18:537.
121. Edwards, *WJE* 18:536.
122. Kang, "Justified by Faith in Christ," 34.
123. Kang, "Justified by Faith in Christ," 34–38.
124. Edwards, *WJE* 20:477–78.

mankind for their encouragement, faith, and comfort."[125] Thus for Edwards, the covenant of grace is "not a different covenant but understood to be the continuation of, or within the scope of, the covenant of redemption." Simply put, the covenant of grace is "but an expression of the eternal covenant of redemption in time."[126]

As Kang correctly points out, the center that unifies the covenant of redemption and the covenant of grace is Jesus Christ. Christ is "a center that holds them together in one perspective."[127] In the same sermon Edwards declares:

> And therefore the fact that Christ never departs from the covenant of redemption, infers that he will never departs from the covenant of grace; for all that was promised to men in the covenant of grace, was agreed on between the Father and the Son in the covenant of redemption.[128]

When the eternal pact was made between the Father and the Son, via the union with Christ, the Father envisaged the entire church elect, saints as the people of God.

> When the promises were made to Christ (the covenant of grace), he was not alone without us in God's mind. Likewise, when the promises are made to us (the covenant of grace), we are not alone without Christ. Thus for Edwards, Christ puts these covenants in one perspective. Also, the fact that the Father made the covenants not directly with us but with Christ highlights that Christ is the center in both covenants. The former is made in eternity and the latter is the manifestation of the former in time.[129]

> The covenant that God made with Christ (covenant of redemption) is in essence no different from the covenant that He made with Christ's spouse (covenant of grace) because Christ (Head) and spouse (member) are united as one in God's sight. The union idea actually binds the covenants into a perspective.[130]

---

125. Edwards, "Sermon on Hebrews 13:8," *WJE* 2:950.
126. Kang, "Justified by Faith in Christ," 35.
127. Kang, "Justified by Faith in Christ," 35.
128. Edwards, "Sermon on Hebrews 13:8," *WJE* 2:950.
129. Kang, "Justified by Faith in Christ," 37.
130. Kang, "Justified by Faith in Christ," 43.

Because Christ is both in covenant with the Father and the church elect at the same time, the covenant of redemption and the covenant of grace are ultimately one covenant.

Edwards also sees the relation between the covenant of grace and the covenant of works in a unified perspective. For Edwards, the covenant of works has never lost its validity. The covenant of works is that "which God entered into with angels and men, is what God will never depart from." It is "an eternal rule of righteousness" that requires "perfect obedience as the condition of eternal life."[131] In fact, Edwards plainly states: "God never made but one with man to wit, the covenant of works; which never yet was abrogated, but is a covenant stands in full force to all eternity without the failing of one tittle."[132] In this sense, the covenant of works as God's law stands forever.

The difference between the covenant of works and the covenant of grace, then, is the agent who fulfills the required legal standard. When humankind fell in sin and failed to honor God's law, the Son of God instead fulfilled the obedience to the divine law on behalf of the elect.

> It therefore became Christ, seeing that in assuming man to himself, he sought a title to this eternal happiness for him, after he had broken the law, that he himself should become subject to God's authority, and be in the form of a servant, that he might do that honor to God's authority for him, by his obedience which God at first required of man, as the condition of his having a title to that reward. Christ came into the world to that end, to render the honor of God's authority and law, consistent with the salvation and eternal life of sinners; he came to save them, and yet withal to assert and vindicate the honor of the Lawgiver, and his holy law.[133]

The works "as the condition to the first Adam is fulfilled by Christ the second Adam's work."[134] Edwards says:

> The covenant of grace is not another covenant made with man upon the abrogation of this, but a covenant made with Christ to fulfill it. And for this end came Christ into the world, to fulfill the law, or covenant of works, for all that receive him.[135]

---

131. Edwards, "God Never Changes His Mind," 5.
132. Edwards, *WJE* 13:217.
133. Edwards, "Justification by Faith Alone," *WJE* 19:188.
134. Kang, "Justified by Faith in Christ," 59.
135. Edwards, *WJE* 13:217.

Trinity and the Covenant of Redemption in Edwards and the Reformed Tradition   75

In sum, "In form and substance, the two covenants are largely continuous, and the second is related to the first as means to end."[136] "Adam's failure as the first head/surety did not nullify headship altogether," Kang summarizes, "The headship is picked up and continued by Christ, thus, our second head/surety."[137]

This understanding of the relation between the covenant of works and the covenant of grace is basically consistent with the broader Reformed and Puritan tradition. William K. B. Stoever sums up the relation between these two covenants:

> In Puritan covenant theology, the terms and the form of God's dealing with mankind for salvation are established in the covenant of works at the foundation of the world, and the covenant of grace functions as a means of applying to the elect the righteousness obtained by Christ, who satisfies the conditions of the first covenant. Under the covenant of grace, obedience is performed for men by Christ, the resulting righteousness belonging personally to Christ and being imputed to men by God."[138]

Therefore, as was in the relation between the covenant of redemption and the covenant of grace, here too, Christ as the second Adam and the surety of the elect holds the covenant of works and the covenant of grace together. Based on the examination above, we can conclude that the covenant of works and the covenant of grace are unfolding and manifesting the eternal covenant of redemption in time. Ultimately, diverse manifestations of covenants in time can be seen as the execution of the eternal covenant of redemption. Jonathan Edwards shares this basic understanding of the *pactum salutis* with his Reformed predecessors.

THE UNITY OF THE IMMANENT AND THE ECONOMIC TRINITY

For the purpose of this study, it is to be noted that Edwards here develops his discussion on the covenant of redemption while he painstakingly makes efforts to underscore the unity between the immanent and the economic Trinity. In this respect too Edwards is consistent with the Reformed tradition where the covenant of redemption functions as a bridge and nexus between the immanent Trinity and the economic Trinity. The following three

---

136. Stoever, *'Faire and Easie Way,'* 87.
137. Kang, "Justified by Faith in Christ," 61.
138. Stoever, *'Faire and Easie Way,'* 96.

examples cumulatively confirm the coherency between the immanent and the economic Trinity in Edwards's theology.

First, even the so-called new arrangement between the Father and the Son subsequent to the covenant of redemption is consistent with the prior natural order of subsistence. As examined in the previous section, the covenant of redemption does involve something new and different from the mere inherent order of subsistence. Nonetheless, Edwards reiterates that even this new scheme takes place in a way consistent with the natural order of subsistence among the persons of the Trinity. For example, with regard to the relation between the Father and the other persons, Edwards states:

> It must be observed that this subordination that two of the persons of the Trinity come into by the covenant of redemption is not contrary to their economical order, but in several respects agreeable to it, though it be new in kind. Thus if either the Father or the Son be brought into the subjection of a servant to the other, it is much more agreeable to the economy of the Trinity that it should be the latter, who by that economy is already under the Father as his head. That the Father should be servant to the Son would be contrary to the economy and natural order of the persons of the Trinity.[139]

> 'Tis fit that the order of the acting of the persons of the Trinity should be agreeable to the order of their subsisting: that as the Father is first in the order of subsisting, so he should be first in the order of acting; that as the other two persons are from the Father in their subsistence, and as to their subsistence naturally originated from him and dependent on him.[140]

When the covenantal pact was made between the Father and the Son, it was fitting that it was not the Father but the Son who took the role of a servant and came down to the world given that the Son is originally under the headship of the Father in their natural order of subsistence. As Studebaker and Caldwell note, "It is the ontological nature of the divine persons that forms the framework for their activity in redemption."[141]

Second, strikingly, Edwards uses the term "economy" even when he describes the natural order of subsistence within the immanent Trinity. For example, when Edwards articulates the basic continuity between the natural order of subsistence in God *ad intra* and the work of redemption *ad extra*,

---

139. Edwards, *WJE* 20:437.
140. Edwards, *WJE* 20:431.
141. Studebaker and Caldwell, *Trinitarian Theology of Jonathan Edwards*, 143.

he emphasizes that obedient works of divine persons in God's redemptive work take place in accord with "*economical* character and station."[142]

> The obedience which the Son of God performs to the Father even in the affair of man's redemption, or as Redeemer or Mediator, before his humiliation, and also that obedience he performs as God-man after his humiliation, when as God-man he is exalted to the glory he had before, is no more than flows from his *economical* office or character, although it be occasioned by the determination or decree of the work of redemption, which is something [new], yea is occasioned by the covenant of redemption. Yet that decree and covenant being supposed, such an obedience as he performs in his divine glory follows of course from his *economical* character and station; nor is it any other kind of obedience than what that character requires.[143]

God's economic work of redemption unfolds in the world in a way that is consistent with the economy of order that already exists within the eternal communion among the three divine persons. The economic Trinity unfolds itself according to the pattern already built in the immanent Trinity.

Third, Edwards clearly sees the correspondence between God *ad intra* and God *ad extra* when he sees a parallel pattern between God and the human. Expounding on God's communication of himself *ad extra*, "which is what is called his glory," Edwards writes:

> This communication is of two sorts: the communication that consists in understanding or idea, which is summed up in the knowledge of God; and the other is in the will, consisting in love and joy, which may be summed up in the love and enjoyment of God. Thus that which proceeds from God *ad extra* is agreeable to the twofold subsistences which proceed from him *ad intra*, which is the Son and the Holy Spirit, the Son being the idea of God or the knowledge of God, and the Holy Ghost which is the love of God and joy in God.[144]

God communicates himself to human beings through their faculties of understanding (knowledge) and will (love and joy) because God himself subsists in the Son as the knowledge of God and in the Holy Spirit as the love and joy of God. Hence, Studebaker summarizes:

---

142. Edwards, *WJE* 20:438 (emphasis mine).
143. Edwards, *WJE* 20:438 (emphasis mine).
144. Edwards, *WJE* 23:153.

> Thus, the immanent identity of the divine persons determines their economic role in the communication of the triune God. Indeed, God created the specific form of the spiritual nature of the human soul to receive the economic communication of the triune God. The human soul consists of understanding and will precisely so that it may receive the communication of divine knowledge and love and in turn know and love the triune God.[145]
>
> The economy of acting derives precisely from the order of subsistence, which in turn is the product of the divine processions; the order of economy reflects the order of the immanent subsistence of the divine persons.[146]

The agreement between the immanent and the economic Trinity in Edwards's theology is distinctly clear.

From these observations, a contemporary reading that the traditional doctrine of the Trinity has become impractical and speculative by detaching the immanent Trinity from the economic Trinity does not hold at least in Edwards's trinitarian theology. For Edwards, as he follows his preceding Reformed tradition, steps to salvation are "the working out of the eternal purpose of an immutable deity."[147] Edwards's doctrine of the covenant of redemption shows that, in a sense, a blueprint of God's work of redemption is already built in the immanent Trinity. If this is the case, then, it is no longer pertinent to claim that the immanent Trinity is abstruse and irrelevant from the concrete Christian life and salvation.

---

145. Studebaker, *Jonathan Edwards's Social Augustinian Trinitarianism*, 201.
146. Studebaker, *Jonathan Edwards's Social Augustinian Trinitarianism*, 205.
147. Gerstner, *Steps to Salvation*, 173.

PART II

4

Covenant of Redemption, Trinity, and Creation

THE COVENANT OF REDEMPTION as the eternal pact between the Father and the Son in the immanent Trinity has a direct connection with creation. Given that history is the outworking of the covenant of redemption in space and time, creation sets up the arena where the divine drama of redemption takes place. In this sense the inherent connection for Edwards between God's plan of redemption from eternity and creation as the stage for the execution of the eternal plan of redemption in temporality is unambiguous. In this chapter, we will examine how the idea of the covenant of redemption in Edwards's trinitarian theology manifests itself in Edwards's doctrine of creation. A survey of Edwards's idealism, typology of nature, issues of panentheism and dispositional ontology will help illumine how in Edwards the covenant of redemption is inherently related to creation.

EDWARDS'S IDEALISM

Creation is, for Edwards, a divine communication stemming directly from God's mind.[1] This divine communication in creation presupposes recipients of the communication. They are agents such as saints and angels[2] who can perceive, understand, and enjoy the communication from God. They are

---

1. Edwards, "End," *WJE* 8:441.
2. Edwards, "Charity and Its Fruits," *WJE* 8:374; "Notes on Scripture," *WJE* 15:386; "True Saints," *WJE* 25:238.

what John J. Bombaro calls "intelligent perceiving minds."[3] Without these sentient beings, the divine communication will not be recognized as such. Even if God's glory is communicated to creation, "there is no glory without perception."[4] Revelation does not take place as revelation without its recipients in creation.

Behind this presupposition lies Edwards's idealism[5] or immaterialism.[6] Edwards believes that ultimately things exist because they exist in consciousness.

> And how doth it grate upon the mind, to think that something should be from all eternity, and nothing all the while be conscious of it. Let us suppose, to illustrate it, that the world had a being from all eternity, and had many great changes and wonderful revolutions, and all the while nothing knew; there was no knowledge in the universe of any such thing. How is it possible to bring the mind to imagine? Yea it is really impossible it should be, that anything should be, and nothing know it. Then you'll say, if it be so, it is because nothing has any existence anywhere else but in consciousness. No, certainly nowhere else but either in created or uncreated consciousness.[7]

The reality of existence ultimately lies in the divine consciousness. All beings are comprehended by God's mind. God is "the infinite, universal and all comprehending existence,"[8] or "*ens entium*."[9] Every existence derives itself from the divine consciousness. In fact, for Edwards, substance in a proper sense exists only in the divine mind. "That which truly is the substance of all bodies is the infinitely exact and precise and perfectly stable idea in God's mind."[10] Things exist because they are in God's consciousness

---

3. Bombaro, *Vision of Reality*, 14.
4. Edwards, *WJE* 13:428.
5. Rupp, "'Idealism' of Jonathan Edwards," 209–26.
6. Anderson, "Immaterialism," 181–200. Anderson provides a comparative study between Edwards and George Berkley. Although Edwards and Berkley independently developed idealism and nuanced differences can be identified, it seems more important to recognize a commonality in their basic attitude of counter-response to the age of Enlightenment. Against the spirit of the age that detaches God's direct influence from the world, they both attempted to reaffirm the world directly upheld by God's power as the idea in the divine mind. For a comparison of Edwards and Berkley, see also Zakai, *Philosophy of Nature*, 266–71.
7. Edwards, "Of Being," *WJE* 6:203–4.
8. Edwards, "Mind," *WJE* 6:381.
9. Edwards, "Things to be Considered," *WJE* 6:238.
10. Edwards, "Mind," *WJE* 6:344.

and because God's consciousness sustains and upholds them in his mind. "So that there is neither real substance nor property belonging to bodies; but all that is real, it is immediately in the first being."[11]

Correspondingly, human beings as intelligent and sentient beings have a special place in creation. In the order of creation, "the more excellent and noble any being is, the more visible and immediate hand of God is there in bringing them into being."[12] According to this chain of being, "the most noble of all, and that which is most akin to the nature of God, viz. the soul of man, is most immediately and directly from him."[13] A human soul in its ontological status has the closest place to God because of its excellence as the image of God.

> In the creation, there is an immediate communication between one degree of being and the next degree of being (every wheel immediately communicates with the next wheel), but man being the top; so that the next immediate step from him is to God. Without doubt, there is an immediate communication between the Creator and this highest of creatures, according to the order of being. So that as the intelligent being is exercised immediately about the Creator, so without doubt the Creator immediately influences the intelligent being, immediately influences the soul; for 'tis but one immediate step from the soul to God.[14]

This central and culminate place of intelligent beings in the order of beings in creation has a moral implication for human beings.

> The last end for which God has made moral agents must be the last end for which God has made all things: it being evident that the moral world is the end of the rest of the world; the inanimate and unintelligent world being made for the rational and moral world, as much as a house is prepared for the inhabitants.[15]

The vocation of human beings is to perceive and enjoy the glory of God diffused and communicated throughout in creation. Edwards declares: "If it were not for men, this world would be altogether in vain, with all the curious workmanship of it and accoutrements about it."[16] Without sentient

---

11. Edwards, "Things to be Considered," *WJE* 6:238.
12. Edwards, *WJE* 18:89.
13. Edwards, *WJE* 18:89.
14. Edwards, *WJE* 13:190–191.
15. Edwards, "True Virtue," *WJE* 8:559.
16. Edwards, *WJE* 13:184.

agents who recognize and appreciate, for this Northampton theologian, the majesty and splendor of created order means nothing.

> What would this vast universe of matter, placed in such excellent order and governed by such excellent rules, be good for, if there was no intelligence that could know anything of it? Wherefore it necessarily follows that intelligent beings are the end of the creation, that their end must be to behold and admire the doings of God, and magnify him for them, and to contemplate his glories in them.[17]

The end of creation is for the intelligent beings to recognize and worship the divine glory in creation. What Edwards calls "religion"[18] or "devotion"[19] to God is the ultimate vocation to which intelligent beings are called.

The fact that human beings have faculties of understanding and will corresponds to God's internal life in which the Son is begotten as the divine understanding and the Holy Spirit proceeds as the divine will. When God communicates himself, intelligent beings receive the knowledge of God in understanding and enjoy it in will.

> God communicates himself to the understanding in the manifestation that is made of the divine excellency and the understanding, idea or view which intelligent creatures have of it. He communicates his glory and fullness to the wills of sensible, willing, active beings in their rejoicing in the manifested glory of God, in their admiring it, in their loving God for it, and being in all respects affected and disposed suitably to such glory, and their exercising and expressing those affections and dispositions wherein consists their praising and glorifying God.[20]

This communication of divine fullness *ad extra* corresponds to the communication of the glory of God *ad intra*. Moreover, the former is the result of the latter. God's work *ad extra* subordinates to God *ad intra* as means to the ultimate end of manifestation of his glory. Edwards explains this parallel relationship as follows:

> This twofold emanation or communication of the divine fullness *ad extra* is answerable to the twofold emanation or going forth of the Godhead *ad intra*, wherein the internal and essential glory and fullness of the Godhead consists, viz. the proceeding

---

17. Edwards, *WJE* 13:184.
18. Edwards, *WJE* 13:185.
19. Edwards, *WJE* 13:186.
20. Edwards, *WJE* 23:213.

of the eternal Son of God, God's eternal idea and infinite understanding and wisdom and the brightness of his glory, whereby his beauty and excellency appears to him; and the proceeding of the Holy Spirit, or the eternal will, temper, disposition of the Deity, the infinite fullness of God's holiness, joy and delight.[21]

As Steven M. Studebaker and Robert W. Caldwell comment, "The structure of the soul reflects the trinitarian God because the intellectual acts of the soul image the two immanent acts of the divine nature from which subsist the Son and the Spirit."[22]

In a similar vein, in miscellany 87 Edwards asks a question: "What could move him to will, that there should be some beings that might know his power and wisdom?"[23]; "what moved God to exercise and make known these attributes?"[24] The answer Edwards has found is that the communication of goodness by its nature requires that the goodness communicated is received, perceived, appreciated, and enjoyed.

> The very notion of wisdom is, wisely contriving for an end; and if there be no end proposed, whatever is done is not wisdom. Wherefore, if God created the world merely from goodness, every whit of this goodness must necessarily ultimately terminate in the consciousness of the creation; for the world is no other way capable of receiving goodness in any measure. But intelligent beings are the consciousness of the world; the end, therefore, of their creation must necessarily be that they may receive the goodness of God, that is, that they may be happy.[25]

Simply put, "It was meet that his attributes and perfections should be expressed. It was the will of God that they should be expressed and should shine forth."[26] Edwards goes so far as to say: "But if the expressions of his attributes ben't known, they are not; the very being of the expression depends on the perception of created understandings."[27] Here Edwards radically means that unless an intelligent sentient being perceives it, even the divine attribute practically does not exist.

Edwards's major treatise on creation recaptures the necessity of sentient beings for the knowledge of the exercise of divine attributes.

21. Edwards, *WJE* 23:213.
22. Studebaker and Caldwell, *Trinitarian Theology of Jonathan Edwards*, 204.
23. Edwards, *WJE* 13:251.
24. Edwards, *WJE* 13:251–52.
25. Edwards, *WJE* 13:252.
26. Edwards, *WJE* 18:200.
27. Edwards, *WJE* 18:200.

> It seems to be a thing in itself fit and desirable, that the glorious perfections of God should be known, and the operations and expressions of them seen by other beings besides himself. If it be fit that God's power and wisdom, etc., should be exercised and expressed in some effects, and not lie eternally dormant, then it seems proper that these exercises should appear, and not be totally hidden and unknown. For if they are, it will be just the same as to the above purpose, as if they were not. God as perfectly knew himself and his perfections, had as perfect an idea of the exercises and effects they were sufficient for, antecedently to any such actual operations of them, as since. If therefore it be nevertheless a thing in itself valuable, and worthy to be desired, that these glorious perfections be actually expressed and exhibited in their correspondent effects; then it seems also, that the knowledge of these perfections, and the expressions and discoveries that are made of them, is a thing valuable in itself absolutely considered; and that 'tis desirable that this knowledge should exist. As God's perfections are things in themselves excellent, so the expression of them in their proper acts and fruits is excellent, and the knowledge of these excellent perfections, and of these glorious expressions of them, is an excellent thing, the existence of which is in itself valuable and desirable.[28]

When the divine perfections are perceived by intelligent beings and these sentient beings esteem, love, and enjoy God's perfections, the communication of divine glory to creation takes place. It is the "manifestation of his internal glory to created understandings," or the "communication of the infinite fullness of God to the creature."[29]

EDWARDS'S TYPOLOGY OF NATURE

One specific instantiation of Edwards's idealism manifests in his typology.[30] Typology is "a mode of biblical interpretation, an ancient science of reading that united the two Testaments."[31] By using this interpretive device,

---

28. Edwards, "End of Creation," *WJE* 8:430–31.
29. Edwards, "End of Creation," *WJE* 8:527.
30. For commentary on typology in the Puritan thought, see Lowance, *Language of Canaan*; Brumm, *American Thought and Religious Typology*; Bercovitch, *Puritan Origins*; *Typology and Early American Literature*; Lewalski, *Protestant Poetics*; Daniel, *Philosophy of Jonathan Edwards*. See also Lane, *Ravished by Beauty*, 170–210; Miller, "Introduction," 1–41.
31. Knight, "Learning the Language of God," 532.

exegetes read the Jewish scripture "in the light of Christian experience," finding in David a type of Messiah, or the Jewish Exodus experience prefiguring Christ's experience in the wilderness.[32] It enabled biblical interpreters to "read specific events and persons of the Old Testament as symbolic prefigurations or types of things fulfilled in the New."[33] However, as Janice Knight points out, Edwards expanded its use beyond the scripture, hearing "God's voice still sounding in nature, in human history, and in the flow of contemporary events."[34]

> Again, it is apparent and allowed that there is a great and remarkable analogy in God's works. There is a wonderful resemblance in the effects which God produces, and consentaneity in his manner of working in one thing and another, throughout all nature. It is very observable in the visible world. Therefore 'tis allowed that God does purposely make and order one thing to be in an agreeableness and harmony with another. And if so, why should not we suppose that he makes the inferior in imitation of the superior, the material of the spiritual, on purpose to have a resemblance and shadow of them? We see that even in the material world God makes one part of it strangely to agree with another; and why is it not reasonable to suppose he makes the whole as a shadow of the spiritual world?[35]

For Edwards, typology was a tool to "unlock God's intentions in the created world and in Scripture."[36]

Edwards lived in the Age of Enlightenment when the reality of God's sovereignty and a sense of direct divine influence began to be relegated to the periphery of the world. It was the age of "mechanical philosophy," "the doctrine that all natural phenomena can be explained and understood by the mere mechanics of matter and motion."[37] In opposition to this influential tide of the age, Edwards attempted to "construct a plausible alternative to the mechanistic interpretation of the essential nature of reality, which

---

32. Knight, "Learning the Language of God," 532.
33. Knight, "Learning the Language of God," 532.
34. Knight, "Learning the Language of God," 532. See also Lowance, "Images or Shadows," 151. Edwards's typological view of history and its connection with typological view of nature will be assessed in chapter 7.
35. Edwards, "Images of Divine Things," *WJE* 11:53.
36. Knight, "Learning the Language of God," 531.
37. Zakai, *Philosophy of Nature*, 9.

would reconstitute the glory of God's absolute sovereignty, power, and will within creation."[38]

For example, against Hobbes's materialism, Edwards claims:

> Contrary to the opinion of Hobbes (that nothing is substance but matter), that no matter is substance but only God, who is a spirit, and that other spirits are more substantial than matter; so also it is true, that no happiness is solid and substantial but spiritual happiness.[39]

Disagreeing with the increasingly popular notion, Edwards tries to reclaim that the spiritual is the actually most substantial, and the material things exist so far as they participate in the spiritual or as long as the spiritual upholds them in power. Through the participation in spiritual things, matters reflect the spiritual realm.

> Accordingly, instead of the New Philosophy's notion of a homogeneous, uniform and symmetrical, one-dimensional world of nature, deprived of theological and teleological considerations and hence could no longer manifest the presence of God, the created order for Edwards was a great treasure of divine signs and metaphors—the whole world is imbued with spiritual, divine meaning and significance.[40]

In this sense, the material can be a window through which the regenerate can witness to the truly substantial reality: God the Trinity as the supreme spiritual being. "Nature reflects transcendent meanings and symbols of divine things beyond and above it."[41]

Instead of a mechanistic, materialistic worldview, as Avihu Zakai puts it, Edwards believes in "*omnia videmus in deo*, or in the active role of God in every aspect of the world."[42] "Given that the being and existence of everything in creation stands under the constant and immediate absolute power and will of God, the whole world of nature is imbued with God's redemptive activity."[43] The created world is suffused and saturated with the glory of the divine Trinity. "Typological exegesis of nature, as was the case with

---

38. Zakai, *Philosophy of Nature*, 9. See also Opie, *Edwards and the Enlightenment*; Moody, *Edwards and the Enlightenment*; Chai, *Edwards and the Limits*.

39. Edwards, *WJE* 13:167. See also Edwards, "Things to be Considered," *WJE* 6:235, 238.

40. Zakai, *Philosophy of Nature*, 237.

41. Zakai, *Philosophy of Nature*, 237.

42. Zakai, *Philosophy of Nature*, 234.

43. Zakai, *Philosophy of Nature*, 257.

Scripture and history, allowed Edwards to interpret the beautiful, Trinitarian harmony he believed permeates all reality."[44]

In fact, because Edwards holds God's immediate sustenance of the world through God's direct power, this New England theologian even espouses the teaching of continuing creation.

> God's *preserving* created things in being is perfectly equivalent to a *continued creation*, or to his creating those things out of nothing at *each moment* of their existence. If the continued existence of created things be wholly dependent on God's preservation, then those things would drop into nothing, upon the ceasing of the present moment, without a new exertion of the divine power to cause them to exist in the following moment.[45]

Put simply, "God's preservation of the world is nothing but a continued act of creation."[46] Zakai summarizes Edwards's project of philosophy of nature as follows:

> His force of mind is evident in his exposition of the poverty of mechanical philosophy and materialism, which radically transformed the traditional Christian dialectic of God's utter transcendence and divine immanence by gradually diminishing divine sovereignty with respect to creation, providence, and redemption, thus leading to the disenchantment of the world. Instead, through idealistic philosophy and natural typology, Edwards sought to mount a counteroffensive to materialist, mechanistic thought. He thus constructed a teleological and theological alternative to the prevailing mechanistic interpretation of the essential nature of reality, whose ultimate goal was the re-enchantment of the world by reconstituting the glory of God's majestic sovereignty, power and will within the order of creation.[47]

Edwards's doctrine of continuing creation can be interpreted as his way of reclaiming God's direct upholding of the world in the Age of Enlightenment where God's direct influence and involvement in the world were increasingly relegated to the periphery.

The Northampton theologian sees these manifestations and reflections of divine glory in creation as "the emanation of God's glory; or the excellent

---

44. Schweitzer, *God Is a Communicative Being*, 49.

45. Edwards, "Original Sin," *WJE* 3:401–2.

46. Edwards, "God Is Everywhere Present," 210. See also Edwards, "Sermon on Psalm 139:7–10," 42.

47. Zakai, *Philosophy of Nature*, 9–10.

brightness and fullness of the divinity diffused, overflowing, and as it were enlarged."[48] In other words, manifestations of divine glory in creation are divine perfections "*existing ad extra.*"[49] For Edwards, God is not the hidden God (*deus absconditus*), but God constantly reveals himself (*deus revelatus*) through creation and history.[50] As noted above, human beings as sentient, intelligent creatures are originally designed to receive, appreciate, and enjoy the beauty and excellence of God revealed in creation and history. This worldview has a practical implication. Because the creation is an arena where God constantly communicates himself through "symmetries and patterns as lower forms of God's love,"[51] human beings are called to take care of this creation with respect and reverence. As Nicola Hoggard Creggan notes, since "the natural world reflects the beauty and the energies and the love of God in physical form," humankind as sentient beings are called to "respect and reverence the earth, not as God but as God's."[52] Interestingly, the covenant of redemption in eternity here echoes down to an ecological and ethical implication for the daily lives of human beings. It would be difficult to claim here that the doctrine of the Trinity or even precisely the immanent Trinity is abstruse and impractical for daily life.

ISSUES OF PANENTHEISM AND DISPOSITIONAL ONTOLOGY

As noted in the previous section, while Edwards maintains that God is in perfect happiness and self-sufficiency, he also claims that unless the expressions of divine attributes are perceived in creation, those attributes practically do not exist. This necessity of the communication of divine goodness seems to indicate the necessity of creation. In addition to the idealistic view of being surveyed above, Edwards seems to use allegedly neo-Platonic languages such as emanation and overflowing fullness in his articulation of God's relation to the world. For example, in his treatise on *The End for which God Created the World*, Edwards comments:

> In the creature's knowing, esteeming, loving, rejoicing in, and praising God, the glory of God is both exhibited and

---

48. Edwards, "End of Creation," *WJE* 8:527.
49. Edwards, "End of Creation," *WJE* 8:527.
50. Zakai, *Philosophy of Nature*, 237.
51. Creegan, "Ecological and Ethical Vision," 49. See also Studebaker and Caldwell, *Trinitarian Theology of Jonathan Edwards*, 208–11.
52. Creegan, "Ecological and Ethical Vision," 51.

acknowledged; his fullness is received and returned. Here is both an *emanation* and *remanation*. The refulgence shines upon and into the creature, and is reflected back to the luminary. The beams of glory come from God, and are something of God, and are refunded back again to their original. So that the whole is *of God*, and *in* God, and *to* God; and God is the beginning, middle and end in this affair.[53]

Because of this nuanced account of God's relation to the world with peculiar languages such as emanation and refulgence, several scholars have charged Edwards as a pantheist, a position that identifies God with the creation.[54] However, it is inaccurate to identify Edwards as a pantheist. Rather, many recent scholars identify Edwards as a panentheist.

In this section, I will first distinguish Edwards's panentheism from pantheism. Then I will review the recent scholarly discussions on Edwards's panentheism with particular attention to Edwards's dispositional ontology. Finally, to make some contribution to the current discussion, I will argue that though Edwards's theology may be called as one version of panentheism, it is not entirely incompatible with classical theism.

First, pantheism and panentheism need to be distinguished from each other. While pantheism nullifies the distinction between the creator and creature and identifies nature itself as divine, panentheism maintains the distinction between the creator and creation but sees the ontologically inclusive relation between the two. Panentheism literally means "all-in-God-ism," or "the doctrine that all is in God."[55] The term means that "God and the world are ontologically distinct and God transcends the world, but the world is in God ontologically."[56] This term was originally introduced by Karl Krause (1781–1832) to "distinguish his own theology from both classical theism and pantheism."[57] Given that this terminology was invented in the nineteenth century, it might not be entirely fair to name Edwards's theology as panentheistic. Still, it would be helpful to identify Edwards's rendition of God's relation to the world as something akin to what is called panentheism today.

Edwards is clear in asserting the distinction between God and creation. For example, Edwards makes efforts painstakingly to differentiate

---

53. Edwards, "End of Creation," *WJE* 8:531.

54. Riley, *American Philosophy*, 126–87; Woodbridge, "Jonathan Edwards," 401, 406; Colacurico, "Example of Edwards," 72; Gerstner, "Jonathan Edwards and God," 7.

55. Cooper, *Panentheism*, 26.

56. Cooper, *Panentheism*, 27.

57. Cooper, *Panentheism*, 26.

himself from a pantheistic scheme when he articulates the participation of the saints in the divine fullness.

> Not that the saints are made partakers of the essence of God, and so are "Godded" with God, and "Christed" with Christ, according to the abominable and blasphemous language and notions of some heretics; but, to use the Scripture phrase, they are made partakers of God's fullness (Eph 3:17–19; John 1:16), that is, of God's spiritual beauty and happiness, according to the measure and capacity of a creature.[58]

In addition, Edwards's seemingly pantheistic language is frequently qualified by such phrases as "as it were," "to the degree of their capacities," or "in some sense."[59] For example, in reference to Matthew 5:16, Edwards says: "Godliness is *as it were* a light that shines in the soul: Christ directs that this light should not only shine within, but that it should shine out before men, that they may see it."[60] When Edwards talks about the multiplication and repetition of divine fullness, Edwards peppers it with qualifying and figurative phrases such as "in some sense" or "as it were."

> And as this fullness is capable of communication or emanation *ad extra*; so it seems a thing amiable and valuable in itself that it should be communicated or flow forth, that this infinite fountain of good should send forth abundant streams, that this infinite fountain of light should, diffusing its excellent fullness, pour forth light all around. And as this is in itself excellent, so a disposition to this in the Divine Being must be looked upon as a perfection or an excellent disposition; such an emanation of good is, *in some sense*, a multiplication of it; so far as the communication or external stream may be looked upon as anything besides the fountain, so far it may be looked on as an increase of good. And if the fullness of good that is in the fountain is in itself excellent and worthy to exist, then the emanation, or that which is *as it were* an increase, repetition or multiplication of it, is excellent and worthy to exist.[61]

When Edwards talks about participation in God's fullness, it does not mean that human nature is somehow transformed into the divine or that human nature is identical with the divine nature.[62] The language of participation

---

58. Edwards, "Religious Affections," *WJE* 2:203.
59. Caldwell, *Communion in the Spirit*, 192.
60. Edwards, "Religious Affections," *WJE* 2:407 (emphasis mine).
61. Edwards, "End of Creation," *WJE* 8:433 (except for "*ad extra*," emphasis mine).
62. Thus, Frederick J. E. Woodbridge's allegation of "mystic pantheism" to Edwards is not entirely accurate. Woodbridge, "Jonathan Edwards," 401, 406.

in Edwards means that, through the indwelling of the Holy Spirit, the saints become a part of the flow of divine self-communication without losing the human nature. Simply put, believers come under the influences of the Holy Spirit.

> Grace in the hearts of the saints, being therefore the most glorious work of God, wherein he communicates of the goodness of his nature, it is doubtless his peculiar work, and in an eminent manner, above the power of all creatures. And the influences of the Spirit of God in this, being thus peculiar to God, and being those wherein God does, in so high a manner, communicate himself, and make the creature partaker of the divine nature (the Spirit of God communicating itself in its own proper nature). This is what I mean by those influences that are divine, when I say that *truly gracious affections do arise from those influences that are spiritual and divine.*[63]

The human nature of the elect is not transformed into a different kind but the way it is exerted comes under the divine influences by participation in the divine nature.[64]

Douglas J. Elwood is one of the earlier scholars who identified Edwards as a panentheist.[65] Yet it was Sang Hyun Lee's dispositional-ontological interpretation of Edwards's theology that made Edwards's panentheistic scheme commonly known. To be sure, Lee does not term Edwards's philosophical theology panentheism. Nonetheless, his interpretation of Edwards is distinctly panentheistic. Lee claims:

> It is my contention that one does not even begin to understand Edwards's world view without noticing that he introduced an essentially new understanding of the very nature of reality, replacing substance metaphysics with a dynamic and relational conception.[66]

Lee thinks that in Edwards a significant conceptual alteration took place that introduces the dispositional view of reality.

> The world . . . is meant to be the spatio-temporal repetition of the prior actuality of the divine being, an everlasting process of God's self-enlargement of what he already is. At this point, Edwards has made a basic modification of the traditional

---

63. Edwards, "Religious Affections," *WJE* 2:203.
64. Withrow, *Becoming Divine*, 136–68.
65. Elwood, *Philosophical Theology of Jonathan Edwards*, 6–7, 21–22.
66. Lee, *Philosophical Theology of Jonathan Edwards*, 47.

> conception of the deity and has introduced an element of dynamic movement into the heart of the divine being. But at the same time, Edwards avoids the failure of contemporary process theology to see God as primordially and fully-self-actualized. And the key to the balancing of being and becoming in Edwards's doctrine of God is the notion of the divine disposition as ontologically productive—that is, as capable of repeating what is already actual and at the same time engaged in a process of self-extension.[67]

In this way, according to Lee, Edwards introduced a dynamic element in God's being without compromising the divine aseity or self-sufficiency.

On this score Lee shares the concern of contemporary theology that through the history of Christian theology, the immanent Trinity has become abstruse and speculative, losing its connection with God's economic work of redemption in the world.

> As the church moved on, however, the theological articulation of the doctrine of the immanent Trinity in particular became philosophically more elaborate and abstruse, with the result that the immanent Trinity's rootedness in the economic Trinity and in the living faith of Christians became largely invisible and ignored. Under the influence especially of Aristotelian conceptions of substance and God, the nature of the Christian God began to be portrayed by most theologians as self-contained, impassable (i.e., unaffected by the changes in history), and remote from what happens in the world.[68]

Instead of this view of the immanent Trinity disconnected from the economy of redemption, Lee argues that Edwards introduced the "dynamic view of the divine being" that sees the "essential nature of God's being as an eternal disposition as well as an actuality, at once fully actual and also continuously tending to further actualizations and thus to further self-enlargement."[69]

In this way, Edwards makes "a new beginning in the development of the doctrine of God in Western theology by re-conceiving God's being as essentially a disposition rather than a substance."[70] Lee thus concludes:

> We can safely say that Edwards clearly left behind the old classical theism's Aristotelian concept of God as the unmoved mover who is absolutely impassible and unaffected by what happens

---

67. Lee, *Philosophical Theology of Jonathan Edwards*, 6.
68. Lee, "Editor's Introduction," *WJE* 21:3.
69. Lee, *Princeton Companion*, 59.
70. Lee, "Does History Matter to God?," 3.

in the world in space and time. Further, whatever Neo-platonic influences there may be in Edwards's thought, his dynamic new thinking on the God-world relation is certainly not one of them.[71]

Because dynamic "becoming" is a part of God's being, the arena of space and temporality in history do matter to God.

> For Edwards, although God does not need temporality for his internal actuality and perfection, God needs or uses the world in space and time to exercise his dispositional essence outside of his own being. What God does in time and space makes time and space important to God. In other words, it is not that the created world as such can increase the divine being; it is rather what God himself does in and through the world in time and space that affects the divine being by adding to his own being. In this specific sense, nevertheless, the world in space and time really matters to God's own life.[72]

Lee believes that Edwards's unique dispositional view of God helps to modify the traditional view of God in classical theism in which God is construed as an impassible, immutable sovereign being who is unaffected by the world.[73]

However, Lee's influential interpretation of Edwards's dispositional ontology has been challenged recently. A question was first raised by Stephen R. Holmes when he pronounced: "it is extremely unlikely that he adopted a novel doctrine of God"[74] like the one Lee suggests. Given that Edwards predominantly inherited the Reformed doctrinal legacy, Holmes concludes: "A 'dispositional' account of God, inasmuch as it demands that there is unfulfilled potential in God's life, and so the possibility of God's 'self-enlargement' or 'increase,' would have been unthinkable to Edwards. Jonathan Edwards did not use a dispositional ontology."[75]

Resonate with Holmes's doubt, Oliver Crisp provides a more refined discussion. While "Lee understands Edwards in places like *End of Creation* to mean that God's *whole nature* is dispositional," Crisp argues that "it is better to think of Edwards as saying God (an immaterial substance) is necessarily disposed to create some world."[76] In other words, rather than reading Edwards as construing God's essence as entirely dispositional, Crisp

71. Lee, "Does History Matter to God?," 10.
72. Lee, "Does History Matter to God?," 10.
73. Lee, "Does History Matter to God?," 10–12.
74. Holmes, "Does Jonathan Edwards," 108.
75. Holmes, "Does Jonathan Edwards," 108.
76. Crisp, "Jonathan Edwards on the Divine Nature," 195.

suggests a more qualified, modest reading that is consistent with the largely Reformed background that Edwards inherited. In another article in which he specifically discussed Lee's argument, Crisp concludes:

> Lee is right in thinking Edwards's ontology is novel in several important respects. But what was novel about it was the way in which he sought to synthesize a commitment to essentialism, idealism, and occasionalism along with his orthodox theological commitments.[77]

Though Edwards implemented some unique rendition of metaphysics, it is an overstatement to conclude with Lee that Edwards departed from western classical theism. Edwards "did not effectively replace the notion of substance with that of disposition, as Lee suggests."[78]

For example, Edwards describes the nature of God as follows:

> It is evident, by both Scripture and reason, that God is infinitely, eternally, unchangeably, and independently glorious and happy: that he stands in no need of, cannot be profited by, or receive anything from the creature; or be truly hurt, or be the subject of any sufferings or *impair* of his glory and felicity from any other being.[79]

For Edwards, God is "the omniscient first cause and supreme disposer of all things who, in one, simple, unchangeable, perpetual view, comprehends all existence in its utmost compass and extent and infinite series."[80] While he has the disposition to communicate himself, he himself is the substance, *ens entium*, or the being of beings.[81] In fact, Edwards declares, "speaking most strictly, there is no proper substance but God himself."[82]

Steven M. Studebaker also views Edwards's trinitarian theology within the broad stream of the Reformed tradition.

> While Edwards may have occasionally employed a modern definition of person in his Trinitarian writings, the overall drift of his trinitarianism reveals a somewhat traditional approach. His take on the numerical oneness of the divine essence, his locating the principle of unity either in the divine essence or in the perichoretic relations of the three, and his affirmation of

77. Crisp, "Jonathan Edwards's Ontology," 15.
78. Crisp, "Jonathan Edwards's Ontology," 15.
79. Edwards, "End of Creation," *WJE* 8:420.
80. Edwards, *WJE* 23:211.
81. Edwards, "Of Atoms," *WJE* 6:215.
82. Edwards, "Of Atoms," *WJE* 6:215.

the complete ontological equality of the three persons together render his trinitarianism at considerable odds with the progressive Trinitarians of his day.[83]

While certainly some idiosyncrasies and ambiguities can be recognized in Edwards, generally "more continuity exists between Edwards's trinitarianism and that of his Reformed scholastic background than is often acknowledged."[84]

Contrary to Holmes, Crisp, and Studebaker, Michael J. McClymond supports the interpretations of Edwards's doctrine of God rendered by Lee and Pauw. McClymond claims: "The Lee-Pauw viewpoint is superior to any alternative offered thus far in that it properly construes Edwards's 'music' and does justice to his soteriology and to his soteriologically oriented doctrine of God and the Trinity."[85] In this way, because of the dispositional ontological interpretation of Edwards's God, the discussion concerning the issue of panentheism has repercussions for Edwards's soteriology.

However, this very interpretation of Edwards's soteriology have been a focal point of discussion recently. While Anri Morimoto and Gerald R. McDermott argue that Edwards's soteriology offers resources for contemporary ecumenical dialogue between Catholics and Protestants on the doctrine of justification[86] or possible salvation of non-Christian believers,[87] questions have been raised whether this interpretation is in line with Edwards's own theological framework.[88]

For example, John Bombaro writes: "Morimoto and McDermott have cast their lines too far from their subject's expressed thought. As a result, their work fails to accurately represent the thought of Jonathan Edwards."[89] After the publication of Lee's dispositional ontological theory and following applications of this interpretation to soteriology, the discussion seems to be moving to qualify Lee's thesis to render it more accurate and in accord with Edwards's own historical context in a way that does justice to his own framework and theological bounds. In response to Lee, Bombaro argues that "Despite his emergent dispositional philosophy, Edwards did not completely depart from the Aristotelian-Scholastic ontology of 'substance,' as

---

83. Studebaker and Caldwell, *Trinitarian Theology of Jonathan Edwards*, 143–44
84. Studebaker and Caldwell, *Trinitarian Theology of Jonathan Edwards*, 144.
85. McClymond, "Hearing the Symphony," 70.
86. Morimoto, *Jonathan Edwards and the Catholic Vision*, 157–63.
87. McDermott, *Jonathan Edwards Confronts Gods*, 130–45.
88. More will be discussed in the next chapter in conjunction with the covenant of redemption and justification.
89. Bombaro, *Jonathan Edwards's Vision of Reality*, 11.

Sang Lee argues."[90] For Bombaro, "neither God nor man is to be thought of *only* in terms of disposition: Edwards retained 'substance' concepts and terminology for both."[91] While Crisp, Studebaker, and Bombaro do not deny that Edwards employs the concept of disposition, the focus of the discussion has moved to the degree and extent of the idea of disposition in Edwards's entire theological framework. For these scholars, it sounds a bit of an overstretch to say that Edwards completely departed from the western classical theism or *actus purus*, substance theism.

One thing these scholars share in common, though, is their assessment that Edwards is, what can be termed today, a panentheist. Crisp says: "Edwards's view turns out to be something like a *pure act panentheism*. God is a pure act but he must create some world because he is essentially creative."[92] Crisp also calls Edwards "an idealist panentheist"[93] in that Edwards's idealism, as God's idea comprehending all things of the world, contributes to Edwards's panentheistic rendition of his theocentrism. Studebaker basically concurs with this diagnosis based on his historical analysis. Studebaker writes: "At most, Edwards's notion is a form of immanentism or panentheism, which affirms that the world is in God and/or God is in the world, yet that God also in some sense transcends the world and should not be conflated with the world."[94] Bombaro also agrees with this conclusion when he says: "his [Edwards's] statements concerning all in God and God in all cannot be taken any other way but panentheistically."[95] Yet they all agree that Edwards's version of panentheism is not something that totally departs from or is incompatible with classical theism.

While panentheism is generally considered to hold the necessity of creation,[96] Edwards does not think that his doctrine makes God dependent on creation. Edwards writes:

> Therefore to speak more strictly according to truth, we may suppose *that a disposition in God, as an original property of his nature, to an emanation of his own infinite fullness, was what*

---

90. Bombaro, *Jonathan Edwards's Vision of Reality*, 13.
91. Bombaro, *Jonathan Edwards's Vision of Reality*, 13.
92. Crisp, "Jonathan Edwards on the Divine," 200.
93. Crisp, *Jonathan Edwards on God*, 159.
94. Studebaker and Caldwell, *Trinitarian Theology of Jonathan Edwards*, 193.
95. Bombaro, *Jonathan Edwards's Vision of Reality*, 299.
96. For more on the issue of the necessity of creation in Edwards, see Crisp, *Jonathan Edwards on God*, 77–93, 138–63; Studebaker and Caldwell, *Trinitarian Theology of Jonathan Edwards*, 197–200; Studebaker, *Jonathan Edwards's Social Augustinian Trinitarianism*, 201–3; Wainwright, "Jonathan Edwards, William Rowe," 119–33.

> excited him to create the word; and so that the emanation itself was aimed at by him as a last end of the creation.[97]

"God's making himself his end," Edwards says, "argues no dependence; but is consistent with absolute independence and self-sufficiency."[98] Because the cause of the creation is God's own dispositional nature, creation of the world does not necessarily make God dependent on the creation. Studebaker and Caldwell note:

> Though he sees the communication of divine goodness in creation as inevitable, he does not believe that it conflicts with God's aseity (God's necessary and full self-existence) because this act of the divine nature is self-caused and the emanation of God in creation has the actualization of the disposition of the divine nature and not creation per se as its proper end.[99]

God's freedom lies in that God acts as he sees fit and according to his own nature of goodness and willingness to communicate himself. Edwards's version of panentheism is not incompatible with God's aseity and independence from the world.

Crisp also agrees that Edwards's panentheism is compatible with the traditional pure act theism. *Actus purus*, or pure act account of the divine nature is a traditional doctrine of God in classical theism. It holds that "a perfect being must exist independent of any other thing (*a se*), must be a necessary being, and must be an entity whose nature is entirely *realized* without remainder."[100] Despite Lee's claim of Edwards's departure from classical theism, evidences indicate that Edwards maintained the basic understanding of classical theism.

For example, when he accounts for the three persons in one divine essence, Edwards articulates it in a traditional way:

> We don't suppose that the Father, the Son, and the Holy Ghost are three distinct beings that have three distinct understandings. It is the divine essence understands, and it is the divine essence is understood; 'tis the divine being that loves, and it is the divine being that is loved. The Father understands, the Son understands, and the Holy Ghost understands, because every

---

97. Edwards, "End of Creation," *WJE* 8:435.
98. Edwards, "End of Creation," *WJE* 8:462.
99. Studebaker and Caldwell, *Trinitarian Theology of Jonathan Edwards*, 198.
100. Crisp, "Jonathan Edwards on Divine Nature," 176.

one is the same understanding divine essence; and not that each of them have a distinct understanding of their own.[101]

Edwards also retains references to God as substance. His "Notes on Knowledge and Existence" indicates that one of the tasks he had in mind was to articulate "How God is as it were the only substance, or rather, the perfection and steadfastness of his knowledge, wisdom, power and will."[102] In *Freedom of the Will*, God is called "the first Being, who is self-existent, independent, of perfect and absolute simplicity and immutability, and the first cause of all things."[103]

Hence, Crisp concludes that, rather than to understand Edwards to mean "that God's *whole nature* is dispositional" as Lee does, it is "better to think of Edwards as saying God (an immaterial substance) is necessarily disposed to create some world."[104] The debate about Edwards's alleged panentheism is moving from Sang Lee's influential dispositional ontological interpretation to efforts to situate Edwards's account of disposition within Edwards's broader traditionally Reformed framework in a more nuanced and accurate way.

This overview of scholarly discussion on Edwards's panentheism indicates that more nuanced recognition of diverse versions of panentheism may be necessary.[105] Charles Hartshorne and William L. Reese make a distinction between modern panentheism (panentheism in that God knows and includes the world) and limited panentheism (panentheism in that God exists "partly exclusive of the world").[106] While both Edwards's version of panentheism and modern process theology can be categorized as panentheism, they are not identical with each other since Edwards's version affirms God's perfection and self-sufficiency prior to the creation of the world whereas process theologians endorse God's self-making in time and space.[107]

Edwards appears to have developed his doctrine of God that includes a dispositional account within the broader framework of his Reformed inheritance. As is manifest in his account of idealism, Edwards's primary concern

101. Edwards, *WJE* 13:392.
102. Edwards, "Notes on Knowledge and Existence," *WJE* 6:398.
103. Edwards, "Freedom of Will," *WJE* 1:377.
104. Crisp, "Jonathan Edwards on Divine Nature," 195.
105. Crisp, "Jonathan Edwards on Divine Nature," 195. Claiming that neo-platonism and panentheism should be distinguished, Robert C. Whittemore argues that Edwards endorses Christian Neo-Platonism but not panentheism. Whittemore, "Jonathan Edwards," 60–75. For the connection between Edwards and the Cambridge Platonists, see Watts, "Jonathan Edwards."
106. Hartshorne and Reese, *Philosophers Speak of God*, 17.
107. For more on this, see Bombaro, *Jonathan Edwards's Vision of Reality*, 297–99.

was to reaffirm God's pervasive sovereignty in the world in the Age of Enlightenment where God was increasingly relegated to the periphery of the world.[108] Whether Edwards's doctrine of God is categorized as panentheism or not, one needs to be very clear about the theological motive behind the way Edwards renders the relation between God and creation. That is to say, Edwards does not have any intention to mitigate divine sovereignty over the entire creation. If by panentheism one means a certain compromise of the distinction between Creator and creation or a certain kind of dependence of God on creation, Edwards does not espouse such a scheme.

> The notion of God's creating the world in order to receive anything properly from the creature is not only contrary to the nature of God, but inconsistent with the notion of creation; which implies a being's receiving its existence, and all that belongs to its being, out of nothing. And this implies the most perfect, absolute and universal derivation and dependence. Now, if the creature receives its all from God entirely and perfectly, how is it possible that it should have anything to add to God, to make him in any respect more than he was before, and so the Creator become dependent on the creature?[109]

Edwards's intention is to establish divine sovereignty and self-sufficiency as opposed to creation and hence the work of creation as God's gracious work entirely.

Besides, terms often alleged as having affinity with panentheism such as "effulgence" or "emanation" can actually be identified in other Puritan writings such as of Richard Sibbes. In contradistinction from Lee who argues that Edwards is more modern than Perry Miller once thought,[110] Janice Knight points out that Edwards dynamism "is rooted in an older tradition of pietism that reaches back to the writings of Sibbes."[111] In his emphasis on "God's dynamic effulgence and on grace as a new perception, as well as his linkage of communication and communalism to the postmillennial reign," Edwards was "far more traditional in these formulations than most scholars acknowledge."[112]

One indicator to diagnose the degree of Edwards's panentheistic leaning is whether Edwards holds creation out of nothing. Given that even

---

108. Zakai, "Jonathan Edwards," 15–41; Zakai, "Theological Origins," 708–24; Zakai, *Jonathan Edwards's Philosophy of Nature*, 231–73.
109. Edwards, "End of Creation," *WJE* 8:421.
110. Lee, *Philosophical Theology of Jonathan Edwards*, 3.
111. Knight, "Learning the Language of God," 544n62.
112. Knight, "Learning the Language of God," 544n62.

panentheism, which distinguishes between Creator and creation, tends to take the being of creation still somewhere from the being of God,[113] it would be helpful to identify exactly where Edwards believes the being of creation comes from. On this score, evidences indicate that Edwards holds the teaching of creation out of nothing without any compromise. Calling the work of creation as God's entirely "arbitrary operation," Edwards says:

> If we ascend with respect to time and go back in the series of existences or events in the order of their succession to the beginning of the creation . . . we shall come to arbitrary operation. The creation of the matter of the material world out of nothing, the creation even of every individual atom or primary particle, was by an operation perfectly arbitrary.[114]

When Edwards articulates the instantaneous nature of conversion, he compares it to creation out of nothing. "In creation, something is brought out of nothing in an instant. God speaks and it is done; he commands and it stands fast. When the dead are raised, it is done in a moment."[115]

> If it be indeed so, as the Scripture abundantly teaches, that grace in the soul, is so the effect of God's power, that it is fitly compared to those effects, which are farthest from being owing to any strength in the subject, such as a generation, or a being begotten, and resurrection, or a being raised from the dead, and creation, or a being brought out of nothing into being, and that it is an effect wherein the mighty power of God is greatly glorified, and the exceeding greatness of his power is manifested.[116]

Furthermore, emphasizing God's ongoing immediate upholding of the universe, Edwards argues:

> If we make no difficulty of allowing that God did immediately make the whole universe at first, and caused it to exist out of nothing, and that every individual thing owes its being to an immediate, voluntary, arbitrary act of almighty power, why should we make a difficulty of supposing that he has still something immediately to do with the things that he has made, and that there is an arbitrary influence still that God has in the creation that he has made?[117]

---

113. See for example, Moltmann, *God in Creation*.
114. Edwards, *WJE* 23:204.
115. Edwards, "Religious Affections," *WJE* 2:161.
116. Edwards, "Religious Affections," *WJE* 2:139.
117. Edwards, "Treatise on Grace," *WJE* 21:177.

> It is most evident by the works of God, that his perfections are infinite, that his understanding and power are infinite; for he that hath made all things out of nothing, and upholds, and governs, and manages all things every day, and every moment, in all ages, without growing weary, must be of infinite power.[118]

It seems clear that Edwards holds the teaching of creation out of nothing without any reservation.

If by panentheism one means crypto-pantheism in which creation takes some *ontological* origin from the being of God, Edwards is not such a panentheist. If by panentheism one means simply an ontologically inclusive relation between God and creation but with a clear distinction between God and creation in terms of each ontological origin, then Edwards may be called a panentheist. The overview of scholarly debate over the allegation of Edwards's panentheism prompts that each scholar needs to provide a more refined definition that clarifies what exactly each scholar means by panentheism and to articulate how that feature manifests in Edwards's theology.

Whatever the conclusion might be, it is important to interpret the relation of God to the world in Edwards's theology within the context of his counteroffensive against the mechanistic view of the world in the Age of Enlightenment. Bombaro writes: "Jonathan Edwards stood as a stalwart, though creative and resourceful, proponent of Christian particularism in the Calvinist tradition."[119] Marsden terms Edwards's theological engagement with the increasingly secular age as "a post-Newtonian statement of classic Augustinian themes."[120] As Studebaker and Caldwell conclude, "Edwards, in short, was a creative and insightful trinitarian theologian of the late Reformed scholastic era who sought new ways within that tradition to communicate the doctrine of the Trinity to an increasingly skeptical and modern world."[121] Rather than rendering Edwards's doctrine of God in relation to creation as exceedingly modern, it seems more consistent with Edwards's own intention and context to interpret it as an attempt to reaffirm the traditional Reformed doctrine in a creative way that would be convincing to the people in an increasingly secular age.

---

118. Edwards, "Sole Consideration," *WJE* 50:41.
119. Bombaro, *Jonathan Edwards's Vision of Reality*, 255.
120. Marsden, *Jonathan Edwards*, 505.
121. Studebaker and Caldwell, *Trinitarian Theology of Jonathan Edwards*, 152.

CREATION AS A TRINITARIAN WORK

The end of the creation is "happiness and the communication of the goodness of God."[122] Edwards holds: "The great and universal end of God's creating the world was to communicate himself. God is a communicative being."[123] This inclination of God's self-communication is underscored by the eternal pact made within the internal communion of divine persons before the foundation of the world. Edwards writes on God's work of redemption.

> Hence it is that in this work, though in no other, God doth distinctly manifest himself in each of the persons of the Godhead, in their mutual relations one to another, and in that economy there is established amongst them, and in their distinct persons appearing in the eternal agreement and covenant these divine persons entered into about this work, and in the several offices and parts which each one bears in it, and how they are therein concerned one with another. 'Tis meet that this should be in the greatest and supreme work of God to which all other works are subordinate.[124]

The work of redemption is the supreme and the greatest work of God. All other decrees such as creation and providence are "subordinate and derivative of" this covenant of redemption.[125] As Bombaro notes, the covenant of redemption, or "the eternal *pactum salutis* possesses, as its substance, a 'confederation' among the members of the triune Godhead" that unfolds the glory of the Trinity through the scheme of redemption in history as the self-repetition of the perfect image of God.[126] The embryonic pattern of the redemption of the world was already in the mind of God in eternity. The universe is "nothing other than the ongoing realization of the divine idea."[127] Creation of the world sets up a stage on which God's eternal covenant of redemption unfolds itself in space and time. As Zakai puts it, Edwards holds "the view that the natural world and its beauty was the theater of God's glory—a special space-time designed from eternity to reveal the glory of God."[128]

---

122. Edwards, *WJE* 13:272.
123. Edwards, *WJE* 13:410.
124. Edwards, *WJE* 18:308.
125. Bombaro, *Jonathan Edwards's Vision of Reality*, 208.
126. Bombaro, *Jonathan Edwards's Vision of Reality*, 208.
127. Schweitzer, *God Is a Communicative Being*, 22.
128. Zakai, *Jonathan Edwards's Philosophy of Nature*, 264.

When Edwards made an entry in his *Blank Bible* on Genesis 1:1, he articulated the creation as the confederation of three divine persons of the Trinity. Based on an exegesis of van Mastricht,[129] Edwards notes that the word for God *Elohim* is plural and thus it signifies "the three persons of the Trinity confederated together as to the grand scheme and design of the creation, as they are in the eternal covenant of redemption."[130] As Stephen J. Stein explains, Edwards's view of the covenant of redemption "clarified by New Testament documents, provided a window back into the origins of the world."[131] Or conversely, Edwards's idea of the eternal covenant of redemption provided the foundation and backbone for the creation of the world.

Edwards's doctrine of the Trinity sets up a stage where God's work of redemption takes place. Creation prepares the arena on which the covenant of redemption made in eternity between the Father and the Son is carried out and put into practice in time. Edwards's idealism, typology of nature, creation as God's self-communication of his goodness and glory, and an importance of ontological status of human beings as sentient, intelligent beings all corroborate this outworking of the divine plan from eternity. As the self-communication of God's glory, the world poses ecological and ethical implications for human beings. Reading Edwards in this covenantal framework also helps to shed a new light on the current discussion on Edwards's alleged panentheism. Because the covenant of redemption has an inherent connection with the creation and ethical life of human beings, the immanent Trinity actually has a highly practical relevance for the believers. In the next chapter, we will turn to the work of redemption in creation specifically applied to an individual believer through justification and sanctification.

---

129. Mastricht, *Theoretico-practica Theologia*, 311–19.
130. Edwards, "Blank Bible," *WJE* 24:123.
131. Stein, "Editor's Introduction," *WJE* 24:26.

5

Covenant of Redemption, Trinity, Justification, and the Christian Life of Piety

As we saw in chapter 3, Jonathan Edwards formulated his doctrine of the covenant of redemption largely in consistence with the broader Reformed tradition. The reality that God's work of redemption was already planned in his eternal intra-trinitarian communion has diverse implications for Christian practical life. In this chapter, we will examine the implication of the covenant of redemption for justification and the Christian life of piety. It will explore the connection between the covenant of redemption and justification, perseverance, and life of Christian piety and practice that manifest in the individual lives of the saints.

In the course of the discussion, I will point out that a part of the reason why Edwards's covenantal theology has been interpreted thus far is due to older scholarship stereotypes of Calvinism. While recent scholarship attempts to examine Protestant orthodoxy in its own historical context and finds more affinity with the traditional Reformed tradition,[1] this recent change in Calvinism studies has been overlooked by many of the studies in Edwards scholarship. More recent studies begin to pay attention to this continuity between Edwards and the covenant theology in the Reformed tradition.

---

1. Muller, *Christ and the Decree*; Muller, *After Calvin*.

COVENANT OF REDEMPTION AND JUSTIFICATION BY FAITH ALONE

While studies on Edwards's doctrine of justification used to be quite limited,[2] since the early 1960s and especially stimulated by post-Vatican ecumenical dialogue, a growing amount of scholarly literature has begun to explore implications of Edwards's teaching on justification.[3] Recently Edwards's doctrine of justification has become "one of the most important interpretive conversations in the field."[4] Among these scholars, Anri Morimoto and Gerald McDermott find in Edwards a resource for a contemporary ecumenical dialogue between Catholics and Protestants.[5] In the most recent overview of Edwards's theology, Gerald McDermott and Michael McClymond declare Edwards as "one modern thinker" who would function "as a point of reference for theological interchange and dialogue."[6] However, as Douglas A. Sweeney points out, it is clear that Edwards did not intend to suggest that his theology might be a bridge between Protestants and Catholics. Edwards "opposed the Catholic Church in a typically old-Protestant way."[7] For example, in his sermon on Revelation 14:3, Edwards terms the Catholic as the "Antichristian church."

> The Antichristian church, or the church of Rome, is in this book called the great whore, but the true church is represented as the faithful spouse of Christ. And so the souls of those men that

---

2. Except for Jan Ridderbos, who treated Edwards's doctrine of justification and suggested a certain degree of affinity with the teaching of Roman Catholics, only a few scholars made a critical engagement with this doctrine. One pioneering work was made by Thomas Schafer. Schafer, "Jonathan Edwards and Justification," 55–67. See Lesser, *Reading Jonathan Edwards*, 682. For Ridderbos's treatment, see Ridderbos, *De Theologie van Jonathan Edwards*, 234–52. See also Sweeney, "Justification by Faith Alone?," 129.

3. Morimoto, *Jonathan Edwards and the Catholic Vision*; McDermott, "Possibility of Reconciliation" 187–91; *Jonathan Edwards Confronts the Gods*; "Jonathan Edwards on Justification," 92–111; McClymond, "Salvation as Divinization," 139–41; Bombaro, "Jonathan Edwards's Vision of Salvation," 45–67; Waddington, "Jonathan Edwards's 'Ambiguous' Doctrine," 357–72; McClenahan, *Jonathan Edwards and Justification*; Withrow, "Jonathan Edwards and Justification (1)," 93–109; Withrow, "Jonathan Edwards and Justification (2)," 98–111; Lee, "Editor's Introduction," *WJE* 21:62–105; *Princeton Companion*, 130–46; Cherry, *Theology of Jonathan Edwards*; Logan, "Doctrine of Justification," 26–52; Moody, *Jonathan Edwards and Justification*; Cho, *Jonathan Edwards on Justification*.

4. Sweeney, "Justification by Faith Alone?," 130.

5. Morimoto, *Jonathan Edwards and the Catholic Vision*, 157–63; McDermott, *Jonathan Edwards Confronts Gods*, 130–45.

6. McClymond and McDermott, *Theology of Jonathan Edwards*, 728.

7. Sweeney, "Justification by Faith Alone?," 132.

> polluted themselves with the idolatries and abominations of the church of Rome, are represented as whorish women that are false to their covenant with him to whom they had been betrothed and prostitute themselves to others.[8]

While it may be possible to explore potential resources for a contemporary ecumenical dialogue on Edwards's theology, I contend that, in a way consistent with Edwards's own historical context, it is still possible to identify helpful implications for contemporary theology today. One of them is the idea of the covenant of redemption that Edwards inherited from his Reformed tradition and delineated in his covenantal framework of his theology.

The proposition that the work of redemption was designed in the intra-trinitarian pact between the Father and the Son underscores the divine work of justification and the total dependence of the elect upon God's grace. In his sermon "Justification by Faith Alone" (1734), Edwards reiterates that God's plan of redemption was preordained in the eternal pact of the covenant of redemption.

> There was a transaction between the Father and the Son, that was antecedent to Christ's becoming man, and being made under the law wherein he undertook to put himself under the law, and both to obey and to suffer; in which transaction these things were already *virtually* done in the sight of God; as is evident by this, that God acted on the ground of that transaction, justifying and saving sinners, as if the things undertaken had been actually performed long before they were performed indeed.[9]

Edwards sees the covenant of redemption as the foundation for the justification of sinners.[10] The justification of sinners is not an emergency measure taken by God after the fall of humans. It was in the eternal pact between the Father and the Son before the foundation of the world. As Sang Lee points out, "God's redemptive activity in the world is the carrying out of the covenant of redemption that had been made by the three persons of the Trinity."[11] As "our surety and representative," Edwards continues, Christ accepted obligation both "to obey the law" and "to suffer the penalty."[12]

---

8. Edwards, "They Sing a New Song," *WJE* 22:227.

9. Edwards, "Justification by Faith Alone," *WJE* 19:192 (emphasis mine).

10. For Edwards's doctrine of sin, see Weddle, "Jonathan Edwards on Man," 155–75; Crisp, *Jonathan Edwards and the Metaphysics*.

11. Lee, "Editor's Introduction," *WJE* 21:77. To be accurate, Edwards articulates the covenant of redemption as the covenant made by two persons, between the Father and the Son. This is a typical articulation of the covenant of redemption in the Reformed tradition as was seen in chapter 2.

12. Edwards, "Justification by Faith Alone," *WJE* 19:192.

> But if we look to that original transaction between the Father and the Son, wherein both these were undertaken and accepted, as virtually done in the sight of the Father, we shall find Christ acting with regard to both, as one perfectly in his own right, and under no manner of previous obligation.[13]

Accordingly, in Edwards, the doctrine of justification is construed within this broader scheme of the eternal pact within the immanent Trinity and its execution in temporality in the world.

As sentient beings that can appreciate and enjoy the beauty and excellence of God, human beings, together with angels, hold a special place in creation. When the elect are justified and their hearts are tuned into the beauty and excellence of God, God is thereby glorified and his internal perfection is repeated *ad extra*. It is important to recognize Edwards's doctrine of justification within this broader framework of God's self-communication. Edwards articulates this point as follows:

> It can't be properly said that the end of God's creating of the world is twofold, or that there are two parallel, coordinate ends of God's creating the world, one to exercise his perfections *ad extra*, another to make his creatures happy. But all is included in one, viz. God's exhibiting his perfections, or causing his essential glory to be exercised, expressed and communicated *ad extra*.[14]

In fact, justification of the elect has a crucial place in God's movement of self-glorification. When the saint receives, appreciates, and enjoys God's glory, which is none other than God's self-communication, God's glory within himself is, so to speak, repeated *ad extra* in the world. Through praise to God by the saint the divine glory communicated to the saint is reflected and returned back to God. In this sense, the justification of sinners is a fulcrum between the emanation and remanation of divine glory. As Morimoto puts it, "Justification occupies a middle step in the economy of salvation, between God's emanation and remanation."[15]

A parallel relation between God and human beings underscores and confirms the fact that human beings, as sentient beings, have a special place in creation in Edwards's theology. Explaining that the difference between the deity and created spirits is not that of contradiction, Edwards writes:

---

13. Edwards, "Justification by Faith Alone," *WJE* 19:192.
14. Edwards, *WJE* 23:150.
15. Morimoto, *Jonathan Edwards and the Catholic Vision*, 101.

> Many have wrong conceptions of the difference between the nature of the Deity and created spirits. The difference is no contrariety, but what naturally results from his greatness and nothing else, such as created spirits come nearer to, or more imitate, the greater they are in their powers and faculties. So that if we should suppose the faculties of a created spirit to be enlarged infinitely, there would be the Deity to all intents and purposes, the same simplicity, immutability, etc.[16]

While this statement seems surprising for a Reformed mind that emphasizes the unequivocal distinction between God and creation, this is Edwards's way of specifying that human beings are created in the image of God. They are hence equipped to perceive God's self-communication in a parallel way that God the Father perceives himself in the Son as his perfect image.

"And this is God's manner," Edwards notes in another place, "to make inferior things shadows of the superior and most excellent, outward things shadows of spiritual, and all other things shadows of those things that are the end of all things and the crown of all things."[17] Because sentient beings are created in God's image and capable of perceiving communication of divine glory, "God glorifies himself and instructs the minds that he has made."[18]

Moreover, Edwards sees that human faculties of understanding and will structurally reflect God's internal communication through the Son in the Holy Spirit. In miscellany 448, Edwards articulates a parallel pattern that can be identified between the way God is glorified within himself and the way God is glorified in relation to creation. First, according to Edwards, God is glorified within himself in two ways: as the perfect idea in the Son and as the delight and enjoyment in the Holy Spirit.

> God is glorified within himself these two ways: (1) by appearing or being manifested to himself in his own perfect idea, or, in his Son, who is the brightness of his glory; (2) by enjoying and delighting in himself, by flowing forth in infinite love and delight towards himself, or, in his Holy Spirit.[19]

Second, corresponding to God's internal pattern of self-communication, intellectual sentient beings have two faculties: understanding and will. As John Bombaro argues, "God's internal relations serve as the archetypal pattern of

---

16. Edwards, *WJE* 13:295.
17. Edwards, *WJE* 13:435.
18. Edwards, *WJE* 13:435.
19. Edwards, *WJE* 13:495.

Covenant of Redemption, Trinity, Justification, and the Christian Life of Piety   111

the inner constitution of man."[20] Each faculty functions as receiver of God's self-communication as the idea and affection. Edwards continues:

> So God glorifies himself towards the creatures also two ways: (1) by appearing to them, being manifested to their understandings; (2) in communicating himself to their hearts, and in their rejoicing and delighting in, and enjoying the manifestations which he makes of himself. They both of them may be called his glory in the more extensive sense of the word, viz. his shining forth, or the going forth of his excellency, beauty and essential glory *ad extra*. By one way it goes forth towards their understandings; by the other it goes forth towards their wills or hearts. God is glorified not only by his glory's being seen, but by its being rejoiced in, when those that see it delight in it: God is more glorified than if they only see it; his glory is then received by the whole soul, both by the understanding and by the heart. God made the world that he might communicate, and the creature receive, his glory, but that it might [be] received both by the mind and heart.[21]

Both of these ways of communication share one motivation in common: "the overflowing of God's internal glory, or an inclination in God to cause his internal glory to flow out *ad extra*."[22]

> And this [is] very consistent with what we are taught of God's being the Alpha and Omega, the first and the last. God made all things; and the end for which all things are made, and for which they are disposed, and for which they work continually, is that God's glory may shine forth and be received. From him all creatures come, and in him their well-being consists; God is all their beginning, and God received is all their end. From him and to him are all things; they are all from him and they are all to be brought to him: but 'tis not that they may add to him, but that God might be received by them.[23]

When believers receive this divine self-communication in understanding and take delight in it, human sentient beings are fulfilling the purpose and *telos* for which they were originally created to be.

However, this fulfillment of the purpose of creation does not take place without cost: the cross of Jesus in his obedience to the will of God the Father

---

20. Bombaro, *Jonathan Edwards's Vision of Reality*, 153.
21. Edwards, *WJE* 13:495.
22. Edwards, *WJE* 13:496.
23. Edwards, *WJE* 13:496.

as the execution of the covenant of redemption. Because human faculties are significantly damaged by the fall, it is not possible in a fallen condition for the unregenerate to understand and take delight in this self-communication of divine glory. Unless God regenerates and justifies the elect and bestows faith on them, a new sense of the communication of divine glory will not take place. In this sense, justification takes a crucial role for redressing human faculties in the right direction. Through the person and work of Jesus Christ in history, Christ purchased salvation for the elect. Christ has carried out the eternal pact in history. This purchase is now applied to each individual through the indwelling of the Holy Spirit. As Kyle Strobel argues, "Edwards's development of soteriological loci occurs under his analysis of the person and work of Christ and the nature and gift of the Spirit,"[24] which indicates Edwards's general agreement with the Augustinian tradition.

Edwards thinks that justification involves "having both a negative, and positive righteousness" belonging to the elect.[25] A "negative righteousness" means freedom from sin and punishment, whereas a "positive righteousness" signifies having real righteousness in God's sight and thereby entitled for a reward. Justification means that God sees a person "as not only quit, or free from any obligation to punishment but also as just and righteous, and so entitled to a positive reward."[26] Since in a fallen state a human being is without righteousness, "the righteousness of some other should be reckoned to his account."[27]

> God neither will nor can justify a person without a righteousness; for justification is manifestly a *forensic* term, as the word is used in Scripture, and the thing a judicial thing, or the act of a judge: so that if a person should be justified without a righteousness, the judgment would not be according to truth: the sentence of justification would be a false sentence, unless there be a righteousness performed that is by the judge properly looked upon as his.[28]

God cannot pronounce sinners as righteous simply by neglecting their inherent ungodliness. God has to see true righteousness in them. This declaration of sinners as righteous can happen only because God sees the elect so united with Christ that God sees Christ's righteousness as their

---

24. Strobel, "By Word and Spirit," 45.
25. Edwards, "Justification by Faith Alone," *WJE* 19:150.
26. Edwards, "Justification by Faith Alone," *WJE* 19:150.
27. Edwards, "Justification by Faith Alone," *WJE* 19:188.
28. Edwards, "Justification by Faith Alone," *WJE* 19:188–89.

own. This union with Christ[29] is a central concept in Edwards's doctrine of justification.

Edwards sees more of the ontological reality that underscores the justification than merely the remission of sin. "Faith gives a title to salvation as it gives an union to Christ, or is in its nature an actual unition of the soul to Christ."[30] As Morimoto points out, Edwards makes efforts to "furnish the legal transaction with an ontological basis."[31] Because the saints are united in Christ so closely as one in unity, God sees the merit of Christ as that of the saints at the same time. Edwards continues: "The soul is saved no otherwise than *in union* with Christ, and so is fitly looked upon [as] his."[32] The term "union" can be equivalent to "relation" for Edwards.[33] In union with Christ, the elect are related so closely to Christ that God sees them as one in which the benefits of Christ also belong to the saints. "This relation or union to Christ, whereby Christians are said to be *in* Christ (whatever it be), is the ground of their right to his benefits."[34]

Morimoto sees in this emphasis on the ontological union of the elect with Christ a doctrine of infusion that resonates with the Catholic teaching on justification. According to Morimoto, generally the Protestant, on one hand, holds that in justification, God imputes Christ's righteousness to a sinner and pronounces the sinner as righteous as a forensic declaration. The Catholic, on the other hand, claims the ontological transformation of the justified through the infusion of grace.[35] Because in Edwards's theological framework a sinner is justified not only by imputation but also by infusion of grace, Morimoto concludes that "Edwards's theories of infused grace exhibit a balanced combination of Protestant and Catholic concerns in one form."[36] In this way, Morimoto finds in Edwards's soteriology a resource for contemporary ecumenical dialogue between the Protestant and the Catholic.

Furthermore, applying Sang Lee's dispositional ontological interpretation to Edwards's soteriology, Morimoto thinks that in Edwards's framework anyone who has disposition to be saved will be saved regardless of

---

29. For recent studies on Calvin's idea of union and participation, see Billings, *Calvin, Participation*; Canlis, *Calvin's Ladder*; Evans, *Imputation and Impartation*.
30. Edwards, *WJE* 18:354.
31. Morimoto, *Jonathan Edwards and the Catholic Vision*, 86.
32. Edwards, *WJE* 18:355.
33. Edwards, "Justification by Faith Alone," *WJE* 19:155–56.
34. Edwards, "Justification by Faith Alone," *WJE* 19:156.
35. Morimoto, *Jonathan Edwards and the Catholic Vision*, 103–30.
36. Morimoto, *Jonathan Edwards and the Catholic Vision*, 68.

their current confessional status. Accordingly, Morimoto even goes so far as to say that Edwards's soteriology is inclusive enough to indicate a possibility of salvation of non-Christian believers.

> Furthermore, salvation as understood in this dispositional view can be extended even beyond the boundary of Judeo-Christian tradition. There is no hard division between Christians and non-Christians in terms of the grounds on which they are saved. Those who do possess the disposition are all saved on account of that disposition, regardless of their explicit or conscious religious affiliation, or lack thereof. This is a paradigm of soteriology that is radically inclusive and yet theologically responsible.[37]

Morimoto finds in Edwards, beyond the intention of Edwards's himself, a resource for contemporary ecumenical dialogue between the Protestant and the Catholic, between Christianity and other religions.[38] In the same way, applying a dispositional interpretation to Edwards's soteriology, McDermott argues that Edwards later in his life conceived a potential of salvation of non-believers. Thus McDermott sees in Edwards a helpful resource for dialogues between Christianity and other religions.[39]

However, if we interpret Edwards in his own context and theological framework, it is clear that "Edwards did theology as a Calvinistic pastor,"[40] or as "a post-Puritan champion of Reformed orthodoxy."[41] A quintessential example can be found in Edwards's covenantal scheme in the development of his soteriology. Perry Miller once argued that Edwards discarded the Reformed covenantal framework.[42] Since then, several scholars have followed this assessment. For example, Shelton Smith argues: "He [Edwards] gave little attention to the federal theory, a fact which probably indicates that he doubted that it sufficiently safeguarded the principle of direct participation."[43] Thomas Schafer comments that in response to the Arminian charge of the unreasonableness of forensic justification, Edwards "recoiled from the merely legal and arbitrary elements in Calvinistic dogma

---

37. Morimoto, *Jonathan Edwards and the Catholic Vision*, 162.

38. To be sure, Morimoto himself acknowledges that it is beyond Edwards's intention that affinities exist between Edwards's soteriology and that of the Roman Catholics. Morimoto, *Jonathan Edwards and the Catholic Vision*, 9.

39. McDermott, *Jonathan Edwards Confronts the God*, 137; McDermott, "Jonathan Edwards, John Henry Newman," 129–30.

40. Sweeney, "Justification by Faith Alone?," 153.

41. Sweeney, "Justification by Faith Alone?," 152.

42. Miller, *Jonathan Edwards*, 30–32, 76–78.

43. Smith, *Changing Conceptions of Original Sin*, 35.

Covenant of Redemption, Trinity, Justification, and the Christian Life of Piety 115

and in the covenant theology."[44] Morimoto basically concurs when he says: "His standard use of the 'federal' vocabulary notwithstanding, Edwards did not make much use of it."[45] Despite these evaluations, which seem to contain the full stereotypes of the Reformed tradition, Edwards actually used this federal theological framework consistently.[46]

For example, Edwards repeatedly points out that it is only through faith alone that the elect are justified.

> We are justified only by faith in Christ, and not by any manner of virtue or goodness of our own.[47]

> Faith is a sensibleness of what is real in the work of redemption; and as we do wholly depend on God, so the soul that believes doth entirely depend on God for all salvation, in its own sense, and act. Faith abases men, and exalts God, it gives all the glory of redemption to God alone.[48]

> There is no one doctrine in the whole Bible is more fully asserted, explained, and urged than the doctrine of justification by faith alone, without any of our own righteousness.[49]

> We are dependent on God's power through every step of our redemption. We are dependent on the power of God to convert us, and give faith in Jesus Christ, and the new nature.[50]

In this exposition, Edwards aligns himself with his Reformed predecessors. While the covenant of works required that human beings obey God's command for their justification, after the fall, humans cannot be justified by their own works of obedience.

---

44. Schafer, "Role of Jonathan Edwards," 215.

45. Morimoto, *Jonathan Edwards and the Catholic Vision*, 84.

46. Part of the reason for this partial assessment is that most of the scholars have focused their analysis on Edwards's well-known discourse *Justification by Faith Alone* and have not paid much attention to the whole spectrum of Edwards's sermons and other exegetical writings. "Nearly everyone who has published on this controversial issue, though, has limited him/herself to Edwards's well-known published discourse, *Justification by Faith Alone* (1738), along with a smattering of statements from his master's thesis at Yale and a few of the theological notebooks where he treated the doctrine famously. None has studied the full array of exegetical writings in which Edwards fleshes out his doctrine of justification further" (Sweeney, "Justification by Faith Alone?," 130–31).

47. Edwards, "Justification by Faith Alone," *WJE* 19:149.

48. Edwards, "God Glorified in Man's Dependence," *WJE* 17:213.

49. Edwards, "Justification by Faith Alone," *WJE* 19:232.

50. Edwards, "God Glorified in Man's Dependence," *WJE* 17:205.

> This is plainly what our divines intend when they say that faith don't justify as a work, or a righteousness, viz. that it don't justify as a part of our moral goodness or excellency, or that it don't justify as a work, in the sense that man was to have been justified by his works by the covenant of works, which was to have a title to eternal life, given him of God in testimony of his pleasedness with his works, or his regard to the inherent excellency and beauty of his obedience.[51]

In his exposition of Rom 1:16–18, Edwards writes that "all are guilty, and in a state of condemnation, and therefore can't be saved by their own righteousness, that it must be by the righteousness of God through Christ received by faith alone."[52] It is only through the union in Christ that the righteousness of Christ is imputed to the elect and thereby they are justified.

Accordingly, Edwards draws a sharp distinction between justification as a reward for the human act of faith and justification by faith as the union in Christ.

> There is a wide difference between its being looked on suitable that Christ's satisfaction and merits should be theirs that believe, because an interest in that satisfaction and merit is but a fit reward of faith, or a suitable testimony of God's respect to the amiableness and excellency of that grace, and its only being looked on suitable that Christ's satisfaction and merits should be theirs, because Christ and they are so united, that in the eyes of the Judge they may be looked upon, and taken, as one.[53]

The elect are justified not because of their inherent moral excellency but because of the union in Christ wrought by faith.

Moreover, Edwards articulates this theme within the framework of federal theology. For instance, in his sermon on the 2 Sam 23:5 in 1729, Edwards explicates justification within the framework of the covenant of works and the covenant of grace. "The Covenant of Grace is that Covenant which G has Revealed to man since he failed of life by the Covenant of works. Promising Justification & Eternal life to all that believe in J.X."[54] Even before the incarnation, saints in the Old Testament were justified by Jesus Christ who was to come.[55] In his biblical exegesis, the Northampton pastor sees in a patriarchs' blessing a type of the covenant of grace in Jesus

---

51. Edwards, "Justification by Faith Alone," *WJE* 19:160.
52. Edwards, "Notes on Scripture," *WJE* 15:294.
53. Edwards, "Justification by Faith Alone," *WJE* 19:158–59.
54. Edwards, "Sermon on 2 Sam 23:5," *WJE* 44:L.3r.
55. Sweeney, "Justification by Faith Alone?," 138.

Christ. "The patriarch's thus blessing their children before their death exhibits to us a type of the covenant of grace, which is as it were Christ's last will and testament to his people. Genesis 27:9."[56] The covenant of grace in Jesus Christ was virtually implied in the Ten Commandments revealed to the people of Israel at Mount Sinai. "The Cov. of Grace is virtually contained in those words in the Preface to the Ten C. Which words G. Spoke at Mt Sinai I am the L. thy G."[57] This economy of redemption stems from the covenant of redemption: the eternal covenant made between the Father and the Son.

> He was appointed to it from Et• in an Eternal Covenant that was between the Father & him. then G• called him & then he undertook to be an high Priest to make attonem• for the sins of men. of this covenant G• speaks in Zech •6• 12• 13• calling it the counsel of Peace that was between G• & him.[58]

Edwards develops his soteriology within the framework of covenant theology that sees the covenant of works and the covenant of grace as the ectypal unfolding of the covenant of redemption.

While Smith, Shafer, and Morimoto seem to think that Edwards's language of participation is not compatible with the scheme of federal theology, Edwards actually develops his language of participation in Christ within the framework of federal theology.

> They are united. union with X is the first & most Immediate Consequence of acceptance of him. Xtians have a vital union with X. they are come to him & are ingrafted onto him & become branches of him members of his body. They are come to him so that he is come to dwell with them & in them by his Holy Spr. . . . There is a Covenant union between & X & the soul of a Xtian they are united by the mutual bed of a Cov. whereby he is theirs and they his there is such an union that they have a mutual propriety in Each other.[59]

In Edwards, covenantal framework and participatory language that describes the elect's union with Christ are not mutually exclusive but rather they intimately go together.

Even Edwards's well-known sermon "Sinners in the Hands of an Angry God" clearly pronounces the damnation of the reprobate who disconnect themselves from the covenant of grace.

56. Edwards, "Blank Bible," *WJE* 24:171.
57. Edwards, "Sermon on Heb 12:22–24 (f)," *WJE* 55:9.
58. Edwards, "Sermon on Heb 9:13–14," *WJE* 53:L.6r.–L.6v.
59. Edwards, "Sermon on Heb 12:22–24 (f)," *WJE* 55:17.

> God has laid himself under *no obligation* by any promise to keep any natural man out of hell one moment. God certainly has made no promises either of eternal life, or of any deliverance or preservation from eternal death, but what are contained in the covenant of grace, the promises that are given in Christ, in whom all the promises are yea and amen. But surely they have no interest in the promises of the covenant of grace that are not the children of the covenant, and that don't believe in any of the promises of the covenant, and have no interest in the *Mediator* of the covenant.[60]

Furthermore, Edwards disapproves of a possibility for the salvation of heathens in the following way:

> Hence we learn that there is nothing appears in the reason and nature of things that can . . . justly lead us to determine that God will certainly reveal Christ and give the necessary means of grace, or some way or other bestow true holiness and saving grace, and so eternal salvation, to those heathen that are sincere . . . in their endeavors to find out the will of the Deity and please him according to that light, that they may escape his future displeasure and wrath and obtain happiness in their future state through his favor.[61]

Rather than plumbing possibilities of ecumenical dialogues or the salvation of non-Christian believers, it seems more faithful to and consistent with Edwards's own theological framework to recapture his federal theology and its practical implications.

JUSTIFICATION AND PERSEVERANCE

Within this covenantal framework, Edwards delineates his doctrine of justification by grace alone through faith alone in Christ alone. The elect are regenerated by the direct influence of the Holy Spirit. The spiritual knowledge that communicates divine excellence and majesty is wrought by the direct work of the Holy Spirit. The spiritual knowledge is "what God is the author of, and none else: he reveals it, and flesh and blood reveals it not."[62] God "imparts this knowledge immediately, not making use of any

---

60. Edwards, "Sinners in the Hands," *WJE* 22:409.
61. Edwards, *WJE* 23:56. See also Bombaro, *Jonathan Edwards's Vision of Reality*, 233–88.
62. Edwards, "Divine and Supernatural Light," *WJE* 17:409.

Covenant of Redemption, Trinity, Justification, and the Christian Life of Piety 119

intermediate natural causes."⁶³ While the Spirit of God acts upon the unregenerate only "as an extrinsic occasional agent" and assists employment of natural faculties, the Spirit "unites himself with the mind of a saint, takes him for his temple, actuates and influences him as a new, supernatural principle of life and action."⁶⁴

Accordingly, there is an unbridgeable gap between the regenerate and the unregenerate in terms of the work of the Holy Spirit. The true regenerate has a "true sense of the divine and superlative excellency of the things of religion."⁶⁵ The regenerate not only rationally understands divine things in understanding, but also has a sense of them because the will is affected by the Spirit of God.

> He don't merely rationally believe that God is glorious, but he has a sense of the gloriousness of God in his heart. There is not only a rational belief that God is holy, and that holiness is a good thing; but there is a sense of the loveliness of God's holiness. There is not only a speculatively judging that God is gracious, but a sense how amiable God is upon that account; or a sense of the beauty of this divine attribute.⁶⁶

The speculative or notional knowledge only apprehends things as theoretical knowledge "in distinction from the will or disposition of the soul,"⁶⁷ while the spiritual knowledge wrought by "the sense of the heart" has "a sense of the beauty, amiableness, or sweetness of a thing; so that the heart is sensible of pleasure and delight in the presence of the idea of it."⁶⁸

> Thus there is a difference between having an opinion that God is holy and gracious, and having a sense of the loveliness and beauty of that holiness and grace. There is a difference between having a rational judgment that honey is sweet, and having a sense of its sweetness. A man may have the former, that knows not how honey tastes; but a man can't have the latter, unless he has an idea of the taste of honey in his mind. So there is a difference between believing that a person is beautiful, and having a sense of his beauty. The former may be obtained by hearsay, but the latter only by seeing the countenance. There is a wide

63. Edwards, "Divine and Supernatural Light," *WJE* 17:409.
64. Edwards, "Divine and Supernatural Light," *WJE* 17:411.
65. Edwards, "Divine and Supernatural Light," *WJE* 17:413.
66. Edwards, "Divine and Supernatural Light," *WJE* 17:413.
67. Edwards, "Divine and Supernatural Light," *WJE* 17:414.
68. Edwards, "Divine and Supernatural Light," *WJE* 17:413. See also Simonson, *Theologian of the Heart*.

> difference between mere speculative, rational judging anything to be excellent, and having a sense of its sweetness, and beauty. The former rests only in the head, speculation only is concerned in it; but the heart is concerned in the latter. When the heart is sensible of the beauty and amiableness of a thing, it necessarily feels pleasure in the apprehension. It is implied in a person's being heartily sensible of the loveliness of a thing, that the idea of it is sweet and pleasant to his soul; which is a far different thing from having a rational opinion that it is excellent.[69]

Citing Matthew 11:27 ("All things are delivered unto me of my Father, and no man knoweth the Son but the Father; neither knoweth any man the Father, save the Son, and he to whomever the Son will reveal him"), Edwards claims that the work of imparting spiritual light is "the arbitrary operation, and gift of God, bestowing this knowledge on whom he will."[70]

The reality that the work of regeneration is God's arbitrary operation means that this divine dispensation is a "covenant of mercy, and way of grace towards his people, as peculiar to the saints, and given only by God."[71] While this sheer dependence of the elect on God's justifying grace is clear in Edwards, this complete dependence does not necessarily mean mere passiveness. While Christ took an active role in becoming a human and fulfilling perfect obedience to the Father's will, the elect also play an active role in the union in Christ. Faith is "the soul's active uniting with Christ, or is itself the very act of union, on their part."[72] Edwards continues:

> God sees it fit, that in order to an union's being established between two intelligent active beings or persons, so as that they should be looked upon as one, there should be the mutual act of both, that each should receive the other, as actively joining themselves one to another. God in requiring this in order to an union with Christ as one of his people, treats men as reasonable creatures, capable of act, and choice; and hence sees it fit that they only, that are one with Christ by their own act, should be looked upon as one in law: what is real in the union between Christ and his people, is the foundation of what is legal; that is, it is something really in them, and between them, uniting them,

---

69. Edwards, "Divine and Supernatural Light," *WJE* 17:414.

70. Edwards, "Divine and Supernatural Light," *WJE* 17:417.

71. Edwards, "Divine and Supernatural Light," *WJE* 17:418. For the morphology of Puritan's doctrine of conversion, see Beeke and Smalley, *Puritan Preparation by Grace*; Pettit, *Heart Prepared*.

72. Edwards, "Justification by Faith Alone," *WJE* 19:158.

that is the ground of the suitableness of their being accounted as one by the Judge.[73]

On the one hand, God brings forth justification of the elect through the perfect obedience of Christ. The elect do not have any inherent value that renders them worthy of justification. Yet on the other hand, since this justification takes place in the elect's union in Christ, it is still an active, willing participation on the part of the elect in the benefits of Christ. Thus, "Edwards's concept of faith is very active and volitional in character."[74] Morimoto points out: "Such an active and voluntary involvement of the believer is important for Edwards, for it expresses an element of human participation in the work of justification."[75]

In fact, Edwards's emphasis on the believers' active role in participating in the benefits of Christ sometimes prompted scholars to think that in his doctrine of justification Edwards inadvertently leaned towards Arminianism, the very opponent he protested. For example, Lawrence R. Rast Jr. argues:

> He [Edwards] wanted to protect the integrity of the human personality and the freedom of the will. He shifted the notion of imputation away from an arbitrary act of God, so that imputation was dependent on an act of the human will, not the decision of God. Imputation depended on faith. In fact, justification depended upon the act of faith. The unintended but real effect was that Edwards stressed the human side in the salvation equation more than the divine. The ironic result was that while Edwards sought to maintain a consistent Calvinism, he opened the door to a full capitulation to the Arminian scheme.[76]

Because Edwards calls the act of faith as "one holy act of ours" and "the condition of our salvation,"[77] some scholars conceived that Edwards ultimately weighed the decision of the human will over against God's gratuitous nature of grace.

However, this interpretation does not take seriously the eternal pact of salvation made between the Father and the Son, or Edwards's understanding of freedom of the will. As was seen before, Edwards's concept of the covenant of redemption virtually contained the salvation of the elect which

---

73. Edwards, "Justification by Faith Alone," *WJE* 19:158. See also Edwards, *WJE* 18:105.

74. Morimoto, *Jonathan Edwards and the Catholic Vision*, 88.

75. Morimoto, *Jonathan Edwards and the Catholic Vision*, 90.

76. Rast, "Jonathan Edwards on Justification," 361.

77. Edwards, *WJE* 20:453.

would be actualized and executed in temporality. Even the willing participation on the part of the believers in the union in Christ was also included in God's eternal plan of redemption. Faith is, in this sense, "an antecedent gift of God."[78] While the believers voluntarily close with Christ in the act of faith, it is at the same time "God that gives faith whereby we close with Christ."[79] Hence for Edwards human free will and God's sovereignty are not exclusive but compatible to each other.[80]

> We are not merely passive in it, nor yet does God do some and we do the rest, but God does all and we do all. God produces all and we act all. For that is what he produces, our own acts. God is the only proper author and fountain; we only are the proper actors. We are in different respects wholly passive and wholly active.[81]

By emphasizing the active participation of the believers in the communion with Christ, Edwards does not undermine the gratuitous nature of divine grace. To be accurate, Edwards emphasizes both the sovereign nature of divine grace and the active participation of the saint in the benefits of Christ's righteousness.

In other words, Edwards sees that the covenant of redemption as God's eternal plan of redemption unfolds in this world in a way that human voluntary acts take a constitutive and indispensable part. Here God rewards the holiness in the elect when that holiness itself is God's gift. Edwards explains: "He [God] has a propensity to reward holiness, but he gives it on purpose that he may reward it; because he loves the creature, and loves to reward, and therefore gives it something that he may reward."[82] "God crowns his own gift of faith with the reward of justification."[83] God gives the gift of faith to the elect and rewards it by himself yet in a way that the elect as an agent of a voluntary decision plays a vital role in that process. In sum, "In faith God's self-communication flows back to God via humanity."[84]

For Edwards, God's sovereign rule and active human involvement in God's grand design of redemption do not exclude but are compatible with each other. Terms such as "action" and "passion" do not signify "opposite

---

78. Morimoto, *Jonathan Edwards and the Catholic Vision*, 97.

79. Edwards, "God Glorified in Man's Dependence," *WJE* 17:202.

80. Guelzo, "Return of the Will," 94; Danaher, *Trinitarian Ethics of Jonathan Edwards*, 168.

81. Edwards, "Efficacious Grace," *WJE* 21:251.

82. Edwards, *WJE* 13:396.

83. Morimoto, *Jonathan Edwards and the Catholic Vision*, 98.

84. Morimoto, *Jonathan Edwards and the Catholic Vision*, 98.

existences," but "only opposite *relations*."[85] In other words, Edwards conceives activeness and passiveness not in absolute sense, but in relational terms. Edwards continues: "The soul may be both active and passive in the same thing in different respects, active with relation to one thing, and passive with relation to another."[86] Thus with the terms "cause" and "effect," Edwards explains, "the same thing may at the same time, in different respects and relations, be both cause and effect."[87] It is possible then that in terms of salvation, the destiny of each human being is constrained and determined, and yet at the same time, in terms of active engagement with objects on which the action is terminated, the person, as the agent, acts actively and freely.

A quintessential example can be found in Edwards's polemical argument against the Arminian interpretation of freedom. In his *Freedom of the Will*, Edwards sees the Arminian notion of freedom as the sheer indifference and equilibrium out of which the agent can choose freely either to do or not to do a certain thing. Since freedom means will's self-determining power, so Arminians argue, any constraint imposed on the agent means necessity that bounds the agent unfree. If the agent is bound to do certain actions necessarily, Arminians believed, then one cannot attribute to the agent virtue and vice, reward and punishment, and praise and blame. In short, for the Arminian notion of freedom, as Edwards so understands, moral agency is incompatible with any idea of necessity and determinism.[88] To this argument, Edwards responds that such a notion of freedom devastates the certainty of salvation itself. If freedom always means openness to conflicting options, then Christ might have failed in sin. Consequently, salvation might not have prevailed. If Christ has a choice to obey the will of the Father or not, there would be a possibility in which Christ failed in his perseverance and obedience to the will of the Father. This uncertainty contradicts with the nature of God's promise because "God's absolute promise of any things makes the things promised *necessary*, and their failing to take place absolutely *impossible*."[89]

In other words, with the Arminian notion of freedom, the idea of a divine decree is untenable. Since Arminian divines also hold the doctrine of

---

85. Edwards, "Freedom of the Will," *WJE* 1:347.
86. Edwards, "Freedom of the Will," *WJE* 1:347.
87. Edwards, "Freedom of the Will," *WJE* 1:347.
88. Edwards, "Freedom of the Will," *WJE* 1:171–74.
89. Edwards, "Freedom of the Will," *WJE* 1:283.

divine decree,⁹⁰ it is their presupposition of freedom itself that Arminians need to reconsider.

> God could not decree before the foundation of the world, to save all that should believe in, and obey Christ, unless he had absolutely decreed that salvation should be provided, and effectually wrought out by Christ. And since (as the Arminians themselves strenuously maintain) a decree of God infers necessity; hence it became necessary that Christ should persevere, and actually work out salvation for us, and that he should not fail by the commission of sin.⁹¹

If, as Arminians argue, moral agency obtains only in a state where the agent has self-determining power to do or not to do certain things, then God, who decrees from eternity that Christ accomplishes salvation without fail would be considered as the amoral agent or the agent morally unaccountable. If Christ was preordained to carry out the Father's will and there was no possibility in which Christ fails to do so, then according to the Arminian definition of freedom, Christ would be unworthy of praise, reward, and virtue. This would be a horrible, blasphemous thought that Arminians themselves would adamantly deny. This logical consequence has to force Arminians to reconsider their notion of free will as a self-determining power exerted from the state of indifference and equilibrium.

It is in this context of attesting the unfailing certainty of salvation that Edwards introduces the idea of the covenant of redemption.

> That it should be possible for Christ to fail of doing his Father's will, is inconsistent with the promise made to the Father by the Son, by the *Logos* that was with the Father from the beginning, before he took the human nature.⁹²

> If the *Logos*, who was with the Father, before the world, and who made the world, thus engaged in covenant to do the will of the Father in the human nature, and the promise, was as it were recorded, that it might be made sure, doubtless it was *impossible* that it should fail; and so it was *impossible* that Christ should fail of doing the will of the Father in the human nature.⁹³

---

90. "Such an absolute decree as this Arminians don't deny" (Edwards, "Freedom of the Will," *WJE* 1:286).

91. Edwards, "Freedom of the Will," *WJE* 1:286.

92. Edwards, "Freedom of the Will," *WJE* 1:287.

93. Edwards, "Freedom of the Will," *WJE* 1:287.

Covenant of Redemption, Trinity, Justification, and the Christian Life of Piety   125

If freedom is will's self-determining power and thus leaves room for failure for Christ to work out redemption for sinners, the whole promise of God's work of salvation would be in jeopardy.

> If it was possible for Christ to have failed of doing the will of his Father, and so to have failed of effectually working out redemption for sinners, then the salvation of all the saints, who were saved from the beginning of the world, to the death of Christ, was not built on a firm foundation. The Messiah, and the redemption which he was to work out by his obedience unto death, was the foundation of the salvation of all the posterity of fallen man, that ever were saved. Therefore, if when the Old Testament saints had the pardon of their sins, and the favor of God promised them, and salvation bestowed upon them, still it was possible that the Messiah, when he came, might commit sin, then all this was on a foundation that was not firm and stable, but liable to fail; something which it was possible might never be. God did as it were trust to what his Son had engaged and promised to do in future time; and depended so much upon it, that he proceeded actually to save men on the account of it, as though it had been already done. But this trust and dependence of God, on the supposition of Christ's being liable to fail of doing his will, was leaning on a staff that was weak, and might possibly break.[94]

> The dependence of those who looked for redemption in Jerusalem, and waited for the consolation of Israel (Luke 2:25, 38), and the confidence of the disciples of Jesus, who forsook all and followed him, that they might enjoy the benefits of his future kingdom, was built on a sandy foundation.[95]

Edwards's point is that since God's promise of salvation should be realized certainly and necessarily without fail, and since even Arminians fully subscribe to this biblical truth, the notion of free will as a self-determining power needs to be reformulated in order to avoid this devastating and infamous consequence. Through this argument of *reductio ad absurdum*, Edwards asserts that the true notion of free will needs to be compatible with the necessity and determinism of God's grand design of redemption.

Does this notion of necessity and determinism frustrate the worthiness of praise and reward for the agent of the action? It should not be so. Even when the action is determined by God's decree, it is still the action of

---

94. Edwards, "Freedom of the Will," *WJE* 1:287–88.
95. Edwards, "Freedom of the Will," *WJE* 1:288.

the agent, the action chosen by the agent who is morally accountable. While actions determined to take place may not be considered as worthy of praise and reward according to the Arminian scheme, the reworked notion of free will should accommodate both this divine necessity and free human moral agency.

> If there be any truth in Christianity or the holy Scriptures, the man Christ Jesus had his will infallibly, unalterably and unfrustrably determined to good, and that alone; but yet he had promises of glorious rewards made to him, on condition of his persevering in, and perfecting the work which God had appointed him.[96]

Even when Christ Jesus was determined to obey the Father's will to accomplish the work of redemption, it was still the action of Jesus as a moral agent and thus accounted for reward and praise. In other words, Christ's obedience to the will of the Father was both necessary and yet meritorious.

The covenant of redemption constitutes the foundation not only for justification of the elect but also for the perseverance of the saints. The benefits that the elect partake of through the union in Christ are not limited to justification. In fact, for Edwards, justification by faith alone as the union in Christ already entails the saint's perseverance as abiding in this communion with Christ.

> So that although the sinner is actually, and finally justified on the first act of faith, yet the perseverance of faith, even then, comes into consideration, as one thing on which the fitness of acceptance to life depends. God the act of justification, which is passed on a sinner's first believing, has respect to perseverance, as being virtually contained in that first act of faith and 'tis looked upon and taken by him that justifies, as being as it were a property in that faith that then is.[97]

Even though the saint's perseverance has not yet actually taken place at the point of justification, it is assumed to ensue because God has intended the perseverance to unfold for the elect. Hence within the justification, the perseverance of the saints is virtually contained and assumed to follow.

> God has respect to the believer's continuance in faith, and he is justified by that, as though it already were, because by divine establishment it shall follow; and it being by divine constitution connected with that first faith, as much as if it were a property

---

96. Edwards, "Freedom of the Will," *WJE* 1:289–90.
97. Edwards, "Justification by Faith Alone," *WJE* 19:203.

in it, it is then considered as such, and so justification is not suspended.[98]

Perseverance indeed comes into consideration even in the justification of a sinner, as one thing on which the fitness of acceptance to life depends. For though a sinner is justified on his first act of faith, yet even then, in that act of justification, God has respect to perseverance, as being virtually in that first act; and 'tis looked upon as if it were a property of the faith, by which the sinner is then justified. God has respect to continuance in faith, and the sinner is justified by that, as though it already were, because by divine establishment it shall follow; and so it is accepted as if it were a property contained in the faith that is then seen.[99]

Because God established the divine constitution in a way that perseverance surely follows justification for the elect, the saints can be assured of the completion of their salvation to the extent that they can see as if perseverance in faith is a property ingrained in the initial faith.

Because of this firm conviction of the divine establishment, Edwards can dare to talk about "final justification" distinguished from the first justification wrought by God's regenerating work.[100] Distinguishing between the first and the second justification, Edwards notes:

The first justification, which is at conversion, is a man's becoming righteous, or his coming to have a righteousness belonging to him, or imputed to him. This is by faith alone. The second is at judgment, which is that by which a man is proved and declared righteous. This is by works, and not by faith only.[101]

In other words, final justification is in a sense pending until the end of time when perseverance in faith will be proved. Also in miscellany 847, Edwards writes:

And even justification itself does in a sense attend and depend upon these after-works of the Spirit of God upon the soul. The condition of justification in a sense remains still to be performed, even after the first conversion, and the sentence of justification in a sense remains still to be passed, and the man remains still in a state of probation for heaven, which could not

98. Edwards, "Justification by Faith Alone," *WJE* 19:203.
99. Edwards, "Miscellany 729," *WJE* 18:354.
100. See Sweeney, "Justification by Faith Alone?," 149.
101. Edwards, "Blank Bible," *WJE* 24:1171.

> be, if his justification did not still depend on what remained to be done.[102]

Yet again, rather than the affinity with the Roman Catholic doctrine of justification, Edwards intends this idea of final justification "to be understood in a Protestant and Calvinistic way."[103] Since God constituted and ordained the sequence of salvation unfailingly, the elect are justified here and now without reservation.

> Though perseverance be not an act performed, till after persons have finished their days; yet perseverance is looked upon as virtually performed in the first act of faith, because that first act is of such a nature as shows the principle to be of a persevering sort.[104]

> But this faith on which salvation thus depends, and the perseverance that belongs to it, is one thing in it that is really a fundamental ground of the congruity that such a qualification gives to salvation. Faith is that which renders it congruous that we should be accepted to a title to salvation. And it is so on the account of certain properties in, or certain things that belong to, it; and this is one of them, viz. its perseverance.[105]

Edwards's intention here is not to emphasize a pending character of justification but the certainty and assurance of salvation of the elect because of the divine constitution made from eternity in the covenant of redemption that carries the elect through perseverance in faith.

In fact, the first act of faith envisions and entails the whole array of God's work of salvation: regeneration, conversion, justification, perseverance, and sanctification. When Edwards elaborates on the covenant of Christ with his people, that is, the covenant of grace, he states:

> It includes sanctification and perseverance; these are included in the enjoyment of Christ and communion with Christ. It includes justification; this also is a part of believers' communion with Christ, for they in their justification are but partakers of

---

102. Edwards, *WJE* 20:74. On the saints' perseverance, see also Edwards, *WJE* 18:276–81, 340–41, 353–57, 403–4.
103. Sweeney, "Justification by Faith Alone?," 149.
104. Edwards, "Persevering Faith," *WJE* 19:601.
105. Edwards, *WJE* 18:354.

Christ's justification. They are pardoned and justified in Christ's acquittance and justification as Mediator.[106]

Faith as the communion in Christ entails justification, sanctification, and perseverance simply because they are all benefits earned by Christ in which the elect partake. In a similar manner, when Edwards describes the benefits intended in the covenant of redemption, he says:

> In the promise of the Father's covenant with the Son are included eternal life, perseverance, justification; and not only so, but regeneration or conversion; the giving faith, and all things necessary in order to faith, [such] as the means of grace, God's Word and ordinances: for all these things are included in the success of what [Christ] has done and suffered and are parts of his reward.[107]

In Edwards, regeneration, justification, perseverance, and sanctification all take place as God's gracious work faithful to his covenant, the covenant of redemption between the Father and the Son, and its ectypal unfolding as the covenant of grace between God and the elect.

CHRISTIAN PIETY AND PRACTICE

The covenant of redemption not only brings forth justification of the elect concomitant with the ensuing perseverance in faith, but also issues into Christian piety and practice. William J. Danaher Jr. notes: "Edwards thus believes that Christian piety and practice flow from the same experience of new being."[108] Because the work of justification and perseverance is wrought utterly by God's grace, the elect experience their utter dependence on God in the divine work of redemption. Edwards writes: "By reason of our so great dependence on God, and his perfections, and in so many respects, he and his glory are the more directly set in our view, which way soever we turn our eyes."[109] As Paul Ramsey points out, "The piety which God requires, the only one he will accept, is one which engages the heart and inclines the self as a whole toward the divine glory in a love which is unmixed"

---

106. Edwards, *WJE* 18:148–49.

107. Edwards, *WJE* 18:149

108. Danaher, *Trinitarian Ethics of Jonathan Edwards*, 149. See also Cherry, *Theology of Jonathan Edwards*, 126–42; Logan, "Justification and Evangelical Obedience," 95–127.

109. Edwards, "God Glorified in Man's Dependence," *WJE* 17:210.

and "the particular change called conversion becomes possible only if the self is affected at the heart."[110] Describing the spiritual knowledge, Edwards remarks:

> This light is such as effectually influences the inclination, and changes the nature of the soul. It assimilates the nature to the divine nature, and changes the soul into an image of the same glory that is beheld; 2 Corinthians 3:18, "But we all with open face beholding as in a glass the glory of the Lord, are changed into the same image, from glory to glory, even as by the Spirit of the Lord." This knowledge will wean from the world, and raise the inclination to heavenly things. It will turn the heart to God as the fountain of good, and to choose him for the only portion. This light, and this only, will bring the soul to a saving close with Christ. It conforms the heart to the gospel, mortifies its enmity and opposition against the scheme of salvation therein revealed: it causes the heart to embrace the joyful tidings, and entirely to adhere to, and acquiesce in the revelation of Christ as our Savior; it causes the whole soul to accord and symphonize with it, admitting it with entire credit and respect, cleaving to it with full inclination and affection. And it effectually disposes the soul to give up itself entirely to Christ.[111]

For Edwards, Christian piety is the full embrace of this divine gracious work on redressing the inclination of the heart through the Holy Spirit, the utter dependence of the saint on God's work of redemption, and the willingness to obey and live out in love God's commandments for the sake of God's glory. Edwards's piety is "an embrace of God in Christ based upon a heartfelt sense of the transcendent beauty of all that God is in himself and all that God has done through Christ for sinful humanity."[112]

For this reason, it is important for Edwards to distinguish between genuine and counterfeit piety. One of the most important signs of genuine piety is, according to Edwards, practice. In fact, all works of redemption: conversion, regeneration, justification, and sanctification should necessarily issue into practice. Edwards concedes:

> Regeneration, which is that work of God in which grace is infused, has a direct relation to practice; for 'tis the very end of it, with a view to which the whole work is wrought: all is calculated

---

110. Smith, "Editor's Introduction," *WJE* 2:15.
111. Edwards, "Divine and Supernatural Light," *WJE* 17:424.
112. Lee, "Editor's Introduction," *WJE* 21:102.

and framed, in this mighty and manifold change wrought in the soul, so as directly to tend to this end.[113]

For Edwards, "The tendency of grace in the heart to holy practice, is very direct, and the connection most natural close and necessary."[114] Only those hearts affected by the direct influence of divine grace bear fruits in "an universal holiness of life"[115] and "a true, gracious and universal obedience."[116]

Edwards describes this natural connection between the infused grace and the ensuing practice with various images of organic association.

'Tis no barren thing; there is nothing in the universe that in its nature has a greater tendency to fruit. Godliness in the heart has as direct a relation to practice, as a fountain has to a stream, or as the luminous nature of the sun has to beams sent forth, or as life has to breathing, or the beating of the pulse, or any other vital act; or as a habit or principle of action has to action: for 'tis the very nature and notion of grace, that 'tis a principle of holy action or practice.[117]

Citing Ephesians 2:10 ("For we are his workmanship, created in Christ Jesus, unto good works") and Titus 2:14 ("Who gave himself for us, that he might redeem us from all iniquity, and purify unto himself a peculiar people, zealous of good works"), Edwards claims: "Yea 'tis the very end of the redemption of Christ."[118] Redemption from the bondage in Egypt also issued into holy practice, signifying that the freedom from bondage by divine grace necessarily issues into holy practice. Exodus 4:23 says: "Let my son go, that he may serve me."[119] Furthermore, bearing the fruit of practice is regarded as "the end of election" as John 15:13 says: "Ye have not chosen me; but I have chosen you, and ordained you, that you go and bring forth fruit, and that your fruit should remain."[120] Hence Edwards concludes: "Holy practice is as much the end of all that God does about his saints, as fruit is the end of all the husbandman does about the growth of his field or vineyard."[121] If

113. Edwards, "Religious Affections," *WJE* 2:398.
114. Edwards, "Religious Affections," *WJE* 2:398. See also Edwards, *WJE* 13:475–76; 18:155–56, 198–99, 222–23, 341–42, 498; 20:119, 493–94.
115. Edwards, "Divine and Supernatural Light," *WJE* 17:424
116. Edwards, "Divine and Supernatural Light," *WJE* 17:425
117. Edwards, "Religious Affections," *WJE* 2:398.
118. Edwards, "Religious Affections," *WJE* 2:398. Other cited scripture passages include 2 Cor 5:15; Heb 9:14; Col 1:21–22; 1 Pet 1:18; Luke 1:74–75.
119. Edwards, "Religious Affections," *WJE* 2:398.
120. Edwards, "Religious Affections," *WJE* 2:398–99. Also cited is Eph 1:4; 2:10.
121. Edwards, "Religious Affections," *WJE* 2:399. Cited passages include Matt 3:10; 13:8, 23, 24–30, 38; 21:19, 33–34; Luke 13:6; John 15:1, 2, 4–6, 8; 1 Cor 3:9; Heb 6:7–8; Isa 5:1–8; Cant 8:11–12; Isa 27:2–3.

this holy practice is the fruit of justification and perseverance, and justification and perseverance have been destined to take place for the elect from eternity in the covenant of redemption, the connection between Christian practice and the covenant of redemption is unmistakable.

This connection between the eternal pact in the immanent Trinity and the holy practice in temporality is further clarified by examining the work of the Holy Spirit as the bond of union between the Father and the Son, and between Christ and the elect. As was seen in chapter 3, the Holy Spirit is the bond of union between the Father and the Son in the immanent Trinity. "The Holy Spirit is," Edwards notes, "the act of God between the Father and the Son infinitely loving and delighting in each other."[122] The Holy Spirit is "the love, the joy, the excellence, the holiness of God"[123] and "that infinite delight there is between the Father and the Son."[124] Hence in the covenant of redemption, the Holy Spirit unites the Father and the Son as the bond of union between these two. "As his nature is the divine love that is between the Father and the Son, he is the bond of union between the two covenanting persons, whereby they with infinite sweetness agree, and are infinitely strongly united as parties joined in covenant."[125]

The work of the Holy Spirit as the bond of union, however, does not remain within the immanent Trinity. When God exerts and communicates himself to the world, the Holy Spirit further works as the bond of union between God and the saints. For Edwards, grace in a soul simply means "the Holy Spirit in man,"[126] or "the Holy Ghost acting in the soul, and there communicating his own holy nature."[127]

As the covenant of redemption functions as the nexus between the immanent Trinity and the economic Trinity, so the Holy Spirit bridges God's inner communion of trinitarian persons and God's work of redemption in temporality. If the covenant of redemption is the divine establishment and framework of God's redemptive work, the Holy Spirit is God enacting and exercising this scheme into practice. When Christ purchased the sum of his salvation, namely, the Holy Spirit, Christ "poured it forth abundantly for the conversion of thousands and millions of souls."[128]

---

122. Edwards, *WJE* 13:260.
123. Edwards, *WJE* 13:410.
124. Edwards, *WJE* 13:261.
125. Edwards, *WJE* 20:443
126. Edwards, *WJE* 13:345.
127. Edwards, "Charity and Its Fruits," *WJE* 8:332.
128. Edwards, *History of the Work*, 375.

> The sum of all that Christ purchased is the Holy Ghost. God is he of whom the purchase is made, God is the purchase and the price, and God is the thing purchased: God is the Alpha and the Omega in this work. The great thing purchased by Jesus Christ for us is communion with God, which is only in having the Spirit; 'tis participation of Christ's fullness, and having grace for grace, which is only in having of that Spirit which he has without measure; this is the promise of the Father.[129]

Through the indwelling of the Holy Spirit, the elect participate in God's fullness and happiness. This means that the disposition of the heart is changed and the elect begins to have a new sense of the heart, or spiritual knowledge.

When grace is infused and the Holy Spirit begins to reside in the heart of the elect, the saint begins to be able to sense spiritual beauty and majesty of God.

> The inward principle from whence they flow, is something divine, a communication of God, a participation of the divine nature, Christ living in the heart, the Holy Spirit dwelling there, in union with faculties of the soul, as an internal vital principle, exerting his own proper nature, in the exercise of those faculties.[130]

As Robert Caldwell notes, "By virtue of this pneumatological union, the Spirit restores the supernatural powers of the soul that were destroyed by the fall."[131] The new principle in the heart begins to exert its power, and the disposition of the heart is reoriented in a way consistent with the divine commands. In this way, this new sense of the heart issues into holy practice. Edwards says: "That spiritual knowledge and understanding, which are the immediate foundation of all true grace in the heart, tends to practice. A true knowledge of God and divine things is a practical knowledge";[132] "Gracious and holy affections have their exercise and fruit in Christian practice."[133] In fact, "Christian practice is the *principal sign* by which Christians are to judge, both of their own and others' sincerity of godliness."[134]

> Indeed the power of godliness is exerted in the first place within the soul, in the sensible, lively exercise of gracious affections

---

129. Edwards, *WJE* 13:466–67.
130. Edwards, "Religious Affections," *WJE* 2:392.
131. Caldwell, *Communion in the Spirit*, 103.
132. Edwards, "Charity and Its Fruits," *WJE* 8:296.
133. Edwards, "Religious Affections," *WJE* 2:383.
134. Edwards, "Religious Affections," *WJE* 2:407.

there. Yet the principal evidence of this power of godliness, is in those exercises of holy affections that are practical, and in their being practical; in conquering the will, and conquering the lusts and corruptions of men, and carrying men on in the way of holiness, through all temptation, difficulty and opposition.[135]

These holy exercises stem from the indwelling of the Holy Spirit in the soul of the elect. As the Holy Spirit unites the Father and the Son as the bond of union, so unites the same Spirit Christ and the elect.

This bonding work of the Holy Spirit is exerted not only to each individual elect but also to the church as God's chosen people as a whole. The covenant of redemption envisions the eternal communion of God with the church elect from before the foundation of the world. This concept can sometimes have repercussions to practical issues such as how to set boundaries in church membership and how to conceive of one's own country. We will explore these implications in the next chapter.

---

135. Edwards, "Religious Affections," *WJE* 2:392.

6

Covenant of Redemption, Trinity, Church Covenant, and National Covenant

JONATHAN EDWARDS'S DOCTRINE OF the covenant of redemption has relevance not only to the doctrine of justification, but also to the doctrine of the church. As the previous chapter examined, the covenant of redemption implies God's decrees of justifying the elect and carrying each as an individual through the perseverance of faith. Yet, beyond the elect as individual believers, the covenant of redemption envisions the church as the communion of the saints, the elect as the whole in unity. The covenant of redemption also has repercussions to the view of one's nation.

At first glance, it might not be entirely clear how the eternal covenant between the Father and the Son relates to seemingly earthly issues such as to whom church membership should be granted or how one should conduct oneself as a citizen of a country. Yet, arguably it is possible to conceive these questions as discerning the relationship between eternity and temporality. How can the saints own their covenant and live out this covenantal fellowship with God on earth? How can one discern and determine church membership on earth when it is supposedly impossible to identify exactly who are the elect within the covenant of grace and who are not? Further, in a society dominantly Christian where the church membership and citizenship were often overlapped, how does the eternal covenantal background influence the view of one's own country and her course of action? How do Christian believers envisage the place and mission of one's nation in light of God's work of redemption in history? In this chapter, I will argue that

Edwards's idea of the covenant of redemption has at least an indirect connection with his view of the church and New England within the history of God's work of redemption.

THE COMMUNION BETWEEN CHRIST AND THE CHURCH

As Douglas Sweeney points out, in spite of his life-long commitment to pastoral ministry, "Edwards's doctrine of the church has gone largely unnoticed by scholars."[1] Partly because Edwards's ecclesiastical writings primarily focus on the qualification of church membership and the related communion controversy, scholarly treatments also tend to be limited to this area.[2] Nonetheless, "inasmuch as these writings deal narrowly with the issue of local church membership, they speak but indirectly to the nature of the Christian church at large."[3] In fact, as will be seen, it is important to see even these narrowly focused issues such as church membership and communion controversy within a larger covenantal framework that stems from eternity in the covenant of redemption. In order to examine the connection between the covenant of redemption and the church covenant, I will first look at the eschatological *telos* of the church in Edwards's thought. Then I will examine how Edwards attempted to discern church membership in a way that is faithful to the covenant between Christ and the church elect. I will then note some practical implications that stem from this covenantal relationship.

First, Edwards sees the goal of the covenant of redemption terminated upon the eternal communion between the Godhead and the church. For Edwards, this church is "the body of Christ, [the] mystical body of Christ."[4] In accordance with the exposition by Thomas Goodwin,[5] Edwards elaborates on the meaning of being chosen *in* Christ as he exegetes Ephesians 1:4: "According as he hath chosen us in him before the foundation of the

---

1. Sweeney, "Church," 167. A few exceptions are Schafer, "Jonathan Edwards's Conception," 51–66; Youngs, "Place of Spiritual Union," 27–47.

2. Hall, "Editor's Introduction," 12:1–90; De Jong, *Covenant Idea*, 136–52; Haroutunian, *Piety Versus Moralism*, 136–52; Cooper, *Tenacious of Their Liberties*; Stuart, "'Mr. Stoddard's Way,'" 243–53; McCoy, "In Defense of the Covenant"; Danaher, "By Sensible Signs Represented," 261–87; Walker, "Jonathan Edwards," 601–14; Jamieson, "Jonathan Edwards's Change of Position," 79–99; Tracy, *Jonathan Edwards, Pastor*; Holmes, *God of Grace*, 169–97; Morgan, *Visible Saints*.

3. Sweeney, "Church," 167.

4. Edwards, "Living to Christ," *WJE* 10:566.

5. Goodwin, *Exposition of the Epistle*, 54–69.

world, that we might be holy and without blame before him in love."[6] To speak of the elect chosen in Christ does not mean that God foresees faith in certain people and therefore chose them to be elect.[7] Nor does the election indicate that God foresaw the merits and satisfactions wrought by Christ as the surety of the elect.[8] They are already chosen in Christ so that they may be holy. The election in Christ has taken place in eternity so that they may be blessed in time. As Edwards notes, "our being looked upon in him is some way the ground of our being chosen from eternity to be holy and happy, as it is the ground of being blessed with spiritual blessings in time."[9] Further, the election of the saints in Christ does not merely mean that they have been elected with Christ. Rather, "Christ, in some respect, is first in this affair, and some way or other the ground of our being chosen, and God's election of him some way or other including and inferring the election of particular saints."[10]

After removing these misinterpretations, Edwards now positively describes the meaning of being chosen in Christ. First, by "in Christ," the Scripture means that all things have been purposed for Christ and they are to be accomplished by Christ. Edwards maintains: "the sum of God's decrees is called the purpose which he purposed in Christ Jesus," signifying that "what God purposed, he purposed for Christ and purposed to accomplish by Christ."[11] Indeed, Christ is "the end of all God's works *ad extra*," and thus "the accomplishment of all was committed to him."[12]

Second, the end of this election in Christ and indeed, the purpose of creation itself, is "to procure a spouse, or a mystical body, for his Son."[13]

> His decree in appointing the individual creatures that were chosen to be members of his body, the accomplishment of God's purposes with respect to which were more especially committed to Christ—I say this purpose may well, in a more peculiar manner, be called a purpose which God purposed in Christ Jesus. And the determination or election of these individual created

---

6. Edwards, *WJE* 23:177.
7. Edwards, *WJE* 23:177.
8. Edwards, *WJE* 23:177.
9. Edwards, *WJE* 23:177.
10. Edwards, *WJE* 23:178.
11. Edwards, *WJE* 23:178.
12. Edwards, *WJE* 23:178.
13. Edwards, *WJE* 23:178.

beings might be called an election in Christ, and they said to be chosen in Christ.[14]

Since the end of creation is to procure a body for the Son, the election in Christ means that God purposed certain people to become members of the body of Christ and that this is to be accomplished in Christ.

Third, because each elect is elected *in* Christ and called to be one with Christ, the church is conceived not as the mere aggregate of individuals but as one body, the organic unity under the headship of Jesus Christ. Edwards describes this unity of the church as the object of God's communication of himself in the love and grace of the Son.

> As God determined in his eternal decrees to create a world, to communicate himself, and his Son might have an object for the object of his infinite grace and love, so God determined that this object should be one. His special aim in all was to procure one created child, one spouse and body of his Son for the adequate displays of his unspeakable and transcendent goodness and grace. Therefore, though many individual persons were chosen, yet they were chosen to receive God's infinite good and Christ's peculiar love in union, as one body, one spouse, all united in one head. Therefore they were all chosen to receive those divine communications no otherwise than in that head.[15]

Because all history is leading to the union in Christ and because Christ brings this into effect according to God's decree, it is fitting to say that the elect are chosen *in* Christ. As the company of people elected and chosen in Christ, the elect are regarded universally as one united with Christ. As Thomas Schafer points out, "The Church, which is elect mankind and the body of Christ, is seen to be a universal, not merely a collection of particulars; it is the new man which is in Christ and, in some sense, *is* Christ."[16]

Fourth, the election in Christ means that Christ is the head of this body. As Edwards notes, "When God had determined that the elect object of his love should be one, all the members one body, united in one head, the first thing was to choose a head, even as when a man goes about to choose materials for a building the first thing is to choose a stone for the foundation."[17] Christ is "the first elect and the head of election" and hence

---

14. Edwards, *WJE* 23:178.
15. Edwards, *WJE* 23:179.
16. Schafer, "Jonathan Edwards's Conception," 54–55.
17. Edwards, *WJE* 23:180.

the participation of individual creatures in God's exaltation is "the fruit of sovereign election."[18]

In this way, the church on earth is called to reflect this eternal and teleological background: the eternal communion between Christ and the elect as his spouse, the organic one body with Christ as her head. "Basic to Edwards's understanding of the nature of the church was his belief that God has 'elected' the church *in* Christ for God's own glory."[19] It is not hard to fathom then why the issue of church membership became an acute and preoccupying subject of discussion among the divines in New England.

THE COMMUNION CONTROVERSY IN LIGHT OF THE COVENANT OF REDEMPTION

Early in March 1742, Edwards drafted a covenant for his congregation and asked members above fourteen years of age to subscribe. Then "on a day of fasting and prayer, all together presented themselves before the Lord in his house, and stood up, and solemnly manifested their consent to it, as their vow to God."[20] As George Marsden points out, "Covenant renewal ceremonies were patterned on the Old Testament, and covenants had been a staple of New England since its founding."[21] One of the uses of the law for the Reformed tradition is the guidance of Christian life as a response to grace. "So Puritans could both preach salvation by wholly unmerited grace and at the same time guide the church with a legal system of the moral law (but not the ceremonial law) that replicated practices of ancient Israel."[22] This Northampton Covenant reiterates the importance of self-examination in light of the covenantal relationship that each saint owns before God. This examination of one's state of the soul was especially instructed before the sacrament of the Lord's Supper.

> And being sensible of our own weakness, and the deceitfulness of our own hearts, and our proneness to forget our most solemn vows and lose our resolutions; we promise to be often strictly examining ourselves by these promises, especially before the sacrament of the Lord's Supper; and beg of God that he would, for Christ's sake keep us from wickedly dissembling in these our solemn vows; and that he who searches our hearts [Romans

18. Edwards, *WJE* 23:180.
19. Sweeney, "Church," 169.
20. Edwards, "To the Reverend Thomas Prince," *WJE* 16:121.
21. Marsden, *Jonathan Edwards*, 261.
22. Marsden, *Jonathan Edwards*, 261.

8:27] and ponders the path of our feet [Proverbs 4:26] would from time to time help us in trying ourselves by this covenant, and help us to keep covenant with him and not leave us to our own foolish, wicked and treacherous hearts.[23]

While the momentum of the revival continued, Edwards attempted to "institutionalize the spirit of the revival."[24] He tried to "transform the volatile euphoria of revival into a more stable spirituality that could be controlled in the fixed channels of the covenant."[25] Edwards had already experienced the spiritual decline of the revival movement in the 1730s and therefore was wrestling this time with a question: "how to keep the revival light from fading once more."[26]

Edwards did not believe that one could decisively distinguish the regenerate and unregenerate on earth. Nonetheless, he believed that "the church should examine candidates for full communicant membership to be sure they showed the visible signs of commitment in their profession and practice."[27] As the discussion of the holy practice in *Religious Affections* in chapter 5 showed, even though it was not possible to conclusively determine who were the regenerate and who were not, still Edwards believed that certain signs or manifestations of the renewal of the heart could be discernible. It was during the communion controversy that this question surfaced most intensely.[28]

Originally the New Englanders baptized children "only if the parents were full communicant members of the church."[29] However, as subsequent generations came along, a question emerged: If baptized children of the full communicant members do not have a conversion experience when they grow up, can the church baptize the children of these half-way baptized church members? After much debate, the synod of clergy came to a conclusion in 1662. The fifth proposition of the result of the synod of 1662 declares:

> Church-members who were admitted in minority, understanding the Doctrine of Faith, and publickly professing their

---

23. Edwards, "To the Reverend Thomas Prince," *WJE* 16:124–25.
24. Marsden, *Jonathan Edwards*, 262.
25. Marsden, *Jonathan Edwards*, 260.
26. Marsden, *Jonathan Edwards*, 262.
27. Marsden, *Jonathan Edwards*, 262.
28. On the communion controversy, see Holifield, *Covenant Sealed*, 197–224; Pope, *Half-Way Covenant*; Marsden, *Jonathan Edwards*, 341–74; Noll, *America's God*, 31–50; Lucas, *God's Grand Design*, 147–60; Gura, *Jonathan Edwards*, 149–64; Grasso, *Speaking Aristocracy*, 86–143.
29. Marsden, *Jonathan Edwards*, 30.

assent thereto; not scandalous in life, and solemnly owning the Covenant before the Church, wherein they give up themselves and their Children to the Lord, and subject themselves to the Government of Christ in the Church, their Children are to be baptized.[30]

This decision clarified that even if parents lack conversion experiences, as long as they affirm the basic doctrine of faith and conduct themselves uprightly, their children shall be baptized.

These believers are called "Confederate visible Believers, though but in the lowest degree such."[31] Since they are children of the covenant and they show "nothing to the contrary," the Synod pronounces, they are "in charity, or to Ecclesiastical reputation, visible Believers."[32] Taking a model from the ancient Israel society where all members of the community were regarded as the people of God, the Synod continues:

> The seed of the Israelites, though many of them were not sincerely godly, yet whilest they held forth the public profession of God's people . . . and continued under the wing of the Covenant, and subjection to the Ordinances, they were still accounted as holy seed.[33]

The clergies of the Synod differentiated "two kinds of holiness and two kinds of covenants," "real holiness and the covenant of grace" on the one hand, and "federal holiness" and "the external covenant" on the other.[34] The church covenant pertains to the latter "federal holiness" and "external covenant." It is "the covenant which God makes with his visible church" and is "the covenant of grace considered in the external dispensation of it, and in the promises and privileges that belong to that dispensation."[35] By making a distinction between the internal and external covenant, the Synod opened a way to the Half-Way Covenant in which all baptized members were invited to the participation in the Lord's Supper whether they had explicit conversion experience or not. Edwards's grandfather Solomon Stoddard called the Lord's Supper as "converting ordinance" and made "the church covenant completely external and sundered it from the covenant of grace."[36]

30. Walker, *Creeds and Platforms*, 328.
31. Walker, *Creeds and Platforms*, 329–30.
32. Walker, *Creeds and Platforms*, 330.
33. Walker, *Creeds and Platforms*, 306.
34. Hall, "Editor's Introduction," *WJE* 12:24.
35. Walker, *Creeds and Platforms*, 321.
36. Schafer, "Jonathan Edwards's Conception," 59. See also Miller, "Solomon

For Edwards, however, the severance between the external and the internal covenant is ultimately untenable. As Frederick W. Youngs notes, Edwards believed that there is "only one major covenant, the covenant of grace."[37]

> He that really complies with the external call, has the internal call; so he that truly complies with the external proposal of God's covenant, as visible Christians profess to do, do indeed perform the inward condition of it. But the New Testament affords no more foundation for supposing two real and properly distinct covenants of grace, than it does to suppose two sorts of real Christians.[38]

Covenant is ultimately one covenant: the covenant of grace. Moreover, as discussed in chapter 3, this covenant of grace stems from the covenant of redemption within the eternal communion of the trinitarian persons. The covenant of redemption and the covenant of grace is one in the sense that the covenant of grace is the ectypal unfolding of the covenant of redemption in time and space.

This ectypal covenantal unfolding is a movement that encloses the elect into the eternal communion between the Father and the Son. Through the spiritual union with Christ, the elect participate in the trinitarian communion.

> For the covenant, to be owned or professed, is God's covenant, which he has revealed as the method of our spiritual union with him, and our acceptance as the objects of his eternal favor; which is no other than the covenant of grace.[39]

In this way, the eternal and spiritual background underscores the owning of the covenant. Public profession of faith and the owning of the covenant have eternal repercussion. This is why, despite his acknowledgment that the distinction between the regenerate and the unregenerate is impossible on this earthly life, Edwards persistently argued for the owning of the covenant with real sincerity of the heart and piety.

Stoddard," 277–320; Gura, "Going Stoddard's Way," 489–98; Stuart, "Mr. Stoddard's Way," 243–53; Schafer, "Solomon Stoddard," 328–61; McDowell, *Beyond the Half-Way Covenant*.

37. Youngs, "Place of Spiritual Union," 36.
38. Edwards, "Humble Inquiry," *WJE* 12:206.
39. Edwards, "Humble Inquiry," *WJE* 12:205.

Edwards's use of the image of marriage is especially pertinent to this emphasis on "a consent of heart."[40] "There is mutual profession in this affair," Edwards says, "a profession on Christ's part, and a profession on our part; as it is in marriage."[41] As Edwards notes in his typological writing, "Marriage signifies the spiritual union and communion of Christ and the church, and especially the glorification of the church in the perfection of this union and communion forever."[42]

> Christ in his Word declares an entire consent of heart as to what he offers; and the

> visible Christian, in the answer that he makes to it in his Christian profession, declares a consent and compliance of heart to his proposal. Owning the covenant is professing to make the transaction of that covenant our own. The transaction of that covenant is that of espousals to Christ; on our part, it is giving our souls to Christ as his spouse: there is no one thing, that the covenant of grace is so often compared to in Scripture, as the marriage covenant; and the visible transaction, or mutual profession there is between Christ and the visible church, is abundantly compared to the mutual profession there is in marriage.[43]

Since through the public profession of faith and owning of the covenant, a believer enters a marital relationship with Christ, "he that professes this towards Christ, professes saving faith."[44]

Saving faith is "the union, cleaving, or joining of that covenant" and "the grand condition of the covenant of Christ, by which we are in Christ: this is what brings us into the Lord."[45]

> To profess the covenant of grace is to profess the covenant, not as a spectator, but as one immediately concerned in the affair, as a party in the covenant professed; and this is to profess that in the covenant which belongs to us as a party, or to profess our part in the covenant; and that is the soul's believing acceptance of the Savior. Christ's part is salvation, our part is a saving faith in him; not a feigned, but unfeigned faith; not a common, but

---

40. Edwards, "Humble Inquiry," *WJE* 12:205.
41. Edwards, "Humble Inquiry," *WJE* 12:205.
42. Edwards, "Images of Divine Things," *WJE* 11:52.
43. Edwards, "Humble Inquiry," *WJE* 12:205.
44. Edwards, "Humble Inquiry," *WJE* 12:205.
45. Edwards, "Humble Inquiry," *WJE* 12:206.

special and saving faith; no other faith than this is the condition of the covenant of grace.[46]

One can recall here that Edwards uses the same image of marriage when he describes the *telos* envisioned in the covenant of redemption from eternity.

> The bridegroom and the bride shall then enter into heaven, both having on their wedding robes, attended with all the glorious angels. And there they enter on the feast and joys of their marriage before the Father; they shall then begin an everlasting wedding day.[47]

Using the parable of the marriage in Matthew 22, Edwards argues: "The wedding garment spoken of as that without which professors will be excluded from among God's people at the day of judgment, is not moral sincerity, or common grace, but special saving grace."[48] In other words, "that true piety, unfeigned faith, or the righteousness of Christ which is upon everyone that believeth, is doubtless the wedding garment intended."[49]

The covenant of grace is destined for the day of judgment and the eternal communion of marriage between Christ and the church elect.[50] Whether the believers's faith is feigned faith or saving faith determines their eternal destiny. The covenant of grace in space and time is the organic development and actualization of the eternal covenant of redemption. Because the believers's eternal destiny was at stake in this way, Edwards was not able to make a compromise on the issue of the qualification of church membership. Sweeney summarizes Edwards's doctrine of the church as follows:

> Before the creation of the world, God chose to shower us with his love, much as a bridegroom showers love upon his bride. But God foreknew that we would fail to reflect his glory, and thus would require a way of salvation. And in keeping with his design to procure a bride for his only Son, God chose some from our fallen race to be reunited with him through the Son, not only selecting them individually but also electing them corporately—as a singular bride for Christ—so that, in Christ, a holy remnant

---

46. Edwards, "Humble Inquiry," *WJE* 12:206.
47. Edwards, "History of Work of Redemption," *WJE* 9:508.
48. Edwards, "Humble Inquiry," *WJE* 12:230.
49. Edwards, "Humble Inquiry," *WJE* 12:230.
50. The connection between the covenant of redemption and Edwards's eschatology will be examined in chapter 7.

would remain in the family of God and would participate in the extension of God's glory in the world.[51]

Indeed, the church's foundation is "God's Eternal decree of election made known to them by the covenant of Grace."[52]

PRACTICAL SIGNIFICANCE OF THE TRINITY FOR THE DOCTRINE OF THE CHURCH

The church is the gathering of the elect decreed by God the Father to be united with the Son to glorify God himself. The church as the people of God is the communication of the divine glory. It is "the church, or those elected by God the Father to be united to his Son, who best represent God's intentions for the creation of the world."[53] Since the elect are eternally decreed to be united with Christ, the eternal foundation of the church issues into practical ramifications such as the church's perseverance to the end of history and the qualification of church membership.

First, because the existence of the church derives from the eternal decree of the trinitarian God, her perseverance to the end is guaranteed by God. As Edwards exposits Psalm 136, he writes: "The main subject of the psalm is the eternity and perpetuity of God's mercy to his church, or his mercy's being forever … his mercy to his church is from everlasting to everlasting, the same, unchangeable."[54] Also, in his preaching on Psalm 106:5, Edwards comforts and encourages the congregation by asking this rhetorical question:

> What can be more stable than what is eternal and has already stood from eternity as God's love to his elect has, which is eternal in the same sense that God's being is eternal and, therefore, is as permanent and immutable as God's being?[55]

In his sermon on Isaiah 32:2, Edwards declares: "Christ has the dispensation of safety and deliverance in his own hands, so that we need not fear but that, if we are united to him, we may be safe."[56] Even when "God's church was

---

51. Sweeney, "Church," 170.
52. Edwards, "Sermon on Psalm 106:5," *WJE* 52:L.31r.
53. Sweeney, "Church," 170.
54. Edwards, *WJE* 18:292.
55. Edwards, "Sermon on Psalm 106:5," *WJE* 52:L.31r. I followed the transcription by Sweeney, "Church," 176.
56. Edwards, "Sermon on Isaiah 32:2," *WJE* 43:L.9r. I followed the transcription by Sweeney, "Church," 176.

almost swallowed up and carried away with the wickedness of the world,"[57] "yet there is a secret life in it that will cause it to flourish again and to take root downward, and bear fruit upward."[58]

Since the church as the elect is destined for life eternal from before the foundation of the world, the saints can be assured that God will carry them through to the fulfillment of redemption whatever trials and tribulations may arise in its process. "God's decree to elect the church in Christ for the advancement of his glory is the church's guarantee that it will 'persevere' to the end."[59]

Second, because the eternal destiny of each individual cannot be definitely discerned, the qualification of church membership became a vexing issue at Edwards's church in Northampton. This may seem contradictory to the first practical implication in which the saints can be assured of their perseverance to the end. Nonetheless, the discrepancy between eternity and time apparently persists. This is why young Edwards struggled with discerning whether he was truly converted.[60] For instance, on May 28, 1725 he wrote in his diary:

> It seems to me, that whether I am now converted or not, I am so settled in the state I am in, that I shall go on in it all my life. But, however settled I may be, yet I will continue to pray to God, not to suffer me to be deceived about it, nor to sleep in an unsafe condition; and ever and anon, will call all into question and try myself, *using for helps, some of our old divines*, that God may have opportunities to answer my prayers, and the Spirit of God to show me my error, if I am in one.[61]

As was discussed in chapter 5, in his pastoral career too Edwards tried to see in holy practice the manifestation and sign of true godliness and regeneration.

It is possible to see these attempts as struggles to discern the invisible state of the heart through visible practices and conditions. Precisely due to the ambiguity in identifying the exact correspondence between eternity and time, the issue of church membership triggered intensive controversies at the church in Northampton costing Edwards his pulpit. While popular

---

57. Edwards, "History of Work of Redemption," *WJE* 9:174.
58. Edwards, "History of Work of Redemption," *WJE* 9:236.
59. Sweeney, "Church," 175.
60. Marsden, *Jonathan Edwards*, 50, 57, 104–5.
61. Edwards, "Diary," *WJE* 16:788.

religion[62] and local history[63] are certainly involved in the ousting of Edwards from his church, "Northampton's controversy," as Sweeney points out, "had *most* to do with the doctrine of the church."[64] The issue was primarily theological—deciphering the invisible business of eternity in life on earth in order to be faithful to the covenant of grace that stems from the covenant of redemption.

NATIONAL COVENANT

Together with the church covenant, the national covenant is another example in which the covenant of redemption has a repercussion in earthly life.[65] To be sure, Edwards seldom makes a direct connection between the covenant of redemption and the national covenant. However, given that for Puritan divines the national covenant was a part of the covenant of grace and the covenant of grace is the ectypal expression of the covenant of redemption, I argue that the national covenant is at least indirectly related to the covenant of redemption.

Though with a bit too broad a stroke, Gerald McDermott explains the national covenant as follows: "In a tradition stretching back to the Reformation and before, God was conceived as entering into covenant with a people or nation, and blessing or punishing that people in proportion to their fidelity to the terms of the covenant."[66] Harry S. Stout argues: "Covenanted peoples like those of ancient Israel and New England were the hub around which sacred (i.e., real) history revolved."[67]

> Such peoples might be ignored or reviled by the world and figure insignificantly in the great empires of profane history, but viewed through the sacred lens of providential history they were seen as God's special instruments entrusted with the task of

---

62. Hall, "Editor's Introduction," *WJE* 12:1–86.
63. Tracy, *Jonathan Edwards, Pastor*, 171–94.
64. Sweeney, "Church," 185.
65. While several scholarly treatments of the national covenant exist, the connection between the covenant of redemption and the national covenant, as far as I know, has not been considered. For general treatment of the national covenant, see Bercovitch, *American Jeremiad*; Stout, *New England Soul*; Heimart, *Religion and the American Mind*. For specifically on Edwards's view of the national covenant, see Mclymond and McDermott, *Theology of Jonathan Edwards*, 332–34; McDermott, *One Holy and Happy Society*; "Poverty, Patriotism, and National Covenant," 229–51; "Jonathan Edwards and the National Covenant," 147–57; Stout, "Puritan and Edwards," 142–59.
66. McDermott, *One Holy and Happy Society*, 12.
67. Stout, *New England Soul*, 7.

> preparing the way for messianic deliverance. As Israel witnessed to God's active involvement with nations in ancient times and brought forth the Christ, so New England's experience confirmed God's continuing involvement with nations that would persist until Christ's return to earth, when history itself would cease and be swallowed up in eternity.[68]

Because this covenant indicates blessings upon the covenantal faithfulness of the chosen people and curses upon unfaithfulness of the same, alluding to Deuteronomy 28, Puritans in New England found their type in the ancient people of Israel for whom their covenantal relationship with God navigated their lives as the chosen people.

> Long before the 1620s, men had begun to think of England as joined in a covenantal relation with the Lord. In this conception the nation was found subject to a Deuteronomic arrangement: obedience to divine law guaranteed favor and prosperity, while disobedience ensured affliction. Puritan interests understandably found the National Covenant a useful weapon in their struggle for religious reform. Fidelity to the covenant came to be defined in terms of the Biblicist program for completing the English reformation.[69]

While some scholars argued that as secularism arose, the national covenant disappeared around the end of the seventeenth century,[70] the idea of the national covenant played an important role in New England to shape and guide the identity of Puritans as the holy nation.[71] From the first generation of Puritans in New England, they believed that their nation was in covenant with God and their destiny depended on their faithfulness to the covenant.

Out of this context emerged a sermonic rhetoric called "jeremiad." Jeremiad refers to a political sermonic discourse that addresses a political and social situation of a specific audience. As the prophet Jeremiah in the Old Testament prophesized to the people of Israel in the Babylonian Captivity divine vengeance and comfort at the same time, so the Puritan preachers in New England carried a message of God's impending wrath and rising hope to their congregations. When they crossed the sea away from religious persecution in England in order to enter the New World, the Puritans compared the experience to the Exodus or liberation from the Babylonian Captivity. In other words, they compared themselves to God's chosen people of Israel.

68. Stout, *New England Soul*, 7.
69. Bozeman, *To Live Ancient Lives*, 98.
70. Miller, *New England Mind*, 447–63.
71. Bercovitch, *American Jeremiad*, 93–131; Stout, *New England Soul*, 140–41.

> All of the Old Testament is an errand to the New; and all of history after the Incarnation, an errand to Christ's Second Coming. It leads from promise to fulfillment: from Moses to John the Baptist to Samuel Danforth; from the Old World to the New from Israel in Canaan to New Israel in America; from Adam to Christ to the Second Adam of the Apocalypse.[72]

By finding its own type in the people of Israel, New England "becomes itself a harbinger of things to come," as "a light proclaiming the latter-day coming of the Messiah, a herald sent to prepare the world to receive His often-promised, long-expected Kingdom."[73]

Yet, rather than the ambitious and self-complacent sense of leadership in the world, the primary focus of the jeremiad for these Puritans was on re-orientating their Christian lives as they repent and return to God in times of political and social troubles. The national covenant and accompanying jeremiad primarily functioned as a guideline for a new life of the immigrating Puritans themselves. The idea of America as the leading nation propagating the Protestant cause for the world was alien for the first-generation Puritans. As Theodore Dwight Boezeman clarified, their chief goal was to recover their identity by retrieving the biblical past.

> Before there could be any question of historical advance, there had to be a secure recovery of origins. Appreciation of that recovery, then, is vital to comprehending the first immigrants' religious purposes. Emigration meant freedom to come to terms with long-lost originals. The impulse was *re*vival, directed to restoration and fulfilling enjoyment of forms ordained in the primal age.[74]

Accordingly, the mentality of the first-generation of Puritan immigrants was "distinctly inhospitable to the crusading exemplarism usually associated with an Errand into the Wilderness" and "Least of all does it provide the originating instance of claims to an American mission on behalf of the world."[75] The national covenant was first and foremost for Puritans themselves as the New Israel to lead the Christian conduct of life before God.

Typically, then, jeremiad involves two aspects. On the one hand, as Perry Miller pointed out, American jeremiad is suffused with impending

---

72. Bercovitch, *American Jeremiad*, 14.
73. Bercovitch, *American Jeremiad*, 14.
74. Bozeman, *To Live Ancient Lives*, 114.
75. Bozeman, *To Live Ancient Lives*, 119.

doom. Puritan prophets of jeremiad emphasize God's looming judgment on the corrupted people of God.

> God avenges the iniquities of a chosen people, and then run down the twelve heads, merely bringing the list up to date by inserting the new and still more depraved practices an ingenious people kept on devising. I suppose that in the whole literature of the world, including the satirists of imperial Rome, there is hardly such another uninhibited and unrelenting documentation of a people's descent into corruption.[76]

However, on the other hand, as Sacvan Bercovitch's revision suggests, jeremiad has "unshakable optimism."[77] Bercovitch writes: "The most severe limitation of Miller's view is that it excludes (or denigrates) this pervasive theme of affirmation and exultation."[78] The American jeremiad sermon typically "inverts the doctrine of vengeance into a promise of ultimate success, affirming to the world, and despite the world, the inviolability of the colonial cause."[79] The severe calamities of a national scale could mean God's chastisement for his people. Thus national trials and hardship actually indicated that New England was the chosen people as the New Israel and the impending judgment was God's awakening call to repent. "God's punishments were *corrective*, not destructive."[80] Puritans used this dual discourse to orientate and navigate their national life as God's chosen people.

For example, in a famous address to the Massachusetts Bay colony, "A Model of Christian Charity," John Winthrop said that the Lord would "expect a strict performance of the articles contained" in his covenant with the New England founders. Winthrop continued: "If we shall neglect the observation of these articles . . . the Lord will surely break out in wrath against us, be revenged of such a perjured people, and make us know the price of the breach of such a covenant."[81] From the first generation, Puritans in New

---

76. Miller, *Errand into the Wilderness*, 8.
77. Bercovitch, *American Jeremiad*, 7.
78. Bercovitch, *American Jeremiad*, 6.
79. Bercovitch, *American Jeremiad*, 7.
80. Bercovitch, *American Jeremiad*, 8.
81. Winthrop, "Model of Christian Charity," 90–91. Other Puritans of the first generation also widely used the national covenant in their orations and writings. Hooker, *Thomas Hooker*, 230–32; Hooke, *New England Teares*, 15, 18–19; Higginson, *Cause of God*, 8; Jameson, *Johnson's Wonder-Working Providence*, 60–121, 238. See also McDermott, *One Holy and Happy Society*, 12.

England regarded themselves as a "peculiar" nation in continuity with Israel, the people of God.[82]

As another example much closer to Edwards, his father Timothy Edwards inherited the Puritan jeremiad and interpreted the national afflictions and calamities as the failing of the New Englanders to faithfully abide by their covenant with God.

> God trys afflictions and the Rods of anger. He makes use of many angry frowning dispensations. [He] chastens, corrects em sends calamitys and Judgments of various Kinds and Sorts ... to bring e'm back from their Sinfull Wanderings unto the Straight path of their duty ... especially those of e'm that he has taken nearest himself, and thus he dealt with that sinfull and Rebellious people of his, the children of Israel.[83]

Yet, trials and tribulations of a national scale as divine judgment "were not signs of divine desertion so much as urgent calls to reformation."[84]

> Sincere Repentance and hearty and Real returning unto God is the proper voice and Loude call of the Judgments of God ... the Judgments of God do with a Loud voice call upon a Sinfull and disobedient people to Repent and Return unto the Lord, God calls upon e'm in every Judgment and in every Affliction.[85]

In this way, "what at first glance seems to be a rhetoric of condemnation and guilt turns out on further analysis to be the necessary first step to deliverance and triumph."[86] In this framework of the national covenant, the divine condemnation to the New England society is instrumental to the repentance and their returning to God. Given that the majority of the New Englanders were church members and the assumption was that the church was almost coextensive with the nation, it was natural for Puritans to see their entire nation in covenant with God. The New England divines believed how they lived out the covenantal relationship with God had necessary consequences in the church membership and the course of the entire nation.

---

82. Stout, "Puritan and Edwards," 144.

83. Stoughton, *"Windsor Farmes,"* 122. The appendix provides Timothy Edwards's sermon notes. Minimum spelling adjustments have been made following Stout, "Puritan and Edwards," 144–45.

84. Stout, "Puritan and Edwards," 145.

85. Stoughton, *"Windsor Farmes,"* 126. Minimum spelling adjustments have been made following Stout, "Puritan and Edwards,"145.

86. Stout, "Puritan and Edwards," 145.

Perry Miller once argued that Edwards departed from this traditional framework of federal covenant. According to Miller, "Every New Englander before Edwards was a 'Federalist,' and because he put aside all this sort of thinking, he became a new point of departure in the history of the American mind."[87] Conrad Cherry basically concurs when he says that federal theology "did not assume for him the same importance for an understanding of the saints' social and political life as it had for his forefathers."[88] Cherry and other scholars found in Edwards's writings only the covenant of grace, and not the national covenant.[89] In McDermott's assessment, "They found, in other words, God's unconditional commitment to give eternal life to individuals but not his conditional ministration of temporal rewards to nations on the basis of obedience to divine law."[90] Here they make a distinction between the covenant of grace and the national covenant. The covenant of grace "concerns individuals, is based on faith, and pertains primarily to the life to come," while the national covenant "concerns nations, is based on works, and pertains to this life only."[91] When scholars approach Edwards's writings based on this distinction, they do not find the national covenant in them.

However, as Harry S. Stout points out, Edwards is in fact "every bit the federal theologian that his Puritan predecessors were."[92] Historians overlooked Edwards's federal theology primarily because the types of the sources they consulted were mostly published sermons. These sermons were mostly "regular" or Sunday sermons where "Comments on the national covenant and corporate morality were generally considered inappropriate" and "naturally did not appear in the text."[93] Rather, an appropriate occasion for "social commentary and discussion of covenant conditions" was "election day" or "fast day" when "communities met during the week to hear about the current state of God's covenant with New England."[94] If we

---

87. Miller, *Jonathan Edwards*, 76.

88. Cherry, "Puritan Notion of the Covenant," 329.

89. Cherry, *Theology of Jonathan Edwards*, 107–23; Heimert, *Religion and the American Mind*, 126; Bogue, *Jonathan Edwards and the Covenant*; Simonson, *Theologian of the Heart*, 140–52; Bryant, "America as God's Kingdom," 63; Jenson, *America's Theologian*, 135–37.

90. McDermott, *One Happy and Holy Society*, 13.

91. McDermott, *One Happy and Holy Society*, 13.

92. Stout, "Puritan and Edwards," 143.

93. Stout, "Puritan and Edwards," 144.

94. Stout, "Puritan and Edwards," 144. Stout notes: "The major distinctions in form, content, and function between regular (Sunday) sermons and occasional (weekday) sermons have not been sufficiently emphasized in studies of Puritan preaching"

Covenant of Redemption, Trinity, Church Covenant, and National Covenant   153

consult these unpublished occasional sermons, traditional Puritan jeremiad is explicit in Edwards's writings.

For example, when Edwards delivered a fast-day sermon on the 2 Chr 23:16 ("And Jehoiada made a covenant between him, and between all the people, and between the king, that they should be the Lord's people") in March 1737, he took ancient Israel as "the model and prototype for all subsequent covenant people"[95] and exposited:

> Some are distinguished of God as a Covenant People. So were that People that were spoken of in the Text God Entered into Covenant with Abraham and Issac and Jacob and brought them out of Egypt and in a solemn manner entered into Covenant with them in the wild and separated them from all the nations in the earth to be a Covenant People a Peculiar People to hims.[96]

Then Edwards turns to his congregation and identifies them as the covenant people in continuity with Israel. "You are a People that have been distinguished of G. as a Covenant People for a long time and have been distinguished in the means that G. has used with you."[97] The preacher continues: "You are a People that have been distinguished of God as a Covenant People for a long time."[98]

The reality that New England[99] is in covenant with God required the New Englanders to conduct themselves in a way faithful to the covenant. Failure to walk obediently in the covenant meant God's impending judgment on the entire nation. In another fast day sermon, Edwards warned his Northampton congregation: "When a covenant people depart from the true God, they ever more go after idols"[100]; "A people may be said to depart

---

(Stout, "Puritan and Edwards," 157–58n4). See also Stout, *New England Soul*, 13–31. "By conflating the themes of regular and occasional preaching, and by emphasizing printed occasional sermons to the virtual exclusion of regular sermon notes, historians have extracted a pattern of meaning that distorts the larger spiritual context in which political ideas were expressed and given meaning" (Stout, *New England Soul*, 6).

95. Stout, "Puritan and Edwards," 148.

96. Edwards, "Sermon on 2 Chr 23:16," *WJE* 52:L.3r. Minimum spelling adjustments have been made following Stout, "Puritan and Edwards," 148, with minor modifications.

97. Edwards, "Sermon on 2 Chr 23:16," *WJE* 52:L.24v.

98. Edwards, "Sermon on 2 Chr 23:16," *WJE* 52:L.24r.

99. Depending on a specific situation in which a sermon is addressed, the exact range of the nation can vary. It can be New England, Northampton, England and England's American colonies, or America in general. According to the specific situation faced, Edwards applied the idea of national covenant to a specific region rather flexibly. McDermott, *One Holy and Happy Society*, 18–19.

100. Edwards, "Indicting God," *WJE* 19:753.

from the Lord when they grow cold and indifferent about the things of God, when they are dull in his service."[101] In the spiritual laxity and leniency the Northampton congregation was going through since the declining of the tide of revival, the preacher pastorally confronted the congregation and provided a dose of spiritual chastisement.

For Edwards too New England is the "city set upon a hill." Yet in his assessment, "a righteous, exemplary city it was not."[102]

> We are as a city set on an hill. We have made an high profession of religion, and the eyes of the world are upon us to observe. And if we lose what we seemed to gain, and depart from what we made an appearance of, and at last prove no better than others, it will be the more abundantly to our reproach. Any ill qualities that are seen in any person or people, is looked upon by the world so much the more to their shame, according as their professions and pretenses of the contrary were higher.[103]

Based on Jeremiah 2:5 ("Thus saith the Lord, What iniquity have your fathers found in me that they are gone far from me, and have walked after vanity, and are become vain?"), Edwards cautioned his congregation that when the covenant people who once cleaved to God backslides into spiritual indifference and self-complacency, it will result in a disastrous sin against God and self-contempt. Edwards said: "So that our backsliding is not only aggravated sin against God, but 'tis exceeding folly towards ourselves. By dishonoring God, we disgrace ourselves and expose ourselves to contempt."[104] The Puritan preacher summoned the congregation to reflect on the seriousness to break the covenant they once made with God: "how greatly may God justly be provoked by such obstinacy, in that which is so reproachful to him, in a people that has [been] so distinguished by his favors."[105]

The assessment of the current state of the Puritan society from a covenantal perspective also comes to the surface when certain natural disasters, war, or other calamities took place. These events function as warning signs from God to his people.

> The Great means G. used with them to reclaim them from their backslidings & wickedness he sent to them by his messengers easing up betimes & sending. He took Great & thorough care to

---

101. Edwards, "Indicting God," *WJE* 19:753.
102. McDermott, *One Happy and Holy Society*, 22.
103. Edwards, "Indicting God," *WJE* 19:767.
104. Edwards, "Indicting God," *WJE* 19:767.
105. Edwards, "Indicting God," *WJE* 19:767.

Covenant of Redemption, Trinity, Church Covenant, and National Covenant 155

counsel reprove & warn them by his messengers which is signified by that Expression of his rising betimes & sending.[106]

A few examples are in order to illustrate this point.

For example, in July 1736, when Northampton was suffering drought, Edwards preached at a private meeting to pray for rain. He perceived this occasion as God's summoning call to search one's own soul and repent. Edwards addressed: "when G. withholds Rain tis a Call of G. to us to search our selves & see whether there bent something."[107] A natural calamity such as drought could be a signal from God for the Northamptonites to check the status of the soul and their conduct as the corporate people of God.

> I don't mean whether there be no Corruption in our Hearts. There is no need of Searching . . . neither whether we bent daily Guilty of sin for neither is there . . . but whether there bent some thing special that we have Reason to think is offensive amonst us a People in which we are sharers.[108]

Thus Edwards drew a lesson:

> Hence we May Learn How much it stands us in hand to use the utmost Care that we be at Good terms with G. that we obey his Command & do those things that please him & Carefully avoid whatsoever is displeasing to him.[109]

For Edwards, a natural calamity is a sign for God's people to examine themselves and call for awakening from spiritual torpor.

In a similar way, when worms devoured the fruits of the land in July 1743, Edwards in his fast day sermon attributed the cause to the stinginess of the Northamptonites to the poor. Edwards claimed: "If a People would but run the venture of giving their temporal good things to G. it would be a sure way to those Judgmts Removed that destroy them & to have a Plenty of them bestowed."[110] Collective experience of hardship occasioned the people in Northampton to reflect on and examine their faithfulness to the covenant with God.

Furthermore, when Edwards preached at a fast day for success in war, he assured the congregation of God's unfaltering care and protection for

---

106. Edwards, "Sermon on 2 Chr 36:15–17," *WJE* 55:L.1v. Transcription mine.
107. Edwards, "Sermon on Deut 28:12," *WJE* 51:L.7v. Transcription mine.
108. Edwards, "Sermon on Deut 28:12," *WJE* 51:L.7v.
109. Edwards, "Sermon on Deut 28:12," *WJE* 51:L.6v.
110. Edwards, "Sermon on Mal 3:10–11" *WJE* 61:L.1v. Transcription mine. See also McDermott, *One Holy and Happy Society*, 11–12.

his covenant people. "God's covenant with them is more stable than the foundation of states and kingdoms,"[111] the preacher comforts his congregation. After citing biblical promises of covenantal protection in 2 Sam 23:5, Ps 89:34, Isa 3:10; 43:2, and Job 5:19–22, the Puritan preacher reiterates the unshakable foundation of covenantal promises for God's people. "These promises stand here, and cannot be removed. God's covenant will remain not only when states and kingdoms are overthrown, but when the everlasting mountains and perpetual hills are removed."[112] Then Edwards cites Isaiah 54:10: "For the mountains shall depart, and the hills be removed; but my kindness shall not depart from thee, neither shall the covenant of my peace be removed, saith the Lord that hath mercy on thee."[113] Hence the doctrine set forth in this sermon is: "In the time of great public commotions and calamities, God will take thorough and effectual care that his servants shall be safe."[114]

When Edwards preached a sermon upon "Fast for success in the expedition against Cape Breton" on April 4, 1745, he supported the dangerous military expedition against the French-fortified town of Louisburg on Cape Breton Island.[115]

> All promises of temporal blessings imply promises of the preservation of the church of God in the world. War is that by which the church of God has been especially endangered; Satan has sought to overthrow it this way. Therefore, the many promises made of defense of God's people.[116]

Hence, as "multitudes of promises that God has made to a covenant people in the Scripture" testify, God is "ready to hear the prayers of his people thus duly offered up in such a case."[117]

These examples show that the idea of covenant played a crucial role in re-orienting the life of the New England society when they were going though troubles and calamities of a national level. As definitions of the national covenant provided by McDermott and Stout indicate, usually scholars make a distinction between the covenant of grace and the national

---

111. Edwards, "God's Care for His Servants," *WJE* 22:347.
112. Edwards, "God's Care for His Servants," *WJE* 22:348.
113. Edwards, "God's Care for His Servants," *WJE* 22:348.
114. Edwards, "God's Care for His Servants," *WJE* 22:346.
115. Edwards, "Duties of Christians," *WJE* 25:127.
116. Edwards, "Duties of Christians," *WJE* 25:136.
117. Edwards, "Duties of Christians," *WJE* 25:136. See also Marsden, *Jonathan Edwards*, 312. On the millennial interpretation of the Louisburg victory in New England, see Hatch, *Sacred Cause of Liberty*, 36–51.

covenant. While the covenant of grace pertains to the eternal salvation, the national covenant pertains only to earthly matters. Thus McDermott and McClymond write: "the national covenant was a conditional agreement and thus was unlike the unconditional covenant of grace to the elect. Furthermore, it pertained to the present life only, and applied to societies rather than to individuals per se."[118] In a similar fashion Stout cites a following passage from Edwards's sermon as evidence that he was "speaking in temporal and collective terms to the people of Northampton, not in eternal terms, and in so doing illustrated the different ends and logics of the two covenants."[119]

> And if a nation or people Are very Corrupt and prove obstinate in their Evil ways God Generally executes these threatening. God is more strict in punishing of a wicked people in this world than a wicked person. God often suffers Particular Persons that Are wicked to prosper in the world and Refers them to Judgment the world to Come. but a people as a people are punished only in this world therefore God will not suffer a people that Grow very Corrupt and Refuse to be Reclaimed to Go Unpunished in this world.[120]

Nonetheless, at least it seems possible to say that even the national covenant has a connection with God's economy stemming from eternity.

While it may be true that the national covenant pertains to only earthly matters, it does not mean that the national covenant has nothing to do with eternity. Rather Edwards discerned earthly phenomena in relation to, and under the spectrum of eternity. For example, in a sermon previously cited on God's care for his servants under public commotions, after emphasizing the secure covenantal foundation, Edwards cautioned that this secure covenantal relationship is valid only for the elect. He warned: "Be not deceived with a vain hope of being converted."[121] If people in Northampton are more concerned in their own "worldly designs and interests" than "the service of God," then, Edwards spoke to the congregation, "you are none of those that have the seal of God set on your forehead, nor will you be owned for one of his, nor are you at all secure from those dreadful judgments that shall come on the wind."[122]

---

118. McClymond and McDermott, *Theology of Jonathan Edwards*, 332.

119. Stout, "Puritan and Edwards," 146.

120. Edwards, "Sermon on Jonah 3:10" *WJE* 42:L.2v. Transcription mine. See also Stout, "Puritan and Edwards," 146.

121. Edwards, "God's Care for His Servants," *WJE* 22:356.

122. Edwards, "God's Care for His Servants," *WJE* 22:356.

> He don't say, "till we have sealed the professors of godliness," or "till we have sealed such as cry, 'Lord, Lord,'" or "till we have sealed all such as have had great affections and great joys, and boast of their great experiences," but "till we have sealed the servants of our God." If you ben't a servant of God, if you seem to be religious, your religion is vain. If you have been never so much affected with sorrow or joy, and whatever experiences you think you have had, you are not marked out for one of God's, to be reserved as one of his children and his jewels.[123]

In this way, Edwards turns an earthly turmoil into an occasion for self-examination of the eternal state of the soul.

> Do you serve God in what you do in religion, or do you only serve yourselves? Is it only or chiefly out of fear of hell, or that you may have good evidence? Inquire how has it been: han't fears carried you further than anything else ever did? While you was under fears of hell and thought yourself in danger of it, was you not willing to do a great deal more in religion than you are since? How does your hope work? Your joys and comforts?[124]

For Edwards, the national covenant at least indirectly related to the covenant of grace in the sense that the former functions as a conduit to the fulfillment of the latter.

This reading also conforms to Edwards's claim that there exist not multiple covenants but only one covenant.[125] For Edwards, the only one covenant: the covenant of grace holds the relationship between God and the elect. As we have seen, this covenant entails the fulfillment of its dimension: the covenant of works.[126] Further, ultimately Edwards thinks that the covenant of grace is identical with the covenant of redemption.[127] The history of the work of redemption is the history of the covenant of grace as the ectypal unfolding of the covenant of redemption. Bercovitch notes on American jeremiad:

> The Puritans' concept of errand entailed a fusion of secular and sacred history. The purpose of their jeremiads was to direct an imperiled people of God toward the fulfillment of their destiny,

---

123. Edwards, "God's Care for His Servants," *WJE* 22:354–55
124. Edwards, "God's Care for His Servants," *WJE* 22:356.
125. See the discussion in chapter 3.
126. Edwards, "Justification by Faith Alone," *WJE* 19:188; *WJE* 13:217.
127. Edwards, *WJE* 20:477–78.

to guide them individually toward salvation, and collectively toward the American city of God.[128]

As a part of the covenant of grace, the national covenant signifies one intersection between the earthly and the eternal. Even in seemingly earthly matters like the national covenant, it seems possible to hear the eternal repercussion of the covenant of redemption.

THE PRACTICAL SIGNIFICANCE OF THE DOCTRINE OF THE TRINITY FOR THE VIEW OF A NATION

In this chapter, despite a standard distinction between the church covenant and the covenant of grace, or between the national covenant and the covenant of grace, I have attempted to show at least an indirect relation between the covenant of grace and these two seemingly earthly covenants. Given that within the visible church on this earth both the regenerate and the unregenerate are mixed together, the church covenant, or church membership is not exactly coextensive with the covenant of grace that pertains to eternal salvation. In the same way, the New England society contained both the regenerate and the unregenerate. Thus, the national covenant applied to the entire nation does not exactly correspond to the covenant of grace. In this sense, certainly the covenant of grace needs to be distinguished from the church covenant and national covenant. Nonetheless, I argue that the reason why the church covenant and the national covenant became such an intense agenda in Edwards's time is precisely because the relation of these covenants to eternal affairs constantly emerged as the vexing issue. Put differently, precisely because the church covenant and the national covenant do not overlap the covenant of grace, Edwards struggled to somehow bridge the gap between these earthly covenants and the covenant of grace.

Indeed, it seems possible to put that Edwards attempted to make the realm of the church and national covenants coextensive with the realm of the covenant of grace. Marsden points out:

> Puritanism and its Reformed-pietist successors constantly vacillated between whether they were rebuilding Christendom by making towns and eventually nations into virtually Christian societies, or whether they were advocating a pure, called-out church. Edwards had strong commitments to both ideals.[129]

---

128. Bercovitch, *American Jeremiad*, 9.
129. Marsden, *Jonathan Edwards*, 350.

In fact, Brandon Withrow, for example, almost identifies the church covenant with the national covenant.

> The concept of a national covenant came from first-generation Puritans, who emphasized the converted soul and required some kind of proof of conversion for obtaining full membership in the church. Puritan covenant theology added to this full membership an additional benefit: these Christians could baptize their children, making the children members of the covenant also. The nation in covenant would therefore consist of numerous churches whose members were personally committed to, and in covenant with, the God they worshipped. This affirmation of the covenant between God and the people meant that they could hope for his blessings on the nation as a whole, so long as the people did not forsake the church.[130]

Edwards's struggles in the communion controversy and jeremiad discourses can be conceived as his attempts to realize a church and a nation coextensive with the realm of the covenant of grace.

On this score, it is possible to say that both Solomon Stoddard and Jonathan Edwards attempted to reconcile the covenant of grace with the church and national covenants. As Marsden notes, "The great problem was how to reconcile the Old and New Testaments."[131] On the one hand, in the case of Stoddard, he "attempted to resolve this dilemma by highlighting the Old Testament model."[132] In Stoddardeanism, "church and town were more or less coextensive" and the Stoddard family "could preside over something like an Old Testament tribe."[133] In this case, "The New Testament agenda of fostering conversions remained a leading goal, but it was pursued in this Old Testament framework."[134] On the other hand, Edwards "can be understood as insisting that the New Testament should have priority if one was attempting to find the model for the church."[135] Facing the same challenge of discerning the visible and invisible church, time and eternity, or earth and heaven, Stoddard chose a way closer to a national church model whereas Edwards adhered to a called-out, spiritual church model.[136]

---

130. Withrow, *Becoming Divine*, 83.
131. Marsden, *Jonathan Edwards*, 351.
132. Marsden, *Jonathan Edwards*, 351.
133. Marsden, *Jonathan Edwards*, 351.
134. Marsden, *Jonathan Edwards*, 351.
135. Marsden, *Jonathan Edwards*, 351.
136. Marsden, *Jonathan Edwards*, 350–51.

This is why, as previously noted, Edwards attempted to require a public covenant to his congregation in 1742. For Edwards, it was "a means of hearty self-dedication to God," and "makes their bonds the stronger and so restrains the conscience."[137] In order to ascertain that the owning of a covenant was genuine and truthful, Edwards required "a heartfelt profession" as "the outward sign of regeneration."[138] He declared: "I think, nothing can be alleged from the Holy Scripture, that is sufficient to prove a profession of godliness to be not a qualification requisite in order to a due and regular participation of the Passover."[139]

True, the church covenant and the national covenant are not identical with the covenant of grace. Because the church and national covenants aim at the mixture of the regenerate and the unregenerate, they need to be distinguished from the covenant of grace that pertains only to the elect or true believers. However, precisely because it became a significant challenge to sort out the relation between these earthly matters and eternal salvation, the church covenant and the national covenant became perplexing subjects in the eighteenth-century New England. Given that the covenant of grace is the *ad extra* unveiling of the trinitarian pact of redemption in eternity, here the doctrine of the Trinity has, so to speak, an unexpected repercussion to seemingly earthly matters such as church membership and the view of a nation. Since the church covenant and the national covenant are areas where eternity and time intersect, it is possible to hear even in this earthly turmoil repercussion echoing down from eternity. Creation, justification and sanctification, issues of church and national membership all take place within history. In the next chapter, we recapture this eternal repercussion of the Trinity by turning to this broader framework: history heading toward eschatological eternity.

---

137. Edwards, "Renewing Our Covenant," *WJE* 22:516.

138. Marsden, *Jonathan Edwards*, 351.

139. Edwards, "Humble Inquiry," *WJE* 12:280. See also Grasso, *Speaking Aristocracy*, 131–36.

7

Covenant of Redemption, Trinity, History, and Eschaton

THE ETERNAL PACT BETWEEN the Father and the Son constitutes the foundation for God's economic work of redemption. We have examined how this covenant of redemption plays itself out in time and space through creation, justification and sanctification, church covenant and national covenant. In this chapter, we will consider how the eternal covenant of redemption unfolds itself in history and culminates in the eschatological communion between God and the elect. The overarching narrative of redemption takes place in history, or time and space in this world.[1] In this sense, history includes creation, the salvation of individual elects, the life of the church, and the view of a national destiny. Accordingly, Edwards's series of sermons *History of the Work of Redemption* covers from the eternal covenant of redemption before the foundation of the world through God's economy of redemption in history to the eschatological culmination in the eternal communion in heaven.

---

1. For a general introduction to Edwards's view of history and eschatology, see Clark, "History of the Work," 45–58; Wilson, "Jonathan Edwards as Historian," 5–18; Goen, "New Departure in Eschatology," 25–40; Zakai, *Jonathan Edwards's Philosophy of History*; Pauw, "'Heaven,'" 392–401; Caldwell, "Brief History of Heaven," 48–71; Ramsey, "Heaven Is a Progressive State," 8:706–38; Delattre, "Beauty and Politics," 20–48; McClymond and McDermott, *Theology of Jonathan Edwards*, 181–90, 195–308, 566–79; Jenson, *America's Theologian*, 177–85; Crisp, *Jonathan Edwards on God*, 164–89; Lucas, *God's Grand Design*; McClymond, *Encounters with God*, 65–79; Bolt, "Glory of Spiders and Politics," 72–80; Stahle, *Great Work of Providence*.

COVENANT OF REDEMPTION AND HISTORY

For Edwards, history includes the fall of human beings to the end of time. As McDermott notes, Edwards sees history as "the larger covenantal story of God's determination to reconcile sinful humanity to himself."[2] Evidences indicate that toward the end of his life he had a plan to write a comprehensive history of the work of redemption. When he replied to the trustees of the College of New Jersey on their request to him to become president, one of the reasons for his hesitation to assume the position was his ongoing project that he was preoccupied with.

> But besides these, I have had on my mind and heart (which I long ago began, not with any view to publication) a great work, which I call *A History of the Work of Redemption*, a body of divinity in an entire new method, being thrown into the form of an history, considering the affair of Christian theology, as the whole of it, in each part, stands in reference to the great work of redemption by Jesus Christ; which I suppose is to be the grand design of all God's designs, and the *summum* and *ultimum* of all the divine operations and degrees; particularly considering all parts of the grand scheme in their historical order. The order of their existence, or their being brought forth to view, in the course of divine dispensations, or the wonderful series of successive acts and events; beginning from eternity and descending from thence to the great work and successive dispensations of the infinitely wise God in time, considering the chief events coming to pass in the church of God, and revolutions in the world of mankind, affecting the state of the church and the affair of redemption, which we have an account of in history or prophecy; till at last we come to the general resurrection, last judgment, and consummation of all things; when it shall be said "It is done. I am Alpha and Omega, the Beginning and the End" [Revelation 22:13]. Concluding my work, with the consideration of that perfect state of things, which shall be finally settled, to last for eternity. This history will be carried on with regard to all three worlds, heaven, earth, and hell: considering the connected, successive events and alterations, in each so far as the Scriptures give any light; introducing all parts of divinity in that order which is most scriptural and most natural.[3]

---

2. McDermott, "Jonathan Edwards on Justification," 108.

3. Edwards, "To the Trustees," *WJE* 16:727–28. Another project Edwards had in mind was *The Harmony of the Old and New Testament*. For more on this project, see Minkema, "Other Unfinished 'Great Work,'" 52–65.

This historically dispensational narrative was a method that appears "the most beautiful and entertaining," Edwards thought, "wherein every divine doctrine, will appear to greatest advantage in the brightest light, in the most striking manner, showing the admirable contexture and harmony of the whole."[4] Although this project did not see its completion due to his unexpected death, it is still possible to reconstruct Edwards's theology of history as an overarching grand narrative of the covenant of redemption from his series of sermons he preached in the late 1730s, which was later published and titled: *A History of the Work of Redemption*.[5]

In the first sermon in *A History of the Work of Redemption*, Edwards defines what he means by this term: the work of redemption. In a more limited sense, the work of redemption signifies "the purchase of salvation," or "a purchase of deliverance"[6]

> It was begun with Christ's incarnation and carried on through Christ's life and finished with his death, or the time of his remaining under the power of death which ended in his resurrection. And so we say that the day of Christ's resurrection is the day when Christ finished the work of our redemption, i.e., then the purchase was finished and the work itself and all that appertained to it was virtually done and finished but not actually.[7]

In this case, the work of redemption was "not so long a-doing but it was begun and finished with Christ's humiliation, or it was all wrought while Christ was upon earth."[8]

In contrast, in a larger sense of the word, the work of redemption signifies "all that God works or accomplishes tending to" the purpose of redemption, "not only the purchasing of redemption but also all God's works that were properly preparatory to the purchase, or as applying the purchase

---

4. Edwards, "To the Trustees," *WJE* 16:728.

5. Wilson, "Editor's Introduction," *WJE* 9:1. Gerald McDermott and Michael McClymond argue that the work Edwards projected later in his life but did not materialize, *A History of the Work of Redemption*, should have been very different from this sermon series he delivered in the 1730s. See McClymond and McDermott, *Theology of Jonathan Edwards*, 284–85. However, given that many of the books written by Reformed scholastics were originally series of sermons and Edwards himself published several books based on his sermons, it is possible that this sermon series constituted the basic framework if this project materialized. At least it is contestable how Edwards's phrase "a body of divinity in an entire new method" should be interpreted. Examples of works based on series of sermons are: Charnock, *Several Discourses*; Willard, *Compleat Body of Divinity*; Ridgley, *Body of Divinity*. See also Neele, "Exchanges," 21–46.

6. Edwards, "History of the Work of Redemption," *WJE* 9:117.

7. Edwards, "History of the Work of Redemption," *WJE* 9:117.

8. Edwards, "History of the Work of Redemption," *WJE* 9:117.

and accomplishing the success of it."⁹ This sense of the term has "respect to [the] church of God or the grand design in general."¹⁰

> It [the work of redemption] is carried on not only by that which is common to all ages [but] by successive works wrought in different ages, all parts of one whole or one great scheme whereby one work is brought about by various steps, one step in each age and another in another.¹¹

It envisions the whole spectrum of God's work of redemption. "So that the whole dispensation as it includes the preparation and the imputation and application and success of Christ's redemption is here called the Work of Redemption."¹² It is primarily this sense of the term that Edwards articulates in this treatise. Critically important for this study is that Edwards envisions this whole grand design of redemption as the outworking of the eternal trinitarian covenant of redemption.

> All that Christ does in this great affair as mediator in any of his offices, either Prophet, Priest or King, either when he was in the world in his human [form], or before or since. And not only what Christ the mediator has done, but also what the Father and the Holy Ghost have done as united or confederated in this design of redeeming sinful men; or in one word, all that is wrought in execution of the eternal covenant of redemption. This is what I called the Work of Redemption in the doctrine, for 'tis all but one work, one design. The various dispensations and works that belong to it are but the several parts of one scheme. 'Tis but one design that is done to which all the offices of Christ do directly tend, and in which all the persons of the Trinity do conspire and all the various dispensations that belong to it are united, as the several wheels in one machine, to answer one end and produce one effect.¹³

Edwards sees the entire course of history, including before and after Christ, under the spectrum of the outworking of the eternal covenant of redemption.

In other words, the whole course of the history of redemption was already conceived in the mind of God in the immanent Trinity or the eternal communion of the three divine persons.

9. Edwards, "History of the Work of Redemption," *WJE* 9:117.
10. Edwards, "History of the Work of Redemption," *WJE* 9:122.
11. Edwards, "History of the Work of Redemption," *WJE* 9:122.
12. Edwards, "History of the Work of Redemption," *WJE* 9:117.
13. Edwards, "History of the Work of Redemption," *WJE* 9:117–18.

> Some things were done before the world was created, yea from all eternity. The persons of the Trinity were as it were confederated in a design and a covenant of redemption, in which covenant the Father appointed the Son and the Son had undertaken their work, and all things to be accomplished in their work were stipulated and agreed.[14]

Kyoung-Chul Jang summarized as follows God's historical work of redemption as the trinitarian undertaking stemming from eternity:

> Edwards's idea of the work of redemption is situated within the framework of the glorification of the triune God. Edwards locates the whole human history within the framework of the trinitrian covenant of redemption. For Edwards, the work of redemption is based upon the agreement made among the divine Persons of the Trinity. Here Edwards says that the work of redemption is grounded in the covenant of redemption among the Persons of the Trinity. According to Edwards, the work of redemption is not the lonely work of Christ, but a trinitarian undertaking.[15]

The work of redemption stipulated and agreed upon in the fellowship of the trinitarian persons now begins to be actualized in history and time.

Not only does Edwards envision the eternal agreement among the three persons of the Trinity preceding the creation and the fall, but also foresees the eternal fruits flourishing beyond the end of the history.

> The glory and blessedness that will be the sum of all the fruits will remain to all eternity after that. The Work of Redemption is not an eternal work, that is, it is not a work always a-doing and never accomplished. But the fruits of this work are eternal fruits. The work has an issue, but in the issue the end will be obtained, which end never will have an end. As things that were in order to this work, as God's electing love and the covenant of redemption never had a beginning, so the fruits of this work that shall be after the end of the work never will have an end.[16]

The eternal pact that has no beginning unfolds itself by way of history and, after the end of the world, goes back into eternity. The eternity of the divine fellowship returns into the eternity with the fruits of the work of redemption

---

14. Edwards, "History of the Work of Redemption," *WJE* 9:118.

15. Jang, "Logic of Glorification," 135–36. Yet note that the primary agents of this covenant are not all three persons but the Father and the Son.

16. Edwards, "History of the Work of Redemption," *WJE* 9:119.

via creation and providence. This time, however, the eternal communion is not only among the three persons of the Trinity, but is also between the triune God and creation represented by the elect. This is, so to speak, an eschatological repercussion of the covenant of redemption. As William M. Schweitzer notes, "In terms of chronological scope, his vision sweeps from eternity past through the whole of human history and into eternity future."[17]

In fact, this participation of creation in the communion of trinitarian persons constitutes the crux of Edwards's theology. Schweitzer identifies the heart of Edwards's theology with God as the communicative being. According to Schweitzer, Edwards conceived all of reality as "the harmonious communication of the Triune divine mind,"[18] or "the ongoing communication of the divine mind."[19] Edwards was preoccupied with a lingering question: If God is self-sufficient and self-contained, why did he create the world? The answer he found was because God is "a communicative being."[20] God in himself is perfectly good and happy. Yet this perfect goodness entails the sharing and enjoying of this goodness with others.

> To be perfectly good is to incline to and delight in making another happy in the same proportion as it is happy itself, that is, to delight as much in communicating happiness to another as in enjoying of it himself, and an inclination to communicate all his happiness; it appears that this is perfect goodness, because goodness is delight in communicating happiness. Wherefore, if this goodness be perfect this delight must be perfect, because goodness and this delight are the same[21]

Because goodness lies in delight in communicating itself, goodness of God also entails the plurality of God. "It appears that there must be more than a unity in infinite and eternal essence, otherwise the goodness of God can have no perfect exercise."[22] Because God enjoys the communication of his goodness within himself in the communion of divine persons, God as the communicative being is inclined to communicate his goodness and happiness to others. Hence, "God's goodness entails his communicativeness, and his communicativeness implies the plurality of the ontological Trinity."[23]

17. Schweitzer, *God Is a Communicative Being*, 3.
18. Schweitzer, *God Is a Communicative Being*, 6.
19. Schweitzer, *God Is a Communicative Being*, 19.
20. Edwards, *WJE* 13:410.
21. Edwards, *WJE* 13:263–64.
22. Edwards, *WJE* 13:263.
23. Schweitzer, *God Is a Communicative Being*, 16.

The communicative unfolding of the eternal covenant takes place in accordance with the communicativeness within the immanent Trinity.

If God's work of redemption is accomplished through the grand design of history in the communication of his goodness, then what exactly is to be accomplished as God's design in this history? Edwards suggests five designs or purposes of the history of redemption. First, God's design of redemption is "to reduce and subdue those enemies of God till they should all be put under God's feet."[24] As Edwards puts it, "It is to put all God's enemies under his feet and that the goodness of God should finally appear triumphing over all evil."[25] God's work of redemption in history involves the subduing of opposing powers and prevailing victory of God's goodness.

The second design in history is the restoration of the ruined world. Edwards sees this restorative work through God's converting work of human souls. "The design was to restore the soul of man in conversion and to restore life to it, and the image of God in conversion and to carry on the restoration in sanctification, and to perfect it in glory."[26] This is God's restorative work that ultimately leads to the creation of "a new heaven and a new earth."[27]

The third design in history conceived by God is "to gather together in one all things in Christ in heaven and on earth."[28] It is the comprehension of all things under the headship of Christ. Edwards portrays: "[This is] to bring all elect creatures in heaven and earth to an union one to another, in one body under one head, and to unite all together in one body to God the Father."[29]

The fourth design of this history is "to complete and perfect the glory of all the elect by Christ."[30]

> He intended to bring them to perfect excellency and beauty in his image and in holiness which is the proper beauty of spiritual beings, and to advance 'em to a glorious degree of honor and also to an ineffable pitch of pleasure and joy. And thus to glorify the whole church of elect men in soul and body, and unite them

---

24. Edwards, "History of the Work of Redemption," *WJE* 9:123.
25. Edwards, "History of the Work of Redemption," *WJE* 9:123.
26. Edwards, "History of the Work of Redemption," *WJE* 9:124.
27. Edwards, "History of the Work of Redemption," *WJE* 9:124.
28. Edwards, "History of the Work of Redemption," *WJE* 9:124.
29. Edwards, "History of the Work of Redemption," *WJE* 9:125.
30. Edwards, "History of the Work of Redemption," *WJE* 9:125.

by the glory of the elect angels to its highest pitch under one head.[31]

It is God's design that all the elect as the image of God will be perfected and completed in glory.

Finally, in all of these designs, God ultimately intends to "accomplish the glory of the blessed Trinity in an exceeding degree."[32] Edwards holds: "God had a design of glorifying himself from eternity, to glorify each person in the Godhead."[33] The ultimate end of God's design is to glorify himself, the Trinity. God has this design of self-glorification "from eternity,"[34] before the creation of the world and within the eternal communion of the three divine persons. The means chosen to accomplish this end was "this great Work of Redemption."[35]

By subduing the enemies, by restoring the image of God, by comprehending all things under the headship of Christ, by completing the glory of the elect, God designs to glorify himself throughout the series of historical development. In this way, the history of redemption actualizes the covenant of redemption.

TYPOLOGY IN HISTORY

While I examined Edwards's typology of nature in chapter 4, Edwards utilizes typology not only in his theological interpretation of nature and creation but also in his theological view of history. As Janice Knight argues, Edwards's use of typology transcends a categorical distinction between typology of nature and typology of history. The central theme of glory in Edwards's theology, Knight points out, "sanctioned the union of neoplatonism with prophetic historicism" and his "conviction of God's essential effulgence produced a theory in which divine communications simply overwhelm the descriptive categories of history and ontology."[36] God's self-communication *ad extra* "consists not just in God's immediate relation with his creature but includes the larger works of creation and redemption."[37] Knight correctly traces the source of this divine communication back to the Trinity.

---

31. Edwards, "History of the Work of Redemption," *WJE* 9:125.
32. Edwards, "History of the Work of Redemption," *WJE* 9:125.
33. Edwards, "History of the Work of Redemption," *WJE* 9:125.
34. Edwards, "History of the Work of Redemption," *WJE* 9:125.
35. Edwards, "History of the Work of Redemption," *WJE* 9:125.
36. Knight, "Learning the Language of God," 546.
37. Knight, "Learning the Language of God," 547.

Implicated in the agreement between God's communications *ad intra* and *ad extra* is the question of how ontology is related to history. The source of the ineffable, indissoluble union of these two modes is contained, though not explained, in the sacred mystery of the Trinity, which not only makes one God three but also insists that priority of existence and equality of essence are eternally joined. History can no more be severed from ontology than the idea of God can be divorced from his love. The coupling of natural and historical types, which does indeed seem anomalous with respect to human reasoning, is resolved *ad intra*, that is, within God's nature.[38]

Because "*Esse* and *Operati* both have a single source in God's love and its Emanation,"[39] Edwards's typology permeates through both nature and history.

However, Knight is not entirely correct when she juxtaposes and contrasts a covenantal framework and an "amorous equation" of emanation and remanation.[40] Knight identifies two major currents in Puritan theologies: the "Intellectual Fathers" and the "Spiritual Brethren."[41] On the one hand, the "Intellectual Fathers" are represented by Thomas Hooker, Thomas Shepard, Peter Bulkeley, and John Winthrop. These preachers, according to Knight, "identified power as God's essential attribute and described his covenant with human beings as a conditional promise."[42] On the other hand, the "Spiritual Brethren" are represented by Richard Sibbes, John Preston, John Cotton, John Davenport, and Henry Vane. Knight says that these preachers are "More emotional and even mystical, their theology stressed divine benevolence over power."[43]

Against the carefully delineated steps and preparations for salvation on the part of humans, these Spiritual Brethren are said to have emphasized "the love of God" and "converted a free testament or voluntary bequeathing of grace for the conditional covenant described by the other orthodoxy."[44] While the "Intellectual Fathers" represented by Richard Hooker emphasize

---

38. Knight, "Learning the Language of God," 547.

39. Knight, "Garden Enclosed," 520.

40. For example, a sentence like the one following that contrasts the covenant with diffusive love sounds puzzling: "Where there is emanation, there is remanation. In that amorous equation—not any contract or covenant—the saint are wedded to God in holiest union" (Knight, "Garden Enclosed," 538).

41. Knight, *Orthodoxies in Massachusetts*, 2.

42. Knight, *Orthodoxies in Massachusetts*, 3.

43. Knight, *Orthodoxies in Massachusetts*, 3.

44. Knight, *Orthodoxies in Massachusetts*, 3.

the covenantal framework, the "Spiritual Brethren" represented by Richard Sibbes emphasize the torrent of love in emanation and remanation, according to Knight.[45]

Yet the fact is that Edwards articulates the communication of diffusive love within his covenantal framework. In Edwards, diffusiveness of love and the covenantal framework are compatible.[46] God communicates himself to the world through a covenantal arrangement made with the elect. As Schweitzer notes, "all of reality is the harmonious communication of the Triune divine mind."[47] Yet only the elect within the covenant of grace can perceive and appreciate this divine communication as God designed. These elects have been ordained to salvation in the mind of God from eternity in the covenant of redemption.

Within the covenantal framework, Edwards articulates God's diffusive and overflowing love and goodness communicated throughout the creation. This means that it is the elect in the covenantal relationship with God who can perceive and appreciate this divine communication in the most proper way. "Grace endows the believer with a capacity to perceive God's presence in his own heart and in the wider world."[48] Even the extrascriptural divine communications are "part of a divinely instituted system of symbols that continuously prefigure and communicate the divine presence in nature and history."[49] God "has constituted the external world in an analogy to things in the spiritual world, in numberless instances."[50] Therefore, it is pleasing to God "to observe analogy in his works, as is manifest in fact in innumerable instances; and especially to establish inferior things in an analogy to superior."[51] This typological analogy is applied not only to the ontological hierarchy of the chain of beings but also to the horizontal development of world history as the history of redemption.

When Edwards applies typology to history, historical types all shadow forth the coming of Jesus Christ. For example, Edwards sees the new earth granted to Noah and his family after the flood as "founded on the covenant

---

45. Knight, *Orthodoxies in Massachusetts*, 2–33, 119, 134.

46. To be fair, Knight herself admits and emphasizes that both the Intellectual Fathers and the Cambridge Brethren talked about diffusive love and covenant and that categorization is a matter of emphasis. See Knight, *Orthodoxies in Massachusetts*, 21, 34.

47. Schweitzer, *God Is a Communicative Being*, 6.

48. Knight, "Learning the Language of God," 533.

49. Knight, "Learning the Language of God," 532.

50. Edwards, "Nature of True Virtue," *WJE* 8:564.

51. Edwards, "Nature of True Virtue," *WJE* 8:564.

of grace."[52] "The sacrifice of Christ was represented by Noah's building an altar to the Lord and offering a sacrifice of every clean beast and every clean fowl."[53] The story of Joseph and salvation of the house of Israel through him is regarded as "a semblance of the salvation of Christ."[54] Israel's exodus from the bondage of Egypt and the passing through the Red Sea signify "The beginning of the application of the redemption of Christ's church in their conversion."[55] Joshua the leader who led Israel into the land of milk and honey is called "an eminent type of Christ."[56] As history makes progress, "The light of the gospel now began to shine much brighter as the time drew nearer that Christ should come."[57] "The light of the gospel," Edwards remarks, "which first began to dawn and glimmer immediately after the fall, gradually increases the nearer we come to Christ's time."[58]

According to Knight, generally speaking, conservative typology is "one of historical existences," while liberal typology is "one of ontological essences."[59] Usually "A type looks forward in time, not upward through the scale of being."[60] However, Edwards defies such a dichotomized categorization. Rather, "Edwards always wove ontological and historical types together in his writings."[61] In one instance, Edwards uses a natural type for typology of history at the same time. When Edwards used an image of the moon "approaching nearer and nearer to her conjunction with the sun" and "her light is still more and more decreasing," he compared it to the "latter end of Solomon's reign," when "the state of things began to darken."[62] Both natural type and historical type here, though from different modes, still point to the same lesson: "that a time of declining light or glory prepares the way, through contrast, for a greater period of illumination with the coming of the Son."[63]

---

52. Edwards, "History of the Work of Redemption," *WJE* 9:152.
53. Edwards, "History of the Work of Redemption," *WJE* 9:152.
54. Edwards, "History of the Work of Redemption," *WJE* 9:171.
55. Edwards, "History of the Work of Redemption," *WJE* 9:184.
56. Edwards, "History of the Work of Redemption," *WJE* 9:192.
57. Edwards, "History of the Work of Redemption," *WJE* 9:170.
58. Edwards, "History of the Work of Redemption," *WJE* 9:189.
59. Knight, "Learning the Language of God," 536.
60. Madsen, "From Shadowy Types to Truth," 99. For an account of the history of typology, see Keach, *Tropologia*.
61. Knight, "Learning the Language of God," 537.
62. Edwards, "History of the Work of Redemption," *WJE* 9:229. See also Knight, "Learning the Language of God," 537.
63. Knight, "Learning the Language of God," 537–38.

While some scholars describe Edwards as divided within himself between his conventional theology and his liberal use of typology,[64] it seems that the fact is, as Knight aptly puts it, "The historical narrative and the natural image were merely alternative ways to understand the work of redemption and to retain it in the mind; the preacher, like God himself, used both to instruct and edify."[65] Given that the same one and only God communicates himself through both nature and history, natural types and historical types both organically work together and complement each other to illustrate the same point in God's work of redemption. In the case of the moon approaching the sun compared to the declining reign of the king Solomon, "the image of the moon blends so organically with the historical type that it argues for an original wholeness in God's communications."[66] John F. Wilson basically concurs when he states:

> For Edwards, nature and history were not alternative sources of knowledge about the Godhead, but each one interpenetrated the other. At his hands, scriptural figures became fused with and elaborated by the images and shadows of nature, and the boundary between them ceased to exist. What remained was an interdependence through which nature and Scripture joined to reveal divine glory. It is not too much to claim that in his Redemption Discourse he so transformed conventional typological assumptions that the discourse became as much a celebration of the God of nature as a hymn to the Lord of history.[67]

Whether in nature or in history, typology enabled Edwards "to find coherence where chaos might otherwise be thought to reign."[68]

THE COVENANTAL DISPENSATION IN HISTORY

In order to accomplish these designs, Edwards maintains, God utilizes the covenantal framework in his way of dealing with his people in history. The covenant of works represents the first covenant that God made with his people. Yet it was "the will of God that it should first appear by the event

---

64. Lewalski, *Protestant Poetics*, 140; Lowance, *Language of Canaan*, 249–76.
65. Knight, "Learning the Language of God," 538.
66. Knight, "Learning the Language of God," 538.
67. Wilson, "Editor's Introduction," *WJE* 9:50. Wilson provides a helpful account on typology in Protestantism and Puritanism as well as in Redemption Discourse in Wilson, "Editor's Introduction," *WJE* 9:40–50, 55–61.
68. Wilson, "Editor's Introduction," *WJE* 9:39.

wherein the first was deficient, or wanting of what man needed."[69] Because in this first covenant "the fulfillment of the righteousness of the covenant, and man's perseverance, was betrusted with man himself, with nothing better to secure it than his own strength," it turned out invalid as the deficiency manifested "in the fall."[70]

> The covenant of works was here exhibited to be as a schoolmaster to lead to Christ, not only for the use of that nation in the age of the Old Testament, but for the use of God's church throughout all ages to the end of the world, as an instrument that the great Redeemer makes use of to convince men of their sin and misery and helplessness and God's awful and tremendous majesty and justice as a lawgiver, and to make men sensible of the necessity of Christ as a savior.[71]

The covenant of works as a schoolmaster led people to know their brokenness and helplessness in the sight of God.

Accordingly, God introduced a "better covenant," or "an everlasting covenant." In this covenant of grace, "that which was wanting in the first covenant would be supplied," and "a remedy should be provided against that which under the first covenant proved man's undoing, viz. man's own weakness and instability."[72] With the failure of humankind in keeping the covenant of works, the purpose of the first covenant has been achieved.

> God did not see it fit that man should be trusted to stand in his own strength a second time. God at first entered into such a covenant with man wherein he was left to stand in his own strength, for that end, that the event might show the weakness and instability of man and his dependence on God. But when the event has once proved this, there is no need of entering into another covenant of the same tenor to manifest it.[73]

In the second covenant, the covenant of grace, God the Father sent the only Son, the mediator who "is the same yesterday, today and forever, who cannot fail, who would undertake for them, who should take the care of them, that is able to save to the uttermost all that come unto God through him, and who ever lives to make intercession for them."[74]

69. Edwards, *WJE* 18:277.
70. Edwards, *WJE* 18:277.
71. Edwards, "History of the Work of Redemption," *WJE* 9:180.
72. Edwards, *WJE* 18:277.
73. Edwards, *WJE* 18:277.
74. Edwards, *WJE* 18:277.

Based on this covenantal framework and utilizing typological interpretation of nature and history, Edwards proposes three progressive stages of history of redemption. The first stage ranges from "the fall of man to Christ's incarnation." The second is "from Christ's incarnation till his resurrection, or the whole time of Christ's humiliation." The third stage ranges from "thence to the end of the world."[75]

Edwards subdivides the first stage between the fall and Christ's incarnation into six periods: from the fall to the flood; from the flood to the calling of Abraham; from Abraham to Moses; from Moses to David; from David to the Babylonian captivity; and from the captivity to the incarnation of Christ.[76] In the first period from the fall to the flood, it is notable that Edwards recognizes the latent work of Christ already beginning immediately since the fall. In Genesis 3:15 ("And I will put enmity between thee and the woman, [and between thy seed and her seed; it shall bruise thy head]") Edwards sees protoevangelism.[77] Upon the fall of human beings, Christ assumed the mediator's office. The preacher says: "Christ immediately on the fall of man entered on that office and began that work to which all the great dispensations that were to be afterwards towards his church to the end of the world do belong."[78] In fact, this promise of another "surety"[79] was "the first revelation of the covenant of grace; this was the first dawning of the light of the gospel on earth."[80] Also, the institution of sacrifice prepared "the way for Christ's coming and working out redemption."[81]

In the second period from the flood to the calling of Abraham, the water that "washed away the filth of the world" is construed as "a type of the blood of Christ that takes away the sin of the world."[82] While a grant of earth was originally made under the covenant of works with Adam in Genesis 1:28 ("Be fruitful and multiply and replenish the earth, and subdue it; and have dominion . . . over every living thing"), Edwards sees in God's covenant with Noah after the flood "the new grant of the earth" "founded on the covenant of grace."[83]

---

75. Edwards, "History of the Work of Redemption," *WJE* 9:127.
76. Edwards, "History of the Work of Redemption," *WJE* 9:129.
77. Edwards, "History of the Work of Redemption," *WJE* 9:132.
78. Edwards, "History of the Work of Redemption," *WJE* 9:132.
79. Edwards, "History of the Work of Redemption," *WJE* 9:132.
80. Edwards, "History of the Work of Redemption," *WJE* 9:133.
81. Edwards, "History of the Work of Redemption," *WJE* 9:137.
82. Edwards, "History of the Work of Redemption," *WJE* 9:151.
83. Edwards, "History of the Work of Redemption," *WJE* 9:152.

In the third period, "a more particular and full revelation and confirmation of the covenant of grace" takes place.[84] God made a covenant with Abraham, promising him that he was Christ's seed and all the families of the earth would enter blessings through Abraham.[85] Circumcision was introduced as "a seal of the covenant of grace," as "a certain sacrament to be a steady seal of this covenant in the visible church till Christ should come."[86] In Abraham's delivering Isaac as a sacrifice to obey the Lord's command,[87] in Jacob's stone and his vision at Bethel,[88] or in Joseph's providential story that turned a tragedy to a drama of saving Israel from famine,[89] Edwards sees God's renewals of the covenant of grace.

During the fourth period, the covenant of works was exhibited at Mount Sinai "as a schoolmaster to lead to Christ," "as an instrument that the great Redeemer makes use of to convince men of their sin and misery and helplessness and God's awful and tremendous majesty and justice as a lawgiver, and so to make men sensible of the necessity of Christ as a savior."[90] Israel's journey through the Red Sea and wilderness and their entry to the land of Canaan indicate God's renewing the covenant of grace.[91] Joshua was "an eminent type of Christ"[92] and judges such as Barak, Jephthah, Gideon, and Samson were "types of the great redeemer and deliverer" of God's church.[93]

Under the fifth period, David became king of Israel as "the greatest personal type of Christ of all under the Old Testament."[94] The city of Jerusalem was "the greatest type of the church of Christ in all the Old Testament."[95] In the promise of the establishment of the throne in 2 Sam 7:16 ("And thy house and thy kingdom shall be established forever before thee; thy throne shall be established forever"),[96] Edwards sees "the fifth solemn establish-

---

84. Edwards, "History of the Work of Redemption," *WJE* 9:160.
85. Edwards, "History of the Work of Redemption," *WJE* 9:161. Edwards cites Gen 12:2; 15:5–6; 22:16–18.
86. Edwards, "History of the Work of Redemption," *WJE* 9:161.
87. Edwards, "History of the Work of Redemption," *WJE* 9:164.
88. Edwards, "History of the Work of Redemption," *WJE* 9:170.
89. Edwards, "History of the Work of Redemption," *WJE* 9:171.
90. Edwards, "History of the Work of Redemption," *WJE* 9:180.
91. Edwards, "History of the Work of Redemption," *WJE* 9:184, 189–90.
92. Edwards, "History of the Work of Redemption," *WJE* 9:192.
93. Edwards, "History of the Work of Redemption," *WJE* 9:196.
94. Edwards, "History of the Work of Redemption," *WJE* 9:204.
95. Edwards, "History of the Work of Redemption," *WJE* 9:213.
96. Edwards, "History of the Work of Redemption," *WJE* 9:214.

ment of the covenant of grace with his church since the fall."[97] Later decline of kingly rule in Israel was "to prepare the way for the spiritual glory of the gospel being more joyfully received."[98]

During the sixth period, the Babylonian captivity took place. This event also prepared "the way for Christ" in that it "showed the necessity of abolishing the Jewish dispensation and introducing a new dispensation of the covenant of grace."[99] Following the conquer of the Persian empire by the Grecian empire, Greek spread as the common language, which prepared a way for "setting up the kingdom <of Christ>, because this was the language in which the New Testament was to be originally written."[100]

Upon the completion of these six periods under the first stage of the work of redemption came Christ's incarnation as the second stage of the history of redemption. Edwards writes on this stage of history: "Though it was but between thirty and forty years, yet more was done in it than had been done from the beginning of the world to that time."[101] All the periods in the first stages and, moreover, the eternal transaction of the covenant of redemption primarily targeted this particular stage of history.

> We have observed that all [things] that had been done before were only preparatory for what was done now, and it may also be observed that all that was done before the beginning of time in the eternal counsels of God, and that eternal transaction there was between the persons of the Trinity, chiefly respected this period.[102]

Because of Christ's humiliation from his incarnation to his resurrection, "the purchase of redemption was made."[103] In Christ the history of redemption sees "the antitype of all that had been done, by all the priests, and in all their sacrifices and offerings, from the beginning of the world."[104]

By Christ's purchase of redemption, two things are intended: "satisfaction" and "merit." First, Christ's death pays "our debt" and thereby satisfies the penalty and punishment the fallen humans owe.[105] The price that Christ paid "satisfies by its intrinsic value and agreement between the Father and

  97. Edwards, "History of the Work of Redemption," *WJE* 9:215.
  98. Edwards, "History of the Work of Redemption," *WJE* 9:231.
  99. Edwards, "History of the Work of Redemption," *WJE* 9:257.
  100. Edwards, "History of the Work of Redemption," *WJE* 9:272.
  101. Edwards, "History of the Work of Redemption," *WJE* 9:294.
  102. Edwards, "History of the Work of Redemption," *WJE* 9:294.
  103. Edwards, "History of the Work of Redemption," *WJE* 9:295.
  104. Edwards, "History of the Work of Redemption," *WJE* 9:318.
  105. Edwards, "History of the Work of Redemption," *WJE* 9:304.

the Son."[106] Second, by the merit of Christ's death, the price "procures a title for us to happiness."[107] While the "satisfaction or propitiation of Christ consists either in his suffering evil, or his being subject to abasement," Christ's obedience to the Father till the death of the cross also has positive merit that earns happiness for the elect.[108]

> But not only proper suffering, but all abasement and depression of the state or circumstance of mankind below its primitive honor and dignity, such as his body's remaining under death, and body and soul remaining separate, and other things that might be mentioned, are the judicial fruits of sin. And all that Christ did in his state of humiliation that had the nature of obedience, or moral virtue, or goodness in it in one respect or another, had the nature of merit in it, and was part of the price with which he purchased happiness for the elect.[109]

In sum, "The satisfaction of Christ is to free us from misery, and the merit of Christ is to purchase happiness for us."[110]

By Christ's obedience Edwards means obedience to "the mediatorial law."[111] Edwards lists three kinds of law that Christ obeyed in his life on earth. First was "those commands that he was subject to merely as man" as stipulated in two tables of stone at Mount Sinai.[112] Second was Jewish ceremonial law.[113] Yet the third kind was "the mediatorial law," "the commands that the Father gave him to teach such doctrines, to preach the gospel, to work such miracles, to call such disciples, to appoint such ordinances, and finally to lay down his life."[114] Particularly Christ's obedience to this mediatorial law was "most meritorious."[115]

> As the obedience of the first Adam, wherein his righteousness would have consisted if he had stood, would have mainly consisted not in his obedience to the moral law that he was subject to as a moral head and surety of mankind, even the command of abstaining from the tree of knowledge <of good and evil>, so

---

106. Edwards, "History of the Work of Redemption," *WJE* 9:304.
107. Edwards, "History of the Work of Redemption," *WJE* 9:304.
108. Edwards, "History of the Work of Redemption," *WJE* 9:305.
109. Edwards, "History of the Work of Redemption," *WJE* 9:305.
110. Edwards, "History of the Work of Redemption," *WJE* 9:304.
111. Edwards, "History of the Work of Redemption," *WJE* 9:310.
112. Edwards, "History of the Work of Redemption," *WJE* 9:309.
113. Edwards, "History of the Work of Redemption," *WJE* 9:309.
114. Edwards, "History of the Work of Redemption," *WJE* 9:310.
115. Edwards, "History of the Work of Redemption," *WJE* 9:310.

the obedience of the second Adam, wherein his righteousness consists, lies mainly not in his obedience to the law that he was subject to merely as man, but to that special law, that which he was subject [to] in his office as mediator and surety for man.[116]

Certainly Christ obeyed the first two kinds of law perfectly. Yet especially in his obedience to this mediatorial law, Christ, as the surety of humankind, fulfilled all the commands he had received from the Father. Because of this merit in Christ's obedience, the elect are not only free from punishment but participate in the felicity of divine life.

After "Christ's purchase of redemption"[117] has been made, the third stage comes that begins with Christ's resurrection to the end of the world. This is the time "for obtaining the end" and "the glorious effect" of Christ's purchase of redemption.[118] This is also the time "wherein the church is under the last dispensation of the covenant of grace that ever will be under on earth."[119] Edwards subdivides this stage into four "great, successive dispensations of providence" all represented in Scripture as "Christ's coming": "setting up the kingdom of Christ and destroying the enemies of his kingdom"; "the destruction of the heathen Roman empire"; "the destruction of Antichrist"; and Christ's "coming to the last judgment."[120] As John F. Wilson notes, these four stages are "cumulative; each successive event incorporates those that went before and issues in yet a further development."[121] In Edwards's own words:

> So far as Christ's kingdom is established, so far are things would up and settled in their everlasting state, and a period put to the course of things in this unchangeable world. So far is the first heavens and the first earth come to an end and the new heavens and new earth, the everlasting heavens and earth, established in their room.[122]

Christ rose from the dead and ascended into heaven. Christ's resurrection means that he rose "from the grave with joy and glory as the joyful bridegroom of the church, as a glorious conqueror to subdue their enemies

---

116. Edwards, "History of the Work of Redemption," *WJE* 9:311
117. Edwards, "History of the Work of Redemption," *WJE* 9:344.
118. Edwards, "History of the Work of Redemption," *WJE* 9:345.
119. Edwards, "History of the Work of Redemption," *WJE* 9:346.
120. Edwards, "History of the Work of Redemption," *WJE* 9:351.
121. Wilson, "Editor's Introduction," *WJE* 9:39.
122. Edwards, "History of the Work of Redemption," *WJE* 9:349–50.

under their feet."[123] Christ's ascension indicates "his solemn enthronization whereby the Father did set him on the throne, and invest him with the glory of his kingdom that he had purchased for himself, and that he might thereby obtain the success of his redemption in conquering all his enemies."[124] Christ rose from the grave and ascended into heaven as "the head of the body and forerunner of all the church" so that the church elect may also rise and ascend with him.[125] History is the spiral and cumulative movement that heads for Christ's kingdom where Christ and the church elect enjoy eternal felicity of communion.

Toward the end of history, the church will experience a time of prosperity. "The success of Christ's purchase has been carried on through the times of the afflicted state of the Christian church," Edwards notes, "from Christ's resurrection till Antichrist is fallen and Satan's visible kingdom on earth is overthrown."[126] After the time of conflicts and afflictions comes the period of time in which the church is in "a state of peace and prosperity."[127] This is the reign of the church for a thousand years called millennium.[128]

The millennium[129] is "a time of great holiness."[130] It is an exceptional time when the knowledge of God permeates the world and universal sanctification takes place.

> Now vital religion shall everywhere prevail and reign. Religion shall not be an empty profession as it now mostly is, but holiness of heart and life shall abundantly prevail. Those times shall be an exception from what Christ says of the ordinary state of the

---

123. Edwards, "History of the Work of Redemption," *WJE* 9:360.
124. Edwards, "History of the Work of Redemption," *WJE* 9:361.
125. Edwards, "History of the Work of Redemption," *WJE* 9:361.
126. Edwards, "History of the Work of Redemption," *WJE* 9:478.
127. Edwards, "History of the Work of Redemption," *WJE* 9:479.
128. Edwards cites Rev 21:1–3: "And I saw an angel . . . having the key of the bottomless pit . . . And he laid hold on the dragon . . . and Satan, and bound him a thousand years, And cast him into the bottomless pit, and shut him up . . . that he should deceive the nations no more, till the thousand years should be fulfilled" (Edwards, "History of the Work of Redemption," *WJE* 9:474).
129. On the millennium, see Capp, *Fifth Monarchy Men*; Hill, *Experience of Defeat*; Smith, "Millenarian Scholarship in America," 535–49; Toon, *Puritans*; Wilson, *Pulpit in Parliament*; Maclear, "New England," 223–60; Gilsdorf, "Puritan Apocalypse"; Rosenmeier, "New England Perfection," 435–59; Rosenmeier, "'Clearing the Medium,'" 577–91; Zakai, *Exile and Kingdom*; Bozeman, *To Live Ancient Lives*; Delbanco, *Puritan Ordeal*. See also Bauckham, *Tudor Apocalypse*; Mede, *Key of the Revelation*; Brightman, *Revelation of St. John*.
130. Edwards, "History of the Work of Redemption," *WJE* 9:481.

church, viz. that there shall be but few [saved], for now holiness shall become general.[131]

During this penultimate time, the Christian church flourishes as the entire world returns to God. As Edwards envisions:

> And then shall all the world be united in peace and love in one amiable society; all nations, in all parts, on every side of the globe, shall then be knit together in sweet harmony, all parts of God's church assisting and promoting the knowledge and spiritual good one of another.[132]

During this period, the world will become "one church, one orderly, regular, beautiful society, one body, all the members in beautiful proportion."[133]

As was the case with justification and sanctification of the elect, here also the work of the Holy Spirit plays an important role. As the Holy Spirit justifies and sanctifies the soul of the elect, so the same Spirit leads the history to consummation. As the Holy Spirit unites the souls of the elect with the divine life and leads the elect souls to participate in the divine trinitarian communion, so the same Spirit leads the history and the entire creation to the participation in the trinitarian communion.[134] According to Avihu Zakai, an important theological endeavor Edwards engaged was "to establish an association between redemptive activity in the soul and its manifestations in time."[135]

> With the drama of salvation and redemption reaching a culmination, the private, existential dimension of conversion became inextricable from the general, external dimension of salvation history. Here lies the close association in Edwards's imagination between historical occurrences and the fate of human beings.[136]

In other words, Edwards's "aim was to transport the dynamism revealed in saving grace from the inner sphere of the soul into the whole realm of history, and thus to show the presence of God's redemptive activity within the whole of history."[137] The existential condition of the humankind is "inextricable from the unfolding revelation of God's work of redemption."[138]

---

131. Edwards, "History of the Work of Redemption," *WJE* 9:481.
132. Edwards, "History of the Work of Redemption," *WJE* 9:483–84.
133. Edwards, "History of the Work of Redemption," *WJE* 9:484.
134. Withrow, *Becoming Divine*, 197–206.
135. Zakai, *Jonathan Edwards's Philosophy of History*, 151.
136. Zakai, *Jonathan Edwards's Philosophy of History*, 280.
137. Zakai, *Jonathan Edwards's Philosophy of History*, 151.
138. Zakai, *Jonathan Edwards's Philosophy of History*, 281.

Edwards's interest in searching for manifestations of God's work of redemption in history dates back to the time shortly after his conversion experience. In *Personal Narrative* that recounts his conversion experience, Edwards notes:

> My heart has been much on the advancement of Christ's kingdom in the world. The histories of the past advancement of Christ's kingdom, have been sweet to me. When I have read histories of past ages, the pleasantest thing in all my reading has been, to read of the kingdom of Christ being promoted. And when I have expected in my reading, to come to any such thing, I have lotted upon it all the way as I read. And my mind has been much entertained and delighted, with the Scripture promises and prophecies, of the future glorious advancement of Christ's kingdom on earth.[139]

When the revival broke out in 1734–1735, Edwards found in it "an important clue to the mystery of salvation history."[140] The Northampton pastor saw the work of redemption "as the great end and drift of all God's works and dispensations from the beginning, and even the end of the work of creation itself."[141]

This outpouring of the Spirit led him to believe that "the operations of saving grace were inextricable from God's great design in time, and that they are not confined only to the private sphere of individual conversions."[142]

> Redemption and history are essentially intermingled because the ultimate mark of history is God's redemptive activity. Not only private conversion and salvation, but the whole internal dynamism behind all historical phenomena is evidence of God's redemptive plan from the beginning to the end of history.[143]

Hence Edwards became convinced that "from the fall of man to this day wherein we live the Work of Redemption in its effect has mainly been carried on by remarkable pourings out of the Spirit of God."[144]

---

139. Edwards, "Personal Narrative," *WJE* 16:800. See also Schweitzer, *God Is a Communicative Being*, 131–33.

140. Zakai, *Jonathan Edwards's Philosophy of History*, 153.

141. Edwards, *WJE* 18:284.

142. Zakai, *Jonathan Edwards's Philosophy of History*, 153.

143. Zakai, *Jonathan Edwards's Philosophy of History*, 153. See also Jang, "Logic of Glorification," 43.

144. Edwards, "History of the Work of Redemption," *WJE* 9:143.

> God, by pouring out his Holy Spirit, shall furnish men to be glorious instruments of carrying on his work; shall fill them with knowledge and wisdom and a fervent zeal for the promoting the kingdom of Christ and the salvation of souls and propagating the gospel in the world.[145]

Indeed, "the way in which the greatest things have been done towards carrying on this work always has been by remarkable pourings out of the Spirit at special seasons of mercy."[146] As William M. Schweitzer puts it, history is "the temporal vehicle for the great work of redemption, that which above all else provides the fullest disclosure of God's character."[147] In sum, the work of the Holy Spirit not only draws the elect souls to communion with God but also drives forth the entire course of history toward the end of time.

This cosmic work of the Holy Spirit is actually in accord with the work of the Spirit within the immanent Trinity. The Spirit works throughout history as well as on individual elect to draw the entire creation to the participation in the divine life because the Holy Spirit is the bond of union between the Father and the Son within the immanent Trinity. The Holy Spirit works as the bond of union between God and the church elect because the same Spirit is originally the bond of union within the divine life. The way the Holy Spirit works in history reflects the way the Holy Spirit subsists in the immanent Trinity. As Robert W. Caldwell notes, "the divine activity of redemption parallels the structure of the immanent divine life."[148]

Moreover, this design of redemption was originally conceived in the covenant of redemption within the communion of divine persons. When the covenant of redemption was made between the Father and the Son, it was conducted in accordance with the way divine persons subsist with each other.

> In conjunction with his eternal disposition to diffuse himself, God plans to glorify himself *ad extra* in a way that will be patterned off of his internal Trinitarian glory. Subsequently, the covenant of redemption is planned between the Father and the Son, as well as the plan to create creatures made in the image of God who are uniquely suited to receive the divine glory.[149]

---

145. Edwards, "History of the Work of Redemption," *WJE* 9:460.
146. Edwards, "History of the Work of Redemption," *WJE* 9:143.
147. Schweitzer, *Communicative Being*, 113.
148. Caldwell, *Communion in the Spirit*, 67.
149. Caldwell, *Communion in the Spirit*, 71.

As John J. Bombaro notes, Edwards's entire theological framework is "to be upon the foundation of the Trinitarian *pactum salutis* for self-glorification."[150] The Holy Spirit maintains "as it were, innertrinitarian covenantal obligations, what Edwards likes to refer to as the eternal confederation within the Godhead."[151] In Knight's words, "The divine impulse precedes the creation of the world and informs the history of redemption."[152] The covenant of redemption is the archetypal blueprint of the history of the work of redemption. The history of redemption is the ectypal outworking of the covenant of redemption. Redemptive history reflects the eternal covenant of redemption. Therefore Edwards declares:

> All decrees may one way or other be referred to the covenant of redemption: the grand subject of [the] revelations that God hath made, [the] subject of the words of God, [the] subject of prophecy, [the] great things insisted on in the contemplations and praises of saints and angels, and will be to all eternity.[153]

All decrees converge as the fulfillment of the covenant of redemption in the eschatological communion of the trinitarian God with the church elect.

ESCHATOLOGICAL COMMUNION AS THE FULFILLMENT OF THE COVENANT OF REDEMPTION

God's eternal decree for the redemption of the elect culminates in the eschatological communion of God with the saints. Although God's economic works in time take diverse manifestations, ultimately, Edwards argues, the end of the whole history is just one. Edwards says: "God's design in all his works is one, and all his manifold and various dispensations are parts of one scheme."[154] While creation takes diverse manifestations in its parts, yet "all bear a relation one to another and all is united together so as to make one frame and to be all together, one building."[155] Likewise, in God's work of providence, "all are the various parts of one scheme, different motions all conspiring together to help one another to bring forth some one great event."[156] As "the different motions of the various parts of a clock, all con-

---

150. Bombaro, *Jonathan Edwards's Vision of Reality*, 286.
151. Bombaro, *Jonathan Edwards's Vision of Reality*, 50.
152. Knight, "Learning the Language of God," 545.
153. Edwards, "Approaching the End," *WJE* 25:119.
154. Edwards, "Approaching the End," *WJE* 25:114.
155. Edwards, "Approaching the End," *WJE* 25:115.
156. Edwards, "Approaching the End," *WJE* 25:115.

spire together to turn one hand and to move one hammer," the entire history heads for one goal.[157] As innumerable streams "all have relation [and] come together [to] make one river," the same goes with "the train and series of the various and manifold works and dispensations of God through all ages of the world."[158]

> Indeed, there are different subordinate designs that God has in his different works, but not different independent designs. All things have one cause—not different beings acting separately and independently that were the efficient causes—but one Being that is the efficient [cause], and so but one Being that is the end of all. All [are] made for his glory as their ultimate end, and not only is the ultimate or last end that God aims at in all his works the same, but the principal means for the obtaining of that end is but one. There is some one grand event that God aims at the bringing to pass in all his works by which he will obtain his glory. The scheme for the obtaining of this great end is but one: all the various works of God have relation one to another and are united one to another as different parts of one scheme, so that the contrivance is but one and the work is one.[159]

Therefore, "the grand design and scheme and work of God in all his manifold works and dispensations is one."[160]

This ultimate end of God's grand design in history is the communion of the elect with the triune God through the union of the elect with Christ. "For it is the union of the elect with Christ that constitutes the essential climax of this dynamic design," Edwards contends. "God's communication of himself and man's enjoyment of him is the realization of God's glory."[161] It is "a vision of the saints' joyful participation in the eternal, overflowing love of the divine life."[162]

As discussed in chapter 6 on the church covenant, Edwards envisioned the eternal felicity in the fulfillment of the marriage covenant of Christ and the church elect.

> The promises of the incarnation of Christ and of his obedience and sacrifice, were included in the covenant between Christ and believers before these things were actually accomplished. These

157. Edwards, "Approaching the End," *WJE* 25:115.
158. Edwards, "Approaching the End," *WJE* 25:115.
159. Edwards, "Approaching the End," *WJE* 25:115.
160. Edwards, "Approaching the End," *WJE* 25:116.
161. Edwards, "Approaching the End," *WJE* 25:111.
162. Pauw, "Edwards on Heaven," 393.

> were included in Christ's promise of giving himself to believers. If he gives himself to believers, as is promised in this marriage covenant, then he must represent them. If Christ gives himself to sinners, of course, justice due to the sinners takes hold on him, and all the sinners' obligations lie upon Christ. These things necessarily follow from Christ's making himself one with them, as he doth in his marriage covenant.[163]

Because Christ has fulfilled all justice and obligations as the head of all the saints and because now these saints are united with Christ in the covenantal marriage, all the merits of Christ at the same time belong to the saints. "That eternal wedding day with his bride that Christ has eagerly awaited throughout all his labors has now been realized in the consummation."[164]

> Thus the grand design of God in all his works and dispensations is to present to his Son a spouse in perfect purity, beauty and glory from amongst [mankind], blessing all [the elect] and destroying those [that oppose], and so to glorify himself through his Jesus Christ, God-man; or in one word, the work of redemption is the grand design of [history], this the chief work of God, [the] end of all other works, so that the design of God is one.[165]

This communion of the elect with Christ is the consummation of the history of the work of redemption. Given that the end of creation is subordinated to the work of redemption, this eschatological communion between the elect and Christ is also the fulfillment of the purpose of creation.

> The creation of the world seems to have been especially for this end, that the eternal Son of God might obtain a spouse, towards whom he might fully exercise the infinite benevolence of his nature, and to whom he might, as it were, open and pour forth all that immense fountain of condescension, love and grace that was in his heart, and that in this way God might be glorified. Doubtless the work of creation is subordinate to the work of redemption: that is called the creation of the *new* heavens and *new* earth, and is represented as so much more excellent than the *old*, that *that*, in comparison of it, is not worthy to be mentioned, or come into mind.[166]

---

163. Edwards, *WJE* 18:148–49.
164. Caldwell, "Brief History of Heaven," 66.
165. Edwards, "Approaching the End," *WJE* 25:119.
166. Edwards, "Church's Marriage," *WJE* 25:187.

Ultimately, the work of redemption as God's self-communication for his own glory is the goal and purpose of the entire history. In this culmination of God's self-communication, creation sees its own fulfillment. "The final result of the accomplishment of God's ultimate purpose to display and communicate His glory," as Craig Biehl summarizes, "is that the holy bride of Christ will spend eternity in ultimate fellowship with God in heaven, the holy abode prepared by God for the enjoyment of Christ and the elect."[167]

The paramount merit that saints can now partake is the communion with the triune God as the Son enjoys the communion with the Father. In this way the elect are welcomed into the trinitarian communion of the divine persons. The joyful feast of the wedding of Christ and the church elect celebrates the eternal union.

> The end of the creation of God was to provide a spouse for his Son Jesus Christ that might enjoy him and on whom he might pour forth his love. And the end of all things in providence are to make way for the exceeding expressions of Christ's love to his spouse and for her exceeding close and intimate union with, and high and glorious enjoyment of, him and to bring this to pass. And therefore the last thing and the issue of all things is the marriage of the Lamb. And the wedding day is the last day, the day of judgment, or rather that will be the beginning of it. The wedding feast is eternal; and the love and joys, the songs, entertainments and glories of the wedding never will be ended. It will be an everlasting wedding day.[168]

God's grand design of redemption is ultimately to "bring all elect creatures in heaven and earth to an union one to another, in one body under one head, and to unite all together in one body to God the Father."[169] The saints in heaven are "partakers with Christ in the joy and glory of the advancement and prosperity of his kingdom of grace on earth, and success of his gospel here."[170] They enjoy "a full view of the state of the church on earth, and a speedy, direct and certain acquaintance with all its affairs, in every part."[171]

The eternal communion of the church elect with Christ as her bridegroom is at the same time the fulfillment of the covenant of redemption

---

167. Biehl, *Infinite Merit of Christ*, 140.
168. Edwards, *WJE* 18:298.
169. Edwards, "History of the Work of Redemption," *WJE* 9:124–25.
170. Edwards, "True Saints," *WJE* 25:237.
171. Edwards, "True Saints," *WJE* 25:237.

as the elect "shall share in Christ's glory as promised by the Father in the covenant of redemption."[172]

> Christ shall enter into heaven with his glorious church every way completed, and shall present them before the Father without spot or {blemish}, having given them that perfect beauty and crowned them with that glory and honor and happiness which was stipulated in the covenant of redemption before the world was, and which he died to procure for them.[173]

In this union, the elect are united with Christ and, through the union with Christ, participate in the divine life. This participatory and communicative relationship between God and the church elect is ever increasing and progressive. The saints will grow constantly in their knowledge and appreciation of God's glory.

> For the sum total of the glory that God is to receive is infinite; for he will be glorified to all eternity, and those that shall render him his tribute of glory will, to eternity, be increasing in their knowledge of his glory, and so in the degree of their love and praise to eternity. So that God's declarative glory, as it is in God's view, is truly an infinitely great thing.[174]

Some streams of traditional western theology tended to portray the eschatological picture as a beatific vision in which the intellect sees and enjoys God as a final and static state of perfection.[175] In contrast, Edwards's eschatological vision has a more dynamic and ever-increasing character.[176]

To be sure, Edwards also talks about beatific vision. Yet as Paul Ramsey points out, "Edwards's account of the progressive end of the happiness of heaven as God's end in creation, providence, and redemption" is "coherent with what he says about the 'Beatifical vision.'"[177]

> Hence that BEATIFICAL VISION that the saints have of God in heaven, is in beholding the manifestations that he makes of himself in the work of redemption: for that arguing of the being and perfections of God that may be a priori, don't seem to be called seeing God in Scripture, but only that which is by [the]

---

172. Biehl, *Infinite Merit of Christ*, 230.
173. Edwards, "Day of Judgment," *WJE* 14:531.
174. Edwards, *WJE* 20:485.
175. Aquinas, *Summa Theologia* 3s.92.1. For the history of the doctrine of the vision of God, see Kirk, *Vision of God*.
176. Ramsey, "Heaven Is a Progressive State," 8:720.
177. Ramsey, "Heaven Is a Progressive State," 8:716.

manifestations God makes of himself in his Son. All other ways of knowing God are by seeing him in Christ the Redeemer, the image of the invisible God, and in his works, or the effects of his perfections in his redemption, and the fruits of it (which effects are the principal manifestation or shining forth of his perfections); and in conversing with them by Christ, which conversation is chiefly about those things done and manifested in this work—if we may judge by the subject of God's conversation with his church—by his work in this world. And so we may infer that [the] business and employment of the saints, so far as it consists in contemplation, praise, and conversation, is mainly in contemplating the wonders of this work, in praising God for the displays of his glory and love therein, and in conversing about things appertaining to it.[178]

The key idea stipulated here is that even in heaven the saints see God only through and in Christ who is the mediator of God and the human. Edwards writes in the same miscellany: "there is no creature can thus have an immediate sight of God, but only Jesus Christ, who is in the bosom of God."[179] As Ramsey notes, "The saints see God through the exalted and glorified one of us men in whom the Son was incarnate (the Father's sending and, by protological covenant, the Son's coming and acting in unison both ad intra and ad extra)."[180] Even in heaven the saints see God through the mediation of Christ the Son incarnated.

> All communicated glory to the creature must be by the Son of God, who is the brightness or shining forth of his Father's glory. And therefore when the external world comes to receive its greatest brightness and glory, it will doubtless [be] by him, and it will be by him as God-man.[181]

Through the union with Christ, the saints participate in the beatific vision of God. Because this vision is mediated by the humanity of the Son incarnate and because they participate in this vision as finite humans, the knowledge of God the saints actively receive will be inexhaustible and infinite. "For perfection in holiness, i.e., a sinless perfection, is not such in those that are finite, but it admits of infinite degrees."[182] Hence, "Properly understood, this means that Edwards's incarnational Christology is essential to his

---

178. Edwards, *WJE* 18:431.
179. Edwards, *WJE* 18:428.
180. Ramsey, "Heaven Is a Progressive State," 8:720.
181. Edwards, *WJE* 20:221.
182. Edwards, *WJE* 20:199.

understanding of Christ as eternally the Mediator of the increase of knowledge, love, and joy in God."[183]

In other words, the distinction between the Creator and creature is unmistakably maintained even in heaven. The union with and in Christ does not violate the Creator-creature distinction. "'Tis God only that is unchangeable. The whole universe, consisting in upper and lower worlds, is in a changing state,"[184] Edwards says. When it comes to the union with God through the elect's union in Christ, "the time will never come when it can be said it has already arrived at this infinite height."[185] In his personal correspondence, the New England divine further expounded his point. When the saints unite with God and become "partakers of his holiness," it means the Holy Spirit "communicates something of to the saints" "without imparting to them his essence."[186] Hence, Ramsey is correct when he says:

> God alone is immutable, unchanging. All creatures are the opposite of that by virtue of their finitude. We ought not to suppose that in the end of the end time of redemption in heaven men become gods and that the good angels . . . also become gods, i.e., become no longer creatures. Therefore we must not suppose that heaven is inherently an unchanging society.[187]

The divine and the human never merge together. Yet the communication of the divine diffusiveness and the elect's participation in God's happiness ever cumulatively increase. Although the divine and the human never merge, they come ever and ever closer. Precisely because God is infinite and the elect are finite human beings, for the elect heaven is full of wonders and new discoveries each day and each moment. Janice Knight writes:

> In place of consummation, Edwards posited an eternal dynamic, in which the bond of attraction between the two entities—God and creature, or more properly the society of the Godhead and the community of saints—grows ever stronger as the mass increases and the distance diminishes.[188]

For Edwards, heaven is never static and motionless. Rather heaven is, from the saints's perspective, full of newness and dynamic dance between the divine and the human.

183. Ramsey, "Heaven Is a Progressive State," 8:730.
184. Edwards, *WJE* 18:408.
185. Edwards, "End of Creation," *WJE* 8:534.
186. Edwards, "Related Correspondence," *WJE* 8:639.
187. Ramsey, "Heaven Is a Progressive State," 8:711.
188. Knight, "Learning the Language of God," 550.

The eschatological fulfillment is also inseparable from the last judgment. Christ as the Son has been appointed as the judge for the coming Day of Judgment. Edwards reasons: "God saw meet that that person that was in the human nature should be the judge of those that had the human nature."[189] As the second person of the Trinity incarnated and assumed human nature, it is appropriate and fitting that Christ the Son sits in the seat of judgment. "Seeing that there is one of the persons in the Trinity united to the human nature," Edwards surmises, "God chooses in all his transactions with mankind to transact by him."[190] Moreover, this arrangement is from eternity as it was "ordained and agreed in the covenant of redemption that he should be."[191] Christ the Son also deserves as the judge of the world "as a suitable reward for his sufferings."[192] The glory as the judge is given to Christ as "a part of Christ's exaltation," "in reward for his humiliation and sufferings."[193] Edwards again ascribes this arrangement to the eternal covenant of redemption: "This was what was stipulated in the covenant of redemption, and we are expressly told that it was given him in reward for that."[194]

On the Last Day of Judgment, both the righteous and the wicked will rise from the graves. They will be brought forth to Christ the Judge and all the works of the righteous and the wicked will be disclosed in light.[195] Then the Book of Scripture will be opened and the people's works will be tested in light of the Word of God.[196] This scrutiny takes place through "the Law" and "the gospel." As for the wicked, it will be "the sentence of the Law that the judge will pronounce upon them."[197] For the righteous, "although their sentence will not be the sentence of the Law, yet it will by no means be such a sentence as shall be inconsistent with it, but such as the Law allows of."[198] Followed by the rule of the Law, the gospel is applied as a "secondary rule of judgment."[199]

> It will be by the gospel, or covenant of grace, that believers shall have eternal blessedness adjudged to them. When it is found

189. Edwards, "Day of Judgment," *WJE* 14:518.
190. Edwards, "Day of Judgment," *WJE* 14:518.
191. Edwards, "Day of Judgment," *WJE* 14:518.
192. Edwards, "Day of Judgment," *WJE* 14:519.
193. Edwards, "Day of Judgment," *WJE* 14:519.
194. Edwards, "Day of Judgment," *WJE* 14:519.
195. Edwards, "Day of Judgment," *WJE* 14:523–28.
196. Edwards, "Day of Judgment," *WJE* 14:528.
197. Edwards, "Day of Judgment," *WJE* 14:528.
198. Edwards, "Day of Judgment," *WJE* 14:528.
199. Edwards, "Day of Judgment," *WJE* 14:529.

> that the Law hinders not, that the curse and condemnation of the Law stands not against them, they shall have the reward of eternal life given them according to the glorious gospel of Jesus Christ: which gospel will be found, as well as the Law, to condemn the ungodly. They, being found not to have believed on the name of the Lord Jesus Christ, shall be condemned according to the tenor of that gospel.[200]

While the wicked will be condemned by the Law, the righteous will participate in the eternal blessedness through the gospel of Jesus Christ who fulfilled the requirement of the Law.

It is notable that here Edwards identifies the gospel with the covenant of grace. The consummation of the covenant of grace is the eternal communion of the elect with Christ and the exclusion of the unregenerate from this eternal blessedness. In proportion to the communion the elect enjoys with Christ, the sentence given to the wicked will be the eternal separation from any kind of communion with God.

> The words of the sentence, they show the greatest abhorrence and wrath. Christ will bid them depart. He'll send them away from his presence, will remove them forever, far out of his sight, into an everlasting separation from God, as those [that] are most loathsome and unfit to be in his presence, and unfit for any sort of communion with him.[201]

When the unregenerate are eliminated from the eternal communion with God and the church elect are embraced into the eternal blessedness of the Trinity, Christ's work as the mediator is fulfilled.

> Then the Mediator will have fully accomplished his work, will have destroyed, and will triumph over, all his enemies. Then Christ will fully have obtained his reward. He will have fully accomplished the design that was upon his heart from all eternity. And then Jesus Christ will rejoice, and his members must needs rejoice with him.[202]

With the consummation of the covenant of grace, Christ's role as the mediator is also fulfilled.

Upon the completion of the mediator's role, Christ delivers the kingdom up to the Father. Citing 1 Cor 15:24, Edwards expounds:

---

200. Edwards, "Day of Judgment," *WJE* 14:529.
201. Edwards, "Day of Judgment," *WJE* 14:529.
202. Edwards, "Day of Judgment," *WJE* 14:534.

> And as Christ when he first entered upon the Work of Redemption, after the fall of man, had the kingdom committed to him of the Father, and took on himself the administration of the affairs of the universe, to manage all so as to subserve to the purposes of this affair; so now that work being finished, he will deliver up the kingdom to the Father.[203]

This does not mean that Christ will "cease to reign or have a kingdom after this," but the meaning is "Christ shall deliver up that kingdom or dominion that he has over the world as the Father's delegate or vicegerent which the Father committed to him to be managed in subserviency to this great design of redemption."[204] The Northampton pastor continues:

> The end of this commission or delegation he had from the Father was to subserve to this particular design of redemption; and therefore when that design is full accomplished the commission will cease, and Christ will deliver it up to the Father from whom he received it.[205]

Upon the completion of the work of redemption comes the eternal felicity of the elect participating in the trinitarian communion.

In this way, "the ultimate purpose of God in displaying and communicating His glory is accomplished."[206] The fulfillment of God's design in his work of redemption is at the same time the fulfillment of the *telos* of all creation. The saints will enjoy the eternal blissfulness in the trinitarian communion.

> Then God will have obtained the end of all his great works that [he] had been doing from the beginning of the world; all the deep designs of God will be unfolded in their events. Then his marvelous contrivance in his hidden, intricate and inexplicable works will appear, their ends being obtained. Then God's glory will more abundantly appear in his works, his works being perfected. This will cause a great occasion of happiness to the saints who behold it. Then God will fully have glorified himself, his Son and the elect. Then he will see that all is very good, and will rejoice in his own works, which will be the joy of all heaven.[207]

---

203. Edwards, "History of Work of Redemption," *WJE* 9:510.
204. Edwards, "History of Work of Redemption," *WJE* 9:510.
205. Edwards, "History of Work of Redemption," *WJE* 9:510.
206. Biehl, *Infinite Merit of Christ*, 248.
207. Edwards, "Day of Judgment," *WJE* 14:534.

> Then God will make more abundant manifestations of his glory and the glory of his Son, and will pour forth more plentifully of his Spirit, and will make answerable additions to the glory of the saints, as will be becoming [to] the commencement of the ultimate and most perfect state of things and as will become such a joyful occasion a the completing of all things. And in this glory and happiness will the saints remain, forever and ever.[208]

The beatific vision takes place as the participation and union in Christ. The ultimate end of this communion is the communion of the church elect with the life of God the Trinity. "God's design" is, Edwards writes, "to admit man as it were to the inmost fellowship with the deity," "an eternal society or family in the Godhead in the Trinity of persons."[209] "That eternal wedding day with his bride that Christ has eagerly awaited throughout all his labors has now been realized in the consummation."[210]

PRACTICALITY OF THE TRINITY IN HISTORY AND ESCHATON

As the account above has showed, the covenant of redemption is inherently connected with God's economic work of redemption in history and its completion. Edwards himself gave an account on how practical the doctrine of the Trinity is. For the New England divine, such doctrines as the Trinity and decrees "are glorious inlets into the knowledge and view of the spiritual world, and the contemplation of supreme things; the knowledge of which I have experienced how much it contributes to the betterment of the heart."[211] In fact, "If such doctrines as these had not been revealed, the church would never have been let half so far into the view of the spiritual world."[212]

On Edwards's appreciation of the doctrine of the Trinity as a highly practical guide, Amy Plantinga Pauw comments: "This may seem surprising, given that the Trinity's reputation as a speculative and arcane doctrine, far removed from the practical concerns of the life of faith."[213] Indeed, the fact was that "Edwards responded to the theological issues prompted by the deepest hopes of Puritan piety with the help of the doctrine of the

---

208. Edwards, "Day of Judgment," *WJE* 14:534.
209. Edwards, *WJE* 18:367.
210. Caldwell, "Brief History of Heaven" 66.
211. Edwards, *WJE* 13:328.
212. Edwards, *WJE* 13:328.
213. Pauw, "'Heaven,'" 393.

Trinity."²¹⁴ The trinitarian theology of Jonathan Edwards is "striking in its concern for the practical matters of the faith, including Christian hopes for the hereafter."²¹⁵

From the eternity of the immanent Trinity, the covenant of redemption was destined to and projected toward the eschatological consummation of the eternal communion of Christ and the church elect in eternal felicity of the wedding banquet. With the ever increasing, dynamic dance between Christ and the church elect in God's kingdom, the purpose of the covenant of redemption is completely fulfilled. The whole history in this world, from creation, through justification and sanctification of the elect, the church, the rise and fall of nations, to the end of time, is the process and arena in which the covenant of redemption made in eternity unfolds itself and is realized in time. Given that all the economic work of redemption was in an inchoate form already conceived from eternity within the immanent Trinity, it is no longer warranted to contend that the immanent Trinity is abstruse and speculatively disconnected from the economic Trinity.

---

214. Pauw, "'Heaven,'" 393. Pauw also comments: "The doctrine of the Trinity, though never denied, was not a moving part in most Puritan theologies" (Pauw, "'Heaven,'" 393). However, given that Edwards seems to theologize within a broader Augustinian and Reformed tradition, the actual case might be that many other Puritans also share this practical view of the doctrine of the Trinity. Further research may be necessary on the doctrine of the Trinity in other Puritan divines.

215. Pauw, "'Heaven,'" 394.

PART III

8

Conclusion
The Significance of the Covenant of Redemption for Trinitarian Theology Today

THIS STUDY HAS EXAMINED the covenant of redemption in the trinitarian theology of Jonathan Edwards. At the end of this study, we return to the trinitarian theology of today. First, I will review the criticism of the immanent Trinity pronounced by contemporary trinitarian theologians. Next, by reviewing the main points of each chapter, I will show that, in light of the covenant of redemption in the trinitarian theology of Jonathan Edwards, the criticism is untenable. I will then close this study by a concluding remark.

A REVIEW OF CONTEMPORARY CRITICISM OF THE IMMANENT TRINITY

At the beginning of this study, I identified the negative assessment of the immanent Trinity in the general trend of contemporary trinitarian theology. As was reviewed in chapter 1, many contemporary trinitarian theologians claim that the immanent Trinity is abstruse and speculative. Most of all, the immanent Trinity is, as they say, impractical because it is detached from God's redemptive work in this world and history.

In reviewing the modern tendency of the marginalization of the Trinity in his book *The Domestication of Transcendence: How Modern Thinking about God Went Wrong*, William C. Placher comments that, by the beginning of the eighteenth century, "the Trinity had, for a great many Christians, simply ceased to be a matter of fundamental importance."[1]

> As the doctrine of the Trinity was moved to the margins of Christian faith, 'God' increasingly referred to the creator of the universe and the basis of moral law. We could know about that God by inference from the order of moral creation, figuring out God's existence and attributes by our reason. We could shape our own lives by living up to the precepts of that God's law, if perhaps with a bit of help or a lowering of standards thanks to grace. Revelation and grace were less important, and the shift away from the God who fits neither human metaphysical schemes nor human ethical systems came all the more naturally. To ask which came first—a change in thinking about the Trinity or a change in thinking about revelation and grace—is like asking about the chicken and the egg. Enough to say that they were happening at roughly the same time, and in complex interrelation.[2]

William S. Babcock makes the same point when he argues a change that took place in the doctrine of the Trinity during the seventeenth century. He writes that in the interval between Calvin's sixteenth century and our time today, "large numbers of Christians seem quietly to have shifted their allegiance to another God, leaving themselves with the doctrine of the Trinity but no longer retaining the God whom it adumbrates."[3]

In Placher's assessment, as reason began to have more and more primacy over grace and revelation during this period, the doctrine of the Trinity proportionately began to lose validity for Christian life. Placher thinks that this shift took place in Protestants as the authority of Scripture, decrees, and covenants came to the center of the debate,[4] and in Catholics as apologetics against atheism began to focus on the existence of God as "the great mover of the universe"[5] rather than the mystery of the Trinity.

> For Protestants the authority of scripture, and decrees and covenants, were replacing the Trinity at the center of theological debate, and reason and the scriptural authority it could warrant were replacing grace and the inner testimony of the Holy Spirit as what energized and undergirded belief. Catholic theologians

---

1. Placher, *Domestication of Transcendence*, 164.
2. Placher, *Domestication of Transcendence*, 165.
3. Babcock, "Changing of the Christian God," 134.
4. Placher, *Domestication of Transcendence*, 169–70.
5. Placher, *Domestication of Transcendence*, 171.

were arguing for the existence of God against atheism in a way that made literal appeal to the particularities of Christian faith. In both cases a marginalization of the Trinity went hand in hand with greater optimism about the use of human reason to move toward God, and greater optimism about the capacity of human moral efforts to cooperate in accomplishing our salvation.[6]

In this way, as they argue, the doctrine of the Trinity is marginalized and relegated to peripheries of Christian discourse.

The assumption behind these arguments appears to be that polemical situations having emerged during the seventeenth century with the ascendance of reason as the adjudicator of truth subtly detached the doctrine of the Trinity from the daily Christian life of piety and practice. As a result, Babcock thinks that the doctrine of the Trinity "occupies a peculiarly ambivalent position in contemporary Western Christianity."[7]

> On the one hand, it is deeply embedded in the Christian doctrinal tradition, far too deeply to be excised without pain or perhaps even to be excised at all; and it certainly maintains a persistent—if hardly vivid—presence in various liturgical formulas and habits of speech that continue to have widespread currency. On the other hand, despite the recent revival of interest in the doctrine on the part of theologians, it seems to exercise little or no control over the complex of ways in which Christians do and do not imagine, do and do not conceive, their God. In this respect, it seems no longer to retain its earlier functions: to identify the God of Christian allegiance; to specify the God whom Christians worship and for whom they yearn; to single out the God who is genuinely God as opposed to the imagined gods whom human beings, whether individually or collectively, devise for themselves.[8]

As Michael J. Buckley puts it, "In the absence of a rich and comprehensive Christology and Pneumatology of religious experience, Christianity entered into the defense of the Christian God without appeal to anything Christian."[9] Patricia Wilson-Kastner also concurs when she worries that the economic work of redemption in Christ and the Holy Spirit was increasingly "reduced to a ghostly whisper."[10]

6. Placher, *Domestication of Transcendence*, 172.
7. Babcock, "Changing of the Christian God," 133.
8. Babcock, "Changing of the Christian God," 133.
9. Buckley, *At the Origins*, 67.
10. Wilson-Kastner, *Faith, Feminism, and the Christ*, 123.

In light of this modern context, it is understandable that an increasing number of contemporary trinitarian theologians endeavor to retrieve the doctrine of the Trinity by accentuating God's trinitarian work in his economic work in history. Nicholas Lash comments:

> I do not see how the doctrine of the Trinity can recover its function of serving as the 'summary grammar' of the mystery of salvation and creation except we speak, from the outset, of Him who is known to us through the Son in the Holy Spirit.[11]

Contemporary trinitarian theology is correct in its striving to reclaim the doctrine of the Trinity inseparably connected with God's saving work in history and in this world.

However, in this effort to recover God the Trinity, it seems that a pendulum has swung to the other extreme. The general trend of contemporary trinitarian theology seems to stress the economic Trinity to the detriment of the immanent Trinity. As a part of the efforts to restore the significance of the doctrine of the Trinity in contemporary theology, some theologies tend to emphasize the economic Trinity as opposed to the immanent Trinity. The emphasis on the economic work of the triune God often comes with the criticism of the abstruse, speculative, and impractical characteristics of the immanent Trinity.

It is true that the so-called Rahner Rule ("The 'economic' Trinity is the 'immanent' Trinity and the 'immanent' Trinity is the 'economic' Trinity")[12] has provided contemporary trinitarian theologians with an inspirational point of departure. As Stanley Grenz observes:

> Although theologians routinely add qualifiers to Rahner's Rule, those working in his wake are conscious of the essential connection between the doctrine of God and soteriology. Moreover, trinitarian thinkers since Rahner seek to give utmost seriousness to the epistemological link between the economic Trinity and the immanent Trinity.[13]

Rahner is right in his efforts to retrieve the inherent bond between the doctrine of the Trinity and soteriology and in his emphasis on an epistemological approach. However, when his dictum is appropriated in a way that practically eliminates the distinction between the immanent and the economic Trinity, the result can endanger the distinction between the triune God and creation in a significant way.

11. Lash, "Considering the Trinity," 188.
12. Rahner, *Trinity*, 22.
13. Grenz, *Social God*, 41.

For example, Joseph A. Bracken claims that mutually relational work of the trinitarian persons entails responses to God from creational entities. The immersion of the economic Trinity into the immanent Trinity amounts to a panentheistic discourse on the doctrine of God.[14] Marjorie Hewitt Suchocki also does not think of the immanent Trinity as a self-closed entity. The immanent Trinity is the God immanent in the world. God as Presence, Power, and Wisdom has an intrinsic relation to the world.[15] Ultimately, the immanent Trinity is absorbed into the economic Trinity.[16]

Several scholars draw similar conclusions from their studies in Christology. Piet J. A. M. Schoonenberg holds that the immanent Trinity can be known only as the economic Trinity and that the immanent-economic distinction is actually a distinction of aspects of the same reality. Consequently any questions on the immanent Trinity apart from the economic Trinity would be illegitimate and unanswerable.[17] Roger Haight argues that what matters is that human beings encounter God in Jesus Christ and the Holy Spirit in the divine economic operation. Whether or not the divine economic works correspond to the self-differentiation within the inner life of God is a question of speculation and is not the point of the Trinity.[18]

Among these scholars who propose the significance of the economic Trinity as opposed to the immanent Trinity, Catherine Mowry LaCugna offers the most extreme case of the Trinity absorbed into the economic Trinity. LaCugna argues that after the period of the Cappadocian fathers, Christian theology has detached *theologia* (God *in se*) from *oikonomia* (God *ad extra*). Because the doctrine of the Trinity has withdrawn into the inner life of God to the detriment of God's economic work of salvation in the world, LaCugna argues, the doctrine of the Trinity today has become highly speculative and irrelevant to Christian practical life.[19] Accordingly, LaCugna holds that the entire frame of theology needs to be reformulated from the vantage point of God's economic work of salvation in the world: God for us.[20] Behind these claims is an assumption that the distinction between the immanent and the economic Trinity has led to the confinement of theology into God in himself detached from his economic work of salvation

---

14. Bracken, "Trinity," 7–22; "Panentheism from a Trinitarian Perspective," 7–28; "Panentheism from a Process Perspective," 95–113. See also Baik, *Holy Trinity*, 163–65.

15. Suchocki, *God-Christ-Church*; "God, Trinity, Process," 169–74.

16. Baik, *Holy Trinity*, 166.

17. Schoonenberg, "Trinity," 111–16. See also Baik, *Holy Trinity*, 181.

18. Haight, *Jesus*, 488.

19. LaCugna, *God For Us*, 250.

20. LaCugna, *God For Us*, 319.

in history, and thereby has resulted in the irrelevance of the doctrine of the Trinity to daily Christian life and practice.[21]

Although these trends rightly emphasize the importance of the economic Trinity as the epistemological link of the human experience of God, sometimes the immanent Trinity is so degraded that the distinction and connection between the immanent and the economic Trinity become blurry. Since the immanent Trinity pertains to the divine perfection in God's self independent from the world and the economic Trinity regards to God's relation to the world, the blurring of the distinction between these two has a direct repercussion in the question of a God-world relationship. Ted Peters summarizes this point succinctly.

> On the one hand, to affirm the immanent-economic distinction risks subordinating the economic Trinity and hence protecting transcendent absoluteness at the cost of genuine relatedness to the world. On the other hand, to collapse the two together risks producing a God so dependent upon the world for self-definition that divine freedom and independence are lost.[22]

Indeed, as Chung-Hyun Baik points out, "both the distinction and unity between the immanent and the economic Trinity need to be acknowledged simultaneously, in order to establish the equilibrium between God's relatedness to the world and God's gracious freedom."[23]

CONCLUDING REMARKS: EDWARDS'S COVENANT OF REDEMPTION AND ITS SIGNIFICANCE FOR TRINITARIAN THEOLOGY TODAY

In this study I have attempted to show that the covenant of redemption in the trinitarian theology of Jonathan Edwards offers a case in which the economic Trinity is aptly emphasized without losing the distinction between the immanent and the economic Trinity. I have attempted to show that the doctrine of the covenant of redemption in the trinitarian theology of Jonathan Edwards indicates that God's plan of redemption is inherently connected with God's plan of redemption eternally set up in the immanent Trinity. If God's economy of redemption in history is inherently connected

---

21. LaCugna, *God For Us*, 1–17.
22. Ted Peters, *GOD*, 108–9.
23. Baik, *Holy Trinity*, 183–84.

with the eternal plan within the immanent Trinity, it is not warranted to hold that the immanent Trinity is impractical and speculative.[24]

In order to show this case, in part 1, consisting of chapters 1 through 3, I tried to show that the doctrine of the covenant of redemption was current among the seventeenth-century Reformed scholastics and Edwards inherited this tradition from these Reformed theological mentors. In chapter 1, I surveyed the current state of discussions on the practicality of the doctrine of the Trinity.

In chapter 2, I tried to show that Edwards theologizes with a broader Reformed theological legacy as his background. The idea of covenant was widely current in Puritan theology in the seventeenth century in England and New England.[25] Puritan theologians such as Samuel Willard, David Dickson, Herman Witsius, Thomas Goodwin, and Petrus van Mastircht all painstakingly articulated the doctrine of the covenant of redemption in its inherent relation to God's economy of redemption in the world. Edwards read Puritan theologians such as Petrus van Mastricht, Stephen Charnock, Samuel Willard, Herman Witsius, Thomas Goodwin, and John Gill. The Northampton theologian built up his theology on this broader Reformed foundation. Edwards inherited his covenant theology from a broader Reformed tradition current in the international Reformed communities in his time.

In chapter 3, I constructively described Edwards's doctrine of the covenant of redemption. In line with his Reformed legacy, Edwards articulated the covenant of redemption as the eternal pact between the Father and the Son before the foundation of the world.

In part 2, consisting of chapters 4 through 7, I attempted to show some manifestations of practicality of the doctrine of the Trinity in various aspects of Edwards's theology. Through examining Edwards's doctrine of creation, justification and sanctification, church and national covenants, and history, I tried to show the connection between these theological aspects and the eternal covenant of redemption.

In chapter 4, I described the relation between the covenant of redemption and creation. Creation sets up the arena where the covenant of redemption is carried into practice in time. The Creation of the world is tied to the plan of redemption from eternity.

In chapter 5, I explored the relation between the covenant of redemption and God's work of justification and sanctification. The reality that the

---

24. Recent works by Michael Horton indicates that retrieval of the covenant idea in contemporary theology is a promising project. See Horton, *God of Promise*; *Lord and Servant*; *Covenant and Salvation*; *Covenant and Eschatology*; *People and Place*.

25. Beeke and Jones, *Puritan Theology*, 203–318.

salvation of the elect has been decreed from eternity in the covenant of redemption gives assurance and comfort to the elect. It is also the foundation of the saints's perseverance in faith.

In chapter 6, I examined the relation between the covenant of redemption and the church and national covenants. While the issue of church membership or the view of one's country seems to be irrelevant to the eternity of the immanent Trinity, I tried to show that it is possible to see at least indirectly a repercussion of the eternal covenant in Edwards's efforts to defend the covenant. As a church leader, Edwards tried to make sure that his congregation maintained their covenantal identity in their church membership and as the New Israel.

In chapter 7, I scrutinized Edwards's view of history and the eschaton. Given that the entire history is the ectypal unfolding of the covenant of redemption eternally made within the immanent Trinity, the relationship between the immanent and the economic Trinity is quintessentially apparent in history and its consummation. History is the covenant of grace as the actualization of the eternal covenant of redemption through time. The eschaton is the fulfillment of the eternal covenant of redemption in the marital communion of the trinitarian God and the church elect through union with Christ.

In part 3, in this concluding chapter, after reviewing the contemporary discussion on the immanent Trinity, I reiterate the thesis of this study. A Reformed idea of the covenant of redemption instantiated in the trinitarian theology of Jonathan Edwards indicates that an inherent connection exists between God's economic work of redemption and the eternal transaction made in eternity. *Pactum salutis* is the nexus between the immanent Trinity and the economic Trinity. Hence, it is important to maintain the distinction and connection between the immanent and economic Trinity. Since the entire plan of redemption was already made eternally in the immanent Trinity, it is not plausible to contend that the immanent Trinity is impractical and speculative. Far from being impractical, the inner-trinitarian pact between the Father and the Son has practical relevance for salvation and the Christian life.

Scholarship on Edwards has fluctuated in its assessment of Edwards's place in modern intellectual history. On the one hand, scholarship since Perry Miller's influential study tended to emphasize the remarkable modernity of Edwards's theology. As Miller puts it, Edwards was so ahead of time in his modernity that even modern scholars can hardly catch up with it.[26] On the other hand, Peter Gay portrays Edwards as an anachronistic

---

26. Miller, *Jonathan Edwards*, xxxii.

figure left behind.[27] However, as George Marsden notes, the truth was that "Edwards was a thoroughly eighteenth-century figure who used many of the categories and assumptions of his era to criticize its trends."[28] In other words, "Edwards's genius was to show how his core theological views were intellectually viable in the Enlightenment era."[29] If we find creative insights in Edwards, it is "not because he was so far ahead of his time, but rather because his rigorous Calvinism—and his position in a distant province—put him in a position to critically scrutinize his own era."[30] Edwards appropriated his Reformed legacy but creatively articulated it for his time of the eighteenth-century Enlightenment. Conversely, Edwards may have innovatively updated his Reformed tradition, but he did so deeply rooted in his own Reformed legacy. Past scholarship tended to stress Edwards's modernity sometimes to the extent of indicating his departure from his Puritan and Reformed tradition. This study has tried to redress the balance by situating Edwards squarely in covenant theology in the Reformed tradition he inherited from previous generations.

Since Edwards inherited the doctrine of the covenant of redemption from his preceding Puritan divines and many of them held this doctrine and perceived its connection with Christian life and piety, this study also poses a question to the current criticism of the speculative and abstruse character of the immanent Trinity. At least future historical and theological studies need to examine to what extent this critical assessment of the immanent Trinity is accurate in light of the history of the doctrine of the Trinity. Further studies of the doctrine of the covenant of redemption among Puritan divines might indicate that the doctrine of the Trinity was actually a vibrant part of the "doctrine for life."[31]

---

27. Gay, *Loss of Mastery*, 116.
28. Marsden, *Jonathan Edwards*, 471.
29. Marsden, *Jonathan Edwards*, 458.
30. Marsden, *Jonathan Edwards*, 471.
31. Beeke and Jones, *Puritan Theology*, 6.

Bibliography

Alexander, T. Desmond. "Genesis 22 and the Covenant of Circumcision." *Journal for the Study of the Old Testament* 25 (1983) 17–22.

Anderson, Wallace E. "Immaterialism in Jonathan Edwards's Early Philosophical Notes." *Journal of the History of Ideas* 25.2 (1964) 181–200.

Aquinas, Thomas. *Summa Theologia*. Translated by Fathers of the English Dominican Province. 5 vols. New York: Benziger Bros., 1948.

Asselt, William J. van. *The Federal Theology of Johannes Cocceius (1603–1669)*. Translated by Raymond A. Blacketer. Studies in the History of Christian Thought. Edited by Robert J. Bast. Leiden: Brill, 2001.

———. "The Fundamental Meaning of Theology: Archetypal and Ectypal Theology in Seventeenth-Century Reformed Thought." *Westminster Theological Journal* 64 (2002) 319–35.

Asselt, William J. van, and E. Dekker, eds. *Reformation and Scholasticism: An Ecumenical Enterprise*. Grand Rapids: Baker, 2001.

Awart, Jannie, et al. "Toward a Missional Theology of Participation: Ecumenical Reflections on Contributions to Trinity, Mission, and Church." *Missiology: An International Review* 37.1 (2009) 75–87.

Babcock, William S. "A Changing of the Christian God: The Doctrine of the Trinity in the Seventeenth Century." *Interpretation* 45.2 (1991) 133–46.

Baik, Chung-Hyun. *The Holy Trinity—God for God and God for Us: Seven Positions on the Immanent-Economic Trinity Relation in Contemporary Trinitarian Theology*. Princeton Theological Monograph. Eugene, OR: Pickwick, 2011.

Ball, John. *A Treatise of the Covenant of Grace*. London: Simeon Ash, 1645.

Ballor, Jordan J. *Covenant, Causality, and Law: A Study of Wolfgang Musculus*. Göttingen: Vandenhoeck & Ruprecht, 2012.

Barnes, Michael René. "Augustine in Contemporary Trinitarian Theology." *Theological Studies* 56 (1995) 237–50.

———. "De Régnon Reconsidered." *Augustinian Studies* 26.2 (1995) 51–79. Bauckham, Richard. *Tudor Apocalypse: Sixteenth Century Apocalypticism, Millennarianism, and the English Reformation—From John Bale to John Foxe and Thomas Brightman*. Oxford: Sutton Courtenay, 1978.

Beach, J. Mark. "The Doctrine of the *Pactum Salutis* in the Covenant Theology of Herman Witsius." *Mid-America Journal of Theology* 13 (2002) 101–42.

Beckwith, Roger T. "The Unity and Diversity of God's Covenants." *Tyndale Bulletin* 38 (1987) 93–118.

Beeke, Joel R. *An Analysis of Herman Witsius's The Economy of the Covenants between God and Man, Comprehending a Complete Body of Divinity.* Grand Rapids: Reformed Heritage, 2002.

———. *Puritan Preparation by Grace.* Grand Rapids: Reformed Heritage, 2012.

Beeke, Joel R., and Mark Jones. *A Puritan Theology: Doctrine for Life.* Grand Rapids: Reformation Heritage, 2012.

Berger, David. "Jewish-Christian Relations: A Jewish Perspective." *Journal of Ecumenical Studies* 20.1 (1983) 5–32.

Bercovitch, Sacvan. *The American Jeremiad.* Madison: University of Wisconsin Press, 1978.

———. *The Puritan Origins of the American Self.* New Haven: Yale University Press, 1975.

———, ed. *Typology and Early American Literature.* Amherst: University of Massachusetts Press, 1972.

Biehl, Craig. *The Infinite Merit of Christ: The Glory of Christ's Obedience in the Theology of Jonathan Edwards.* Jackson, MS: Reformed Academic, 2009.

Bierma, Lyle D. "Covenant or Covenants in the Theology of Olevianus." *Calvin Theological Journal* 22.2 (1987) 228–50.

———. *German Calvinism in the Confessional Age: The Covenant Theology of Casper Olevianus.* Grand Rapids: Baker, 1996.

Billings, J. Todd. *Calvin, Participation, and the Gift: The Activity of Believers in Union with Christ.* New York: Oxford University Press, 2007.

Bird, Michael F., and Robert Shillaker. "Subordination in the Trinity and Gender Roles: A Response to Recent Discussion." *Trinity Journal* 29.2 (2008) 267–83.

Boardman, George Nye. *A History of New England Theology.* New York: A. D. F. Randolph, 1899.

Boff, Leonardo. *Trinity and Society.* Translated by Paul Burns. Maryknoll, NY: Orbis, 1988.

Bogue, Carl W. *Jonathan Edwards and the Covenant of Grace.* Cherry Hill, NJ: Mack, 1975.

Bolt, John. "The Glory of Spiders and Politics." *Calvin Theological Journal* 46 (2011) 72–80.

Bombaro, John J. *Jonathan Edwards's Vision of Reality: The Relationship of God to the World, Redemption History, and the Reprobate.* Princeton Theological Monograph Series. Edited by K. C. Hanson, et al. Eugene, OR: Pickwick, 2012.

———. "Jonathan Edwards's Vision of Salvation." *Westminster Theological Journal* 65 (2003) 45–67.

Boston, Thomas. *Human Nature in its Four-Fold State.* Edinburgh: James Mceuen and Co., 1720.

Bozeman, Theodore Dwight. "Federal Theology and the 'National Covenant: An Elizabethan Presbyterian Case Study." *Church History* 61.4 (1992) 392–407.

———. *To Live Ancient Lives: The Primitivist Dimension in Puritanism.* Chapel Hill: University of North Carolina Press, 1988.

Bracken, Joseph A. *The One and the Many: A Contemporary Reconstruction of the God-World Relationship.* Grand Rapids: Eerdmans, 2001.

———. "Panentheism from a Process Perspective." In *Trinity in Process: A Relational Theology of God*, edited by Joseph A. Bracken and Marjorie Hewitt Suchocki, 95–113. New York: Continuum, 1997.

———. "Panentheism from a Trinitarian Perspective." *Horizons* 22 (1995) 7–28.
———. "Trinity: Economic and Immanent." *Horizons* 25 (1998) 7–22.
———. *The Triune Symbol: Persons, Process, and Community*. Lanham: University Press of America, 1985.
Breen, T. H. *The Character of the Good Ruler: A Study of Puritan Political Ideas in New England, 1630–1730*. New Haven: Yale University Press, 1970.
Brightman, Thomas. *The Revelation of St. John, illustrated with analysis and scholions: wherein the fence is opened by the scripture, and the events of things foretold, shewed by histories*. Amsterdam: Thomas Stafford, 1644.
Brown, Sally A. "Speaking Again of the Trinity." *Theology Today* 64 (2007) 145–58.
Brueggemann, Walter. "*Covenanting as Human Vocation: A Discussion of the Relation of Bible and Pastoral Care*." *Interpretation* 33.2 (1979) 115–29.
———. "A Shape for Old Testament Theology: 1, Structure Legitimation; 2, Embrace of Pain." *Catholic Biblical Quarterly* 47.1 (1985) 28–46.
Brumm, Ursula. *American Thought and Religious Typology*. Translated by John Hoaglund. New Brunswick: Rutgers University Press, 1970.
Bryant, M. Darrol. "America as God's Kingdom." In *Religion and Political Society*, Edited by Jürgen Moltmann, et al., 49–94. Translated by The Institute of Christian Thought. New York: Harper & Row, 1974.
Bucanus, Gulielmus. *Institutions of Christian Religion*. Vol. 2. London: Daniel Pakeman, Abel Roper, and Richard Tomlins, 1659.
Buckley, Michael J. *At the Origins of Modern Atheism*. New Haven: Yale University Press, 1987.
Bulkeley, Peter. *The Gospel-Covenant, or, The Covenant of Grace opened . . . preached in Concord in New-England*. London: MS, 1646.
Burgess, Anthony. *The True Doctrine of Justification Asserted & Vindicated from the Errours of many, and more especially Papists and Socinians*. London: Anchor and Bible, 1654.
Bushnell, Horace. *Christ in Theology*. Hartford: Brown and Parsons, 1851.
Caldwell, Robert W., III. "A Brief History of Heaven in the Writings of Jonathan Edwards." *Calvin Theological Journal* 46 (2011) 48–71.
———. *Communion in the Spirit: The Holy Spirit as the Bond of Union in the Theology of Jonathan Edwards*. Studies in Evangelical History and Thought. Eugene, OR: Wipf & Stock, 2007.
Campbell, William S. "Christianity and Judaism: Continuity and Discontinuity." *International Bulletin of Missionary Research* 8.2 (1984) 54–58.
Canlis, Julie. *Calvin's Ladder: A Spiritual Theology of Ascent and Ascension*. Grand Rapids: Eerdmans, 2010.
Capp, Bernard S. *The Fifth Monarchy Men: A Study in Seventeenth-Century English Millenarianism*. London: Faber, 1972.
Carr, Anne. *The Transforming Grace: Christian Tradition and Women's Experience*. San Francisco: Harper & Row, 1998.
Chai, Leon. *Jonathan Edwards and the Limits of Enlightenment Philosophy*. New York: Oxford University Press, 1998.
Chapman, Mark D. "The Social Doctrine of the Trinity: Some Problems." *Anglican Theological Review* 83.2 (2001) 239–54.

Charnock, Stephen. *Several Discourses upon the Existence and Attributes of God.* London: D. Newman, T. Cockerill, Benj. Griffin, T. Simmons, and Benj. Alsop, 1682.

Charry, Ellen T. *By the Renewal of Your Minds: The Pastoral Function of Christian Doctrine.* New York: Oxford University Press, 1997.

Cherry, Conrad. "The Puritan Notion of the Covenant in Jonathan Edwards's Doctrine of Faith." *Church History* 34.3 (1965) 328–41.

———. *The Theology of Jonathan Edwards: A Reappraisal.* Garden City, NY: Doubleday, 1966.

Cho, Hyun-Jin. *Jonathan Edwards on Justification: Reformed Development of the Doctrine in Eighteenth-Century New England.* Lanham: University Press of America, 2012.

Clark, Stephen M. "Jonathan Edwards: The History of the Work of Redemption." *Westminster Theological Journal* 56 (1994) 45–58.

Coakley, Sarah. "Living into the Mystery of the Holy Trinity: Trinity, Prayer, and Sexuality." *Anglican Theological Review* 80.2 (1998) 223–332.

———, ed. *Re-thinking Gregory of Nyssa.* Malden, MA: Blackwell, 2003.

———. "Why Three? Some Further Reflections on the Origins of the Doctrine of the Trinity." In *The Making and Remaking of Christian Doctrine: Essays in Honour of Maurice Wiles*, edited by Sarah Coakley and David A. Pailin, 29–56. Oxford: Clarendon, 1993.

Coccejus, Johannes. *De leer van het verbond en het testament van God.* Translated by W. J. van Asselt and H. G. Renger. Kampen: de Groot-Goudriaan, 1990.

Cohen, Charles Lloyd. *God's Caress: The Psychology of Puritan Religious Experience.* New York: Oxford University Press, 1986.

Colacurico, Michael. "The Example of Edwards: Idealist Imagination and the Metaphysics of Sovereignty." In *Puritan Influences in American Literature*, edited by Emory Elliott, 55–106. Illinois Studies in Language and Literature 65. Urbana, IL: University of Illinois Press, 1979.

The Congregational Churches in England. *A Declaration of the Faith and Order owned and practiced in the Congregational Churches in England agreed upon, and confessed to, by their Elders and Messengers, in their Meeting at the Savoy.* London: D. Midwinter and J. Clarke, 1745.

Cooper, James F., Jr. *Tenacious of Their Liberties: The Congregationalists in Colonial Massachusetts.* Religion in America Series. New York: Oxford University Press, 1999.

Cooper, John W. *Panentheism: The Other God of Philosophers.* Grand Rapids: Baker, 2006.

Coyle, Suzanne Murphy. "A Covenanting Process in Pastoral Home Visits." *Journal of Pastoral Care* 39.2 (1985) 96–109.

Creegan, Nicola Hoggard. "Jonathan Edwards's Ecological and Ethical Vision of Nature." *Stimulus: The New Zealand Journal of Christian Thought and Practice* 15.4 (2007) 49–51.

Crisp, Oliver D. *Jonathan Edwards and the Metaphysics of Sin.* Burlington, VT: Ashgate, 2005.

———. "Jonathan Edwards on Divine Nature." *Journal of Reformed Theology* 3.2 (2009) 175–201.

———. *Jonathan Edwards on God and Creation.* New York: Oxford University Press, 2012.

———. "Jonathan Edwards's Ontology: A Critique of Sang Hyun Lee's Dispositional Account of Edwardsean Metaphysics." *Religious Studies* 46 (2010) 1–20.
Cunningham, David S. *These Three Are One: The Practice of Trinitarian Theology.* Oxford: Blackwell, 1998.
Danaher, William J., Jr. "By Sensible Signs Represented: Jonathan Edwards's Sermons on the Lord's Supper." *Pro Ecclesia* 7.3 (1998) 261–87.
———. *The Trinitarian Ethics of Jonathan Edwards.* Columbia Series of Reformed Theology. Louisville, KY: Westminster John Knox, 2004. Daniel, Stephen H. *The Philosophy of Jonathan Edwards: A Study in Divine Semiotics.* The Indiana Series in the Philosophy of Religion. Edited by Merold Westphal. Bloomington and Indianapolis: Indiana University Press, 1994.
D'Costa, Gavin. *The Meeting of Religions and the Trinity.* Maryknoll: Orbis, 2000.
De Jong, Peter Y. *The Covenant Idea in New England Theology, 1620–1847.* Grand Rapids: Eerdmans, 1945.
De Régnon, Théodore. *Études de théologie positive sur la Sainte Trinité.* 4 vols. Paris: Victor Retaux, 1892–1898.
Delattre, Roland André. "Beauty and Politics: A Problematic Legacy of Jonathan Edwards." In *American Philosophy from Edwards to Quine*, edited with an introduction by Robert W. Shahan and Kenneth R. Merrill, 20–48. Norman: University of Oklahoma Press, 1977.
———. *Beauty and Sensibility in the Thought of Jonathan Edwards: An Essay in Aesthetics and Theological Ethics.* The Jonathan Edwards Classic Studies Series 4. 1968. Reprint, Eugene, OR: Wipf & Stock, 2006.
———. "Beauty and Theology: A Reappraisal of Jonathan Edwards." *Soundings* 51.1 (1968) 60–79.
Delbanco, Andrew. *The Puritan Ordeal.* Cambridge: Harvard University Press, 1989.
Dickson, David. *Therapeutica sacra.* Edinburgh: Evan Tyler, 1664.
Dickson, David, and James Durham. *The Summe of Saving Knowledge, with the Practical Use thereof.* Edinburgh: George Swintoun and Thomas Brown, 1659.
Diodati, Jean. *Pious and Learned Annotations upon the Holy Bible, plainly Expounding the Most Difficult Places Thereof.* 3rd ed. London: James Flesher, 1651.
Donovan, Mary Ann. "The Trinity, Pastoral Theology, and Catherine LaCugna: The Trajectory." *Horizons* 27.2 (2000) 354–59.
Edwards, Jonathan. *The Apocalyptic Writings.* Vol. 5 of *The Works of Jonathan Edwards.* Edited by Stephen J. Stein. New Haven: Yale University Press, 1977.
———. *The "Blank Bible."* Vol. 24 of *The Works of Jonathan Edwards.* Edited by Stephen J. Stein. New Haven: Yale University Press, 2006.
———. *Catalogues of Books.* Vol. 26 of *The Works of Jonathan Edwards.* Edited by Peter J. Thuesen. New Haven: Yale University Press, 2008.
———. *Ecclesiastical Writings.* Vol. 12 of *The Works of Jonathan Edwards.* Edited by David D. Hall. New Haven: Yale University Press, 1994.
———. *Ethical Writings.* Vol. 8 of *The Works of Jonathan Edwards.* Edited by Paul Ramsey. New Haven: Yale University Press, 1989.
———. *The Freedom of the Will.* Vol. 1 of *The Works of Jonathan Edwards.* Edited by Paul Ramsey. New Haven: Yale University Press, 1957.
———. "God Is Everywhere Present." In *Jonathan Edwards: Containing 16 Sermons Unpublished in Edwards's Lifetime*, edited by Don Kistler, 207–22. The Puritan Pulpit: The American Puritans. Morgan: Soli Deo Gloria, 2004.

———. "God Never Changes His Mind." In *Jonathan Edwards: Containing 16 Sermons Unpublished in Edwards's Lifetime*, edited by Don Kistler, 1–13. The Puritan Pulpit: The American Puritans. Morgan: Soli Deo Gloria, 2004.

———. *A History of the Work of Redemption*. Vol. 9 of *The Works of Jonathan Edwards*. Edited by John F. Wilson. New Haven: Yale University Press, 1989.

———. *Images or Shadows of Divine Things*. New Haven: Yale University Press, 1948.

———. *Letters and Personal* Writings. Vol. 16 of *The Works of Jonathan Edwards*. Edited by Georges S. Claghorn New Haven: Yale University Press, 1998.

———. *The "Miscellanies": 501–832*. Vol. 18 of *The Works of Jonathan Edwards*. Edited by Ava Chamberlain. New Haven: Yale University Press, 2000.

———. *The "Miscellanies": 833–1152*. Vol. 20 of *The Works of Jonathan Edwards*. Edited by Amy Plantinga Pauw. New Haven: Yale University Press, 2002.

———. *The "Miscellanies": 1153–1360*. Vol. 23 of *The Works of Jonathan Edwards*. Edited by Douglas A. Sweeney. New Haven: Yale University Press, 2004.

———. *The "Miscellanies": a–z, aa–zz, 1–500*. Vol. 13 of *The Works of Jonathan Edwards*. Edited by Thomas A. Schafer. New Haven: Yale University Press, 1994.

———. *Observations concerning the Scripture Oeconomy of the Trinity and Covenant of Redemption*. With an introduction and appendix by Egbert C. Smyth. New York: Scribner's Sons, 1880.

———. *Original Sin*. Vol. 3 of *The Works of Jonathan Edwards*. Edited by Clyde A. Holbrook. New Haven: Yale University Press, 1970.

———. *Religious Affections*. Vol. 2 of *The Works of Jonathan Edwards*. Edited by John E. Smith. New Haven: Yale University Press, 1959.

———. *Scientific and Philosophical Writings*. Vol. 6 of *The Works of Jonathan Edwards*. Edited by Wallace Anderson. New Haven: Yale University Press, 1980.

———. "Sermon on Hebrews 13:8 (April 1738)." In *The Works of Jonathan Edwards, AM*, edited by Edward Hickman, 2:949–54. With an introduction by Henry Rogers and Sereno E. Dwight. 2 vols. London: John Childs and Son, 1865.

———. *Sermons and Discourses, 1720–1723*. Vol. 10 of *The Works of Jonathan Edwards*. Edited by Wilson H. Kimnach. New Haven: Yale University Press, 1992.

———. *Sermons and Discourses, 1723–1729*. Vol. 14 of *The Works of Jonathan Edwards*. Edited by Kenneth P. Minkema. New Haven: Yale University Press, 1997.

———. *Sermons and Discourses, 1730–1733*. Vol. 17 of *The Works of Jonathan Edwards*. Edited by Mark Valeri. New Haven: Yale University Press, 1999.

———. *Sermons and Discourses, 1734–1738*. Vol. 19 of *The Works of Jonathan Edwards*. Edited by M. X. Lesser. New Haven: Yale University Press, 2001.

———. *Sermons and Discourses, 1739–1742*. Vol. 22 of *The Works of Jonathan Edwards*. Edited by Harry S. Stout, et al. New Haven: Yale University Press, 2003.

———. *Sermons and Discourses, 1743–1758*. Vol. 25 of *The Works of Jonathan Edwards*. Edited by Wilson H. Kimnach. New Haven: Yale University Press, 2006.

———. *Sermons, Series II, 1723–1727*. Vol. 42 of *The Works of Jonathan Edwards Online*. Edited by Jonathan Edwards Center. Jonathan Edwards Center: Yale University, 2008. http://edwards.yale.edu/research/browse.

———. *Sermons Series II, 1728–1729*. Vol. 43 of *The Works of Jonathan Edwards Online*. Edited by Jonathan Edwards Center. Yale University, 2008. http://edwards.yale.edu/research/browse.

———. *Sermons Series II, 1729*. Vol. 44 of *The Works of Jonathan Edwards Online*. Edited by Jonathan Edwards Center. Jonathan Edwards Center: Yale University, 2008. http://edwards.yale.edu/research/browse.

———. *Sermons Series II, 1736*. Vol. 51 of *The Works of Jonathan Edwards Online*. Edited by Jonathan Edwards Center. Jonathan Edwards Center: Yale University, 2008. http://edwards.yale.edu/research/browse.

———. *Sermons Series II, 1737*. Vol. 52 of *The Works of Jonathan Edwards Online*. Edited by Jonathan Edwards Center. Jonathan Edwards Center: Yale University, 2008. http://edwards.yale.edu/research/browse.

———. *Sermons Series II, 1738, and undated, 1734–1738*. Vol. 53 of *The Works of Jonathan Edwards Online*. Edited by Jonathan Edwards Center. Jonathan Edwards Center: Yale University, 2008. http://edwards.yale.edu/research/browse.

———. *Sermons Series II, January–June 1740*. Vol. 55 of *The Works of Jonathan Edwards Online*. Edited by Jonathan Edwards Center. Jonathan Edwards Center: Yale University, 2008. http://edwards.yale.edu/research/browse.

———. *Sermons Series II, 1743*. Vol. 61 of *The Works of Jonathan Edwards Online*. Edited by Jonathan Edwards Center. Jonathan Edwards Center, Yale University, 2008. http://edwards.yale.edu/research/browse.

———. *Treatise on Grace and Other Posthumously Published Writings*. Edited with an introduction by Paul Helm. Cambridge and London: James Clarke, 1971.

———. *Typological Writings*. Vol. 11 of *The Works of Jonathan Edwards*. Edited by Wallace E. Anderson, et al. New Haven: Yale University Press, 1993.

———. *Writings on the Trinity, Grace, and Faith*. Vol. 21 of *The Works of Jonathan Edwards*. Edited by Sang Hyun Lee. New Haven: Yale University Press, 2003.

Elwood, Douglas J. *The Philosophical Theology of Jonathan Edwards*. New York: Columbia University Press, 1960.

Emory, Elliott. *Puritan Influences in American Literature*. Illinois Studies in Language and Literature. Urbana, IL: University of Illinois Press, 1979.

Eron, Lewis John. "You Who Revere the Lord, Bless the Lord." *Journal of Ecumenical Studies* 18.1 (1981) 63–73.

Evans, William B. "Déjà vu All Over Again?: The Contemporary Reformed Soteriological Controversy in Historical Perspective." *Westminster Theological Journal* 72 (2010) 135–51.

———. *Imputation and Impartation: Union with Christ in American Reformed Theology*. Studies in Christian History and Thought. Eugene, OR: Wipf & Stock, 2008.

Farrelly, John. "Trinity as Salvific Mystery and Historical Consciousness." In *Culture, Evangelization, and Dialogue*, edited by Antonio Gallo, et al., 95–110. Washington, DC: Council for Research in Values and Philosophy, 2003.

Fiddes, Paul. *Participating in God: A Pastoral Doctrine of the Trinity*. Louisville, KY: Westminster John Knox, 2000.

Fiering, Norman. *Jonathan Edwards's Moral Thought and Its British Context*. With a new foreword by Oliver Crisp. The Jonathan Edwards Classic Studies Series 3. 1981. Reprint, Eugene, OR: Wipf & Stock, 2006.

Forrer, Richard. "Puritan Religious Dilemma: The Ethical Dimensions of God's Sovereignty." *Journal of the American Academy of Religion* 44.4 (1976) 613–28.

Gay, Peter. *A Loss of Mastery: Puritan Historians in Colonial America*. Berkeley: University of California Press, 1966.

Gerstner, John H. "Jonathan Edwards and God." *Tenth: An Evangelical Quarterly* 10.1 (1980) 2–71.

———. *The Rational Biblical Theology of Jonathan Edwards*. 3 vols. Powhatan, VA: Berea, 1991–1993.

———. *Steps to Salvation: The Evangelistic Message of Jonathan Edwards*. Philadelphia: Westminster, 1959.

Gill, John. *A Complete Body of Doctrinal and Practical Divinity*. 3 vols. London: W. Winterbotham, 1796.

Gilsdorf, Joy. "The Puritan Apocalypse: New England Eschatology in the Seventeenth Century." PhD diss., Yale University, 1965.

Goen, C. C. "Jonathan Edwards: A New Departure in Eschatology." *Church History* 28.1 (1959) 25–40.

Goodwin, Thomas. *The Works of Thomas Goodwin*. Vol. 1. London: J. D. and S. R., 1681.

———. *The Works of Thomas Goodwin*. Vol. 5. 1861–1866. Reprint, Grand Rapids: Reformed Heritage, 2006.

Goudriaan, Aza. *Reformed Orthodoxy and Philosophy, 1625–1750: Gisbertus Voetius, Petrus van Mastricht, and Anthonius Driessen*. Edited by Wim Janse. Brill's Series in Church History 26. London: Brill, 2006.

Grasso, Christopher. *A Speaking Aristocracy: Transforming Public Discourse in Eighteenth-Century Connecticut*. Chapel Hill: University of North Carolina Press, 1999.

Grenz, Stanley J. *The Named God and the Question of Being: A Trinitarian Theo-Ontology*. Louisville, KY: Westminster John Knox, 2005.

———. *Rediscovering the Triune God: The Trinity in Contemporary Theology*. Minneapolis, MN: Fortress, 2004.

———. *The Social God and the Relational Self: A Trinitarian Theology of the Imago Dei*. Louisville, KY: Westminster John Knox, 2001.

Guelzo, Allen C. "Return of the Will: Jonathan Edwards and the Possibilities of Free Will." In *Edwards in Our Time: Jonathan Edwards and the Shaping of American Religion*, edited by Sang Hyun Lee and Allen C. Guelzo, 87–110. Grand Rapids: Eerdmans, 1999.

Gura, Philip F. *Jonathan Edwards: America's Evangelical. An American Portrait*. New York: Hill and Wang, 2005.

———. "Going Stoddard's Way: William Williams on Church Privileges, 1693." *William and Mary Quarterly* 45.3 (1988) 489–98.

Haight, Roger. *Jesus: Symbol of God*. Maryknoll, NY: Orbis, 1999.

———. "Trinity and Religious Pluralism." *Journal of Ecumenical Studies* 44.4 (2009) 525–40.

Hall, David D. "Editor's Introduction." In *Ecclesiastical Writings*, edited by David D. Hall, 1–90. Vol. 12 of *The Works of Jonathan Edwards*. New Haven: Yale University Press, 1994.

Haroutunian, Joseph. *Piety Versus Moralism: The Passing of the New England Theology*. Studies in Religion and Culture, American Religion Series 4. New York: H. Holt, 1932.

Harrison, Nonna Vema. "Human Community as an Image of the Holy Trinity." *St. Vladimir's Theological Quarterly* 46.4 (2002) 347–64.

Hart, D. G., et al. *The Legacy of Jonathan Edwards: American Religion and the Evangelical Tradition*. Grand Rapids: Baker Academic, 2003.

Hartshorne, Charles, and William L. Reese. *Philosophers Speak of God*. Chicago: University of Chicago Press, 1953.
Hatch, Nathan O. *The Sacred Cause of Liberty: Republican Thought and the Millennium in Revolutionary New England*. New Haven: Yale University Press, 1977.
Hatch, Nathan O., and Harry S. Stout. *Jonathan Edwards and the American Experience*. New York: Oxford University Press, 1988.
Heim, A. Mark. *The Depth of the Riches: A Trinitarian Theology of Religious Ends*. Grand Rapids: Eerdmans, 1998.
Heimart, Alan. *Religion and the American Mind from the Great Awakening to the Revolution*. The Jonathan Edwards Classic Studies Series 5. 1966. Reprint, Eugene, OR: Wipf & Stock, 2006.
Heimart, Alan, and Andrew Delbanco, eds. *The Puritans in America: A Narrative Anthology*. Cambridge, MA: Harvard University Press, 1985.
Helm, Paul, ed. *Treatise on Grace and Other Posthumously Published Writings*. Cambridge: James Clarke, 1971.
Helm, Paul, and Oliver D. Crisp, eds. *Jonathan Edwards: Philosophical Theologian*. Burlington, VT: Ashgate, 2003.
Heppe, Heinrich. *Reformed Dogmatics: Set Out and Illustrated from the Sources*. With a foreword by Karl Barth. Translated by G. T. Thomson. Edited by Ernst Bizer. London: George Allen & Unwin, 1950.
Hickman, Edward, ed. *The Works of Jonathan Edwards, AM*. With an introduction by Henry Rogers and Sereno E. Dwight. 2 volumes. London: John Childs and Son, 1865.
Higginson, John. *The Cause of God and His People in New-England*. Cambridge: Samuel Green, 1663.
Hill, Christopher. *The Experience of Defeat: Milton and Some Contemporaries*. London: Faber, 1984.
Hinlicky, Paul R. "The Doctrine of the New Birth From Bullinger to Edwards." *Missio Apostolica* 7.2. (1999) 102–19.
Holifield, E. Brooks. *The Covenant Sealed: The Development of Puritan SacramentalTheology in Old and New England, 1570–1720*. New Haven: Yale University Press, 1974.
Holmes, Oliver Wendell. "Jonathan Edwards." *The International Review* 10 (1880) 1–28.
Holmes, Stephen R. *God of Grace and God of Glory: An Account of the Theology of Jonathan Edwards*. Grand Rapids: Eerdmans, 2001.
———. "Does Jonathan Edwards Use a Dispositional Ontology?: A Response to Sang Hyun Lee." In *Jonathan Edwards: Philosophical Theologian*, edited by Paul Helm and Oliver D. Crisp, 99–114. Burlington, VT: Ashgate, 2003.
Hooke, William. *New England Teares, for Old Englands Fears*. London: John Rothwell and Henry Overton, 1641.
Hooker, Thomas. *Thomas Hooker: Writings in England and Holland, 1626–1633*, Edited by George H. Williams, et al. Cambridge: Cambridge University Press, 1975.
Horton, Michael Scott. *Covenant and Eschatology: The Divine Drama*. Louisville, KY: Westminster John Knox, 2002.
———. *Covenant and Salvation: Union with Christ*. Louisville, KY: Westminster John Knox, 2007.
———. *God of Promise: Introducing Covenant Theology*. Grand Rapids: Baker, 2006.

———. *Lord and Servant: A Covenant Christology*. Louisville, KY: Westminster John Knox, 2005.

———. *People and Place: A Covenant Ecclesiology*. Louisville, KY: Westminster John Knox, 2008.

Hubbard, David Allan. "Hope in the Old Testament." *Tyndale Bulletin* 34 (1983) 33–59.

Jamieson, John F. "Jonathan Edwards's Change of Position on Stoddardeanism." *Harvard Theological Review* 74 (1981) 79–99.

Jang, Kyoung-Chul. "The Logic of Glorification: The Destiny of the Saints in the Eschatology of Jonathan Edwards." PhD diss., Princeton Theological Seminary, 1994.

Janzen, J. Gerald. "Metaphor and Reality in Hosea 11." *Semeia* 24 (1982) 7–44.

Jenson, Robert W. *America's Theologian: A Recommendation of Jonathan Edwards*. New York: Oxford University Press, 1988.

———. *The Triune Identity: God According to the Gospel*. Philadelphia: Fortress, 1982.

Jinkins, Michael. "'The Being of Beings': Jonathan Edwards's Understanding of God as Reflected in His Final Treatises." *Scottish Journal of Theology* 46.2 (1993) 161–90.

———. "Mutuality and Difference: Trinity, Creation and the Theological Ground of the Church's Unity." *Scottish Journal of Theology* 56.2 (2003) 148–71.

Johnson, Edwards. *Johnson's Wonder-Working Providence 1628–1651*. Edited by J. Franklin Jameson. Original Narratives of Early American History. 1654. Reprint, New York: Scribner's Sons, 1910.

Johnson, Elizabeth. *She Who Is: The Mystery of God in Feminist Theological Discourse*. New York: Crossroad, 1992.

Kaiser, Walter C., Jr. "Davidic Promise and the Inclusion of the Gentiles (Amos 9:9–15 and Acts 15:13–18): A Test Passage for Theological Systems." *Journal of the Evangelical Theological Society* 20.2 (1977) 97–111.

Kang, Kevin Woongsan. "Justified by Faith in Christ: Jonathan Edwards's Doctrine of Justification in Light of Union with Christ." PhD diss., Westminster Theological Seminary, 2003.

Kärkkäinen, Veli-Matti. "The Trajectories of the Contemporary 'Trinitarian Renaissance' in Different Contexts." *Journal of Reformed Theology* 3 (2009) 7–21.

———. *Trinity and Religious Pluralism: The Doctrine of the Trinity in Christian Theology of Religions*. Aldershot: Ashgate, 2004.

Karlberg, Mark W. "Legitimate Discontinuities Between the Testaments." *Journal of the Evangelical Theological Society* 28.1 (1985) 9–20.

Kaufman, Gordon D. *Systematic Theology: A Historical Perspective*. New York: Scribner's Sons, 1968.

Keach, Benjamin. *Tropologia, or, A key to open Scripture metaphors*. London: John Richardson and John Darby, 1681.

Kevern, John R. "The Trinity and Social Justice." *Anglican Theological Review* 79.1 (1997) 45–54.

Kidd, Thomas S. "From Puritan to Evangelical: Changing Culture in New England, 1689–1740." PhD diss., University of Notre Dame, 2001.

Kimel, Alvin F., Jr., ed. *This Is My Name Forever: The Trinity and Gender Language for God*. Downers Grove: InterVarsity, 2001.

Kirk, Kenneth E. *The Vision of God: The Christian Doctrine of the Summum Bonum*. The Bampton Lectures for 1928. London: Longmans, 1934.

Kirkpatrick, Wm. David. "The Trinity and Christian Spirituality." *Southern Journal of Theology* 45.2 (2003) 48–63.

Kistler, Don, ed. *Jonathan Edwards: Containing 16 Sermons Unpublished in Edwards's Lifetime*. The Puritan Pulpit: The American Puritans. Morgan: Soli Deo Gloria, 2004.

Kloosterman, Nelson D. "The Use of Typology in Post-Canonical Salvation History: An Orientation to Jonathan Edwards's *A History of the Work of Redemption*." *Mid-American Journal of Theology* 14 (2003) 59–96.

Knight, Janice Lynn. "A Garden Enclosed: The Tradition of Heart-Piety in Puritan New England." PhD diss., Harvard University, 1988.

———. "Learning the Language of God: Jonathan Edwards and the Typology of Nature." *William and Mary Quarterly* 48.4 (1991) 531–51.

———. *Orthodoxies in Massachusetts: Rereading American Puritanism*. Cambridge, MA: Harvard University Press, 1994.

LaCugna, Catherine Mowry. *God For Us: The Trinity and Christian Life*. San Francisco: Harper San Francisco, 1991.

———. "Philosophers and Theologians on the Trinity." *Modern Theology* 2.3 (1986) 169–81.

———. "The Practical Trinity." *Christian Century* 109.22 (1992) 678–82.

Lane, Belden C. *Ravished by Beauty: The Surprising Legacy of Reformed Spirituality*. New York: Oxford University Press, 2011.

Lash, Nicholas. "Considering the Trinity." *Modern Theology* 2.3 (1986) 183–96.

Lee, Brian J. "Biblical Exegesis, Federal Theology, and Johannes Cocceius: Developments in the Interpretation of Hebrews 7:1—10:18." PhD diss., Calvin Theological Seminary, 2003.

Lee, Sang Hyun. "Does History Matter to God?" In *Jonathan Edwards at 300: Essays on the Tercentenary of His Birth*, edited by Harry S. Stout, et al., 1–13. Lanham, MD: University Press of America, 2005.

———. "Editor's Introduction." In *Writings on the Trinity, Grace, and Faith*, edited by Sang Hyun Lee, 1–38. Vol. 21 of *The Works of Jonathan Edwards*. New Haven: Yale University Press, 2003.

———. *The Philosophical Theology of Jonathan Edwards*. Expanded ed. Princeton: Princeton University Press, 1988.

———, ed. *The Princeton Companion to Jonathan Edwards*. Princeton: Princeton University Press, 2005.

Lee, Sang Hyun, and Allen C. Guelzo, eds. *Edwards in Our Time: Jonathan Edwards and the Shaping of American Religion*. Grand Rapids: Eerdmans, 1999.

Lesser, M. X. *Reading Jonathan Edwards: An Annotated Bibliography in Three Parts, 1729–2005*. Grand Rapids: Eerdmans, 2008.

Levenson, Jon D. "The Theologies of Commandment in Biblical Israel." *Harvard Theological Review* 73.1–2 (1980) 17–33.

Lewalski, Barbara Kiefer. *Protestant Poetics and the Seventeenth-Century Religious Lyric*. Princeton: Princeton University Press, 1979.

Logan, Samuel T., Jr. "The Doctrine of Justification in the Theology of Jonathan Edwards." *Westminster Theological Journal* 46.1 (1984) 26–52.

Loonstra, Bert. *Verkiezing, verzoening, verbond: beschrijving en beoordeling van de leer van het "pactum salutis" in de gereformeerde theologie*. Den Haag: Boekencentrum, 1990.

Lowance, Mason I., Jr. "Images or Shadows of Divine Things: The Typology of Jonathan Edwards." *Early American Literature* 5.1 (1970) 141–81.

———. *The Language of Canaan: Metaphor and Symbol in New England from the Puritans to the Transcendentalists*. Cambridge, MA: Harvard University Press, 1980.

Lucas, Sean Michael. *God's Grand Design: The Theological Vision of Jonathan Edwards*. Wheaton, IL: Crossway, 2011.

Maclear, James. "New England and the Fifth Monarchy: The Quest for the Millennium in Early American Puritanism." *William and Mary Quarterly* 32 (1975) 223–60.

Madsen, William G. "From Shadowy Types to Truth." In *Milton*, edited by Alan Rudrum, 219–32. New York: Macmillan, 1968.

Marsden, George M. "The Edwardsean Vision." *Reformed Journal* 39.6 (1989) 23–25.

———. *Jonathan Edwards: A Life*. New Haven: Yale University Press, 2003.

Mastricht, Petrus Van. *Beschouwende en praktikale godgeleerdheit*. Translated by Henricus Pontanus. 4 vols. Utrecht: Jan Jacob van Poolsum, 1749–1753.

———. *Theoretico-practica theologia*. Utrecht, 1699.

———. *Theoretico-practica theologia*. Amsterdam, 1715.

———. *A Treatise on Regeneration*. Edited by Brandon Withrow. Morgan, PA: Soli Deo Gloria, 2002.

McClenahan, Michael. *Jonathan Edwards and Justification by Faith*. Burlington, VT: Ashgate, 2012.

McClymond, Michael J. *Encounters with God: An Approach to the Theology of Jonathan Edwards*. New York: Oxford University Press, 1998.

———. "Hearing the Symphony: A Critique of Some Critics of Sang Lee's and Amy Pauw's Accounts of Jonathan Edwards' View of God." In *Jonathan Edwards as Contemporary: Essays in Honor of Sang Hyun Lee*, edited by Don Schweitzer, 67–92. New York: Peter Lang, 2010.

———. "Salvation as Divinization: Jonathan Edwards, Gregory Palamas, and the Theological Use of Neoplatonism." In *Jonathan Edwards: Philosophical Theologian*, edited by Paul Helm and Oliver D. Crisp, 139–60. Burlington, VT: Ashgate, 2003.

McClymond, Michael J., and Gerald R. McDermott. *The Theology of Jonathan Edwards*. New York: Oxford University Press, 2012.

McCormack, Bruce, ed. *Engaging the Doctrine of God: Contemporary Protestant Perspectives*. Grand Rapids: Baker; Edinburgh: Rutherford House, 2008.

McCoy, Michael Ryan. "In Defense of the Covenant: The Sacramental Debates of Eighteenth-Century New England (Puritanism)." PhD diss., Emory University, 1986.

McDermott, Gerald R. "Holy Pagans: Could a Person Be Saved without an Explicit Knowledge of Christ? Among the Stockbridge Indians, Edwards Began to Entertain the Possibility." *Christian History* 77 (2002) 38–39.

———. "Jonathan Edwards and the National Covenant: Was He Right?" In *The Legacy of Jonathan Edwards: American Religion and the Evangelical Tradition*, edited by D. G. Hart, et al., 147–57. Grand Rapids: Baker Academic, 2003.

———. "Jonathan Edwards and the Salvation of Non-Christians." *Pro Ecclesia* 9.2 (2000) 208–227.

———. "Jonathan Edwards, the City on a Hill, and the Redeemer Nation: A Reappraisal." *American Presbyterians* 69.1 (1991) 33–47.

———. *Jonathan Edwards Confronts Gods: Christian Theology, Enlightenment Religion, and Non-Christian Faiths*. New York: Oxford University Press, 2000.

———. "Jonathan Edwards, Deism, and the Mystery of Revelation." *Journal of Presbyterian History* 77.4 (1999) 211–24.

———. "Jonathan Edwards, John Henry Newman, and non-Christian Religions." In *Jonathan Edwards: Philosophical Theologian*, edited by Paul Helm and Oliver D. Crisp, 127–37. Burlington, VT: Ashgate, 2003.

———. "Jonathan Edwards on Justification by Faith—More Protestant or Catholic?" *Pro Ecclesia* 17.1 (2008) 92–111.

———. *One Holy and Happy Society: The Public Theology of Jonathan Edwards*. University Park, PA: Pennsylvania State University Press, 1992.

———. "A Possibility of Reconciliation: Jonathan Edwards and the Salvation of Non-Christians." In *Edwards in Our Time: Jonathan Edwards and the Shaping of American Religion*, edited by Sang Hyun Lee and Allen C. Guelzo, 173–202. Grand Rapids: Eerdmans, 1999.

———. "Poverty, Patriotism, and National Covenant: Jonathan Edwards and Public Life." *Journal of Religious Ethics* 31.2 (2003) 229–51.

McDowell, David Paul. *Beyond the Half-Way Covenant: Solomon Stoddard's Understanding of the Lord's Supper as a Converting Ordinance*. Eugene, OR: Wipf & Stock, 2012.

McGiffert, Michael. "Grace and Works: The Rise and Division of Covenant Divinity in Elizabethan Puritanism." *Harvard Theological Review* 75.4 (1982) 463–502.

McKee, William Wakefield. "The Idea of Covenant in Early English Puritanism (1580–1643)." PhD diss., Yale University, 1948.

McWilliams, Warren. "Only the Triune God Can Help: The Relation of the Trinity to Theodicy." *Perspectives in Religious Studies* 33.3 (2006) 345–59.

Mede, Joseph. *The Key of the Revelation, searched and demonstrated out of the natural and proper characters of the visions*. Translated by Richard More. With a preface by Twisse. London, 1643.

Metzger, Paul Louis, ed. *Trinitarian Soundings in Systematic Theology*. London: T&T Clark, 2005.

Migliore, Daniel L. "The Trinity and Human Liberty." *Theology Today* 36.4 (1980) 488–97.

Miller, Perry. *Errand into the Wilderness*. Cambridge, MA: Belknap, 1956.

———. "Introduction." In *Images or Shadows of Divine Things*, by Jonathan Edwards, 1–41. New Haven: Yale University Press, 1948.

———. *Jonathan Edwards*. With an introduction by Donald Weber. Amherst, MA: University of Massachusetts Press, 1981.

———. *The New England Mind: From Colony to Province*. Cambridge, MA: Harvard University Press, 1953.

———. "Solomon Stoddard, 1643–1729." *Harvard Theological Review* 34.4 (1941) 277–320.

Minkema, Kenneth P. "The Other unfinished 'Great Work': Jonathan Edwards, Messianic Prophecy, and 'The Harmony of the Old and New Testaments.'" In *Jonathan Edwards's Writings: Text, Context, Interpretation*, edited by Stephen J. Stein, 52–65. Bloomington, IN: Indiana University Press, 1996.

Mitchell, Louis J. "The Theological Aesthetics of Jonathan Edwards." *Theology Today* 64.1 (2007) 36–46.

Mohler, R. Albert, Jr., et al. "The SBJT Forum: The Relevance of the Trinity." *The Southern Baptist Journal of Theology* 10.1 (2006) 86–101.

Moltmann, Jürgen. *God in Creation: A New Theology of Creation and the Spirit of God.* Translated by Margaret Kohl. Minneapolis, MN: Fortress, 1993.

———. "The Unity of the Triune God: Remarks on the Comprehensibility of the Doctrine of the Trinity and its Foundation in the History of Salvation." *St. Vladimir's Theological Quarterly* 28.3 (1984) 157–71.

Moody, Josh. *Jonathan Edwards and the Enlightenment: Knowing the Presence of God.* Lanham, ML: University Press of America, 2005.

———, ed. *Jonathan Edwards and Justification.* Wheaton, IL: Crossway, 2012.

Morgan, Edmund S. *Visible Saints: The History of a Puritan Idea.* New York: New York University Press, 1963.

Morimoto, Anri. *Jonathan Edwards and the Catholic Vision of Salvation.* University Park, PA: Pennsylvania University Press, 1995.

———. "Salvation as Fulfillment of Being: The Soteriology of Jonathan Edwards and Its Implications for Christian Mission." *Princeton Seminary Bulletin* 20.1 (1999) 13–23.

Morris, William S. *The Young Jonathan Edwards: A Reconstruction.* With a foreword by Kenneth P. Minkema. The Jonathan Edwards Classic Studies Series 1. PhD diss., University of Chicago, 1955. Reprint, Eugene, OR: Wipf & Stock, 2005.

Mount, Eric, Jr. "Homing In On Family Values: The Family, Religion, and Culture Series." *Theology Today* 55.1 (1998) 77–89.

Muller, Richard. *After Calvin: Studies in the Development of a Theological Tradition.* New York: Oxford University Press, 2003.

———. "Calvin and the 'Calvinists': Assessing Continuities and Discontinuities between the Reformation and Orthodoxy." *Calvin Theological Journal* 30 (1995) 345–75.

———. "Calvin and the 'Calvinists': Assessing Continuities and Discontinuities between the Reformation and Orthodoxy." *Calvin Theological Journal* 31 (1996) 125–60.

———. *Christ and the Decree: Christology and Predestination in Reformed Theology from Calvin to Perkins.* Grand Rapids: Baker, 2008.

———. "God as Absolute and Relative, Necessary, Free, and Contingent: the Ad Intra Ad Extra Movement of Seventeenth-Century Reformed Language About God." In *Always Reformed: Essays in Honor of W. Robert Godfrey*, edited by R. Scott Clark and Joel E. Kim, 56–73. Escondido, CA: Westminster Seminary California, 2010.

———. *Post-Reformation Reformed Dogmatics: The Rise and Development of Reformed Orthodoxy, ca. 1520 to ca. 1725.* 4 vols. Grand Rapids: Baker, 2003.

———. "Toward the *Pactum Salutis*: Locating the Origins of a Concept." *Mid-America Journal of Theology* 18 (2007) 11–65.

Naughton, E. R. "Panentheism." In *Oxford Encyclopedia of the Reformation*, 1:943–45. 4 vols. Oxford: Oxford University Press, 1996.

Neele, Adriaan C. *The Art of Living to God: A Study of Method and Piety in the Theoretico-practica theologia of Petrus van Mastricht (1630–1706).* Edited by J. W. Hofmeyr. Perspectives on Christianity 1. Pretoria: University of Pretoria, 2005.

———. "Exchanges in Scotland, the Netherlands, and America: The Reception of the *Theoretico-practica theologia* and *A History of the Work of Redemption*." In

Jonathan Edwards and Scotland, edited with an introduction by Kelly Van Andel, et al., 21–46. Edinburgh: Dunedin Academic, 2011.

———. *Petrus van Mastricht (1630–1706) Reformed Orthodoxy: Method and Piety*. Edited by Wim Janse. Brill's Series in Church History 35. Leiden: Brill, 2009.

Newbigin, Lesslie. *The Open Secret*. Rev. ed. Grand Rapids: Eerdmans, 1995.

Nicole, Roger R. "Covenant, Universal Call and Definitive Atonement." *Journal of the Evangelical Theological Society* 38.3 (1995) 403–11.

Niebuhr, H. Richard. "The Doctrine of the Trinity and the Unity of the Church." *Theology Today* 3.3 (1946) 371–84.

Noll, Mark. *America's God: From Jonathan Edwards to Abraham Lincoln*. New York: Oxford University Press, 2002.

Opie, John, ed. *Jonathan Edwards and the Enlightenment, Problems in American Civilization*. Lexington, MA: Raytheon Education, 1969.

Oxford-Carpenter, Rebecca. "Gender and the Trinity." *Theology Today* 41.1 (1984) 7–25.

Panikkar, Raimundo. *The Trinity and the Religious Experience of Man: Icon-Person-Mystery*. Mayknoll, NY: Orbis, 1973.

Park, Edwards A. "Remarks of Jonathan Edwards on the Trinity." *Bibliotheca Sacra* 38 (1881) 147–87, 333–69.

Pauw, Amy Plantinga. "'Heaven Is a World of Love': Edwards on Heaven and the Trinity." *Calvin Theological Journal* 30 (1995) 392–401.

———. "'One Alone Cannot Be Excellent': Edwards on Divine Simplicity." In *Jonathan Edwards: Philosophical Theologian*, edited by Paul Helm and Oliver D. Crisp, 115–25. Burlington, VT: Ashgate, 2003.

———. *The Supreme Harmony of All: The Trinitarian Theology of Jonathan Edwards*. Grand Rapids: Eerdmans, 2002.

Pembroke, Neil Francis. "Trinity, Polyphony and Pastoral Relationships." *The Journal of Pastoral Care & Counseling* 58.4 (2004) 351–61.

Perkins, William. *The Works of That Famous and Worthie Minister of Christ*. Vol. 1. Cambridge: John Legatt, 1635.

Peters, Ted. *GOD—The World's Future: Systematic Theology for a Postmodern Era*. Minneapolis: Fortress, 1992.

Pettit, Norman. *The Heart Prepared: Grace and Conversion in Puritan Spiritual Life*. New Haven: Yale University Press, 1966.

Phelan, Jon. "Unity in Trinity: Some Reflections on the Doctrine of the Trinity in Jewish-Christian Relations." *Dialogue & Alliance* 17.1 (2003) 37–50.

Pierce, Richard D. "A Suppressed Edwards Manuscript on the Trinity." *The Crane Review* 1 (1959) 68–76.

Piscator, Johannes. *Analysis logica evangelii secundum Lucam*. London: Excudebat Richardus Field, 1596.

Placher, William C. *The Domestication of Transcendence: How Modern Thinking about God Went Wrong*. Louisville, KY: Westminster John Knox, 1996.

Pope, Robert G. *The Half-Way Covenant: Church Membership in Puritan New England*. Princeton: Princeton University Press, 1969.Preston, John. *The New Covenant or the Saints Portion*. London: I. D., 1639.

Rahner, Karl. *The Trinity*. 1970. Reprint, London: Continuum, 2001.

Ramsey, Paul. "Editor's Introduction." In *Ethical Writings*, edited by Paul Ramsey, 1–121. Vol. 8 of *The Works of Jonathan Edwards*. New Haven: Yale UniversityPress, 1989.

———. "Heaven Is a Progressive State." In *Ethical Writings*, edited by Paul Ramsey, 706–38. Vol. 8 of *The Works of Jonathan Edwards*. New Haven: Yale University Press, 1989.

Richardson, Cyril C. *The Doctrine of the Trinity*. Nashville: Abingdon, 1958.

Richardson, Herbert W. "The Glory of God in the Theology of Jonathan Edwards: A Study in the Doctrine of the Trinity." PhD diss., Harvard University, 1962.

Ridderbos, Jan. *De Theologie van Jonathan Edwards*. Hague: Johan A. Nederbragt, 1907.

Ridgley, Thomas. *A Body of Divinity: Wherein the Doctrines of the Christian Religion are Explained and Defended, being the Substance of Several Lectures on the Assembly's Larger Catechism*. 2 vols. London: Daniel Midwinter, Aaron Ward, John Oswald, and Richard Hett, 1731–1733.

Rightmire, R. David. "The Sacramental Theology of Jonathan Edwards in the Context of Controversy." *Fides et Historia* 21.1 (1989) 50–60.

Riley, I. Woodbridge. *American Philosophy: The Early Schools*. New York: Dodd, Mead, and Co., 1907.

Robertson, O. Palmer. *The Christ of the Covenants*. Philippsburg, NJ: Presbyterian and Reformed, 1980.

Rosenmeier, Jesper. "'Clearing the Medium': A Reevaluation of the Puritan Plain Style in Light of John Cotton's *A Practicall Commentary upon the First Epistle Generall of John*." *William and Mary Quarterly* 37 (1980) 577–91.

———. "New England Perfection: The Image of Adam and the Image of Christ in the Antinomian Crisis, 1634–1638." *William and Mary Quarterly* 27 (1970) 435–59.

Row, William L. "Jonathan Edwards on Divine and Human Freedom." In *Can God Be Free?*, by William L. Row, 54–73. New York: Oxford University Press, 2004.

Rupp, George. "The 'Idealism' of Jonathan Edwards." *Harvard Theological Review* 62 (1969) 209–26.

Sairsingh, Krister. "Jonathan Edwards and the Idea of Divine Glory: His Foundational Trinitarianism and Its Ecclesial Import." PhD diss., Harvard University, 1986.

Sanders, Fred. "The State of the Doctrine of the Trinity in Evangelical Theology." *Southwestern Journal of Theology* 47.2 (2005) 153–75.

Schafer, Thomas A. "Jonathan Edwards and Justification by Faith." *Church History* 20 (1951) 55–67.

———. "Jonathan Edwards's Conception of the Church." *Church History* 24.1 (1955) 51–66.

———. "The Role of Jonathan Edwards in American Religious History." *Encounter* 30.3 (1969) 212–22.

———. "Solomon Stoddard and the Theology of the Revival." In *A Miscellany of American Christianity: Essays in Honor of H. Shelton Smith*, edited by Stuart C. Henry, 328–61. Durham, NC: Duke University Press, 1963.

Schaff, Philip. *The Evangelical Protestant Creeds, with translations*. Vol. 3 of *The Creeds of Christendom, with a History and Critical Notes*. New York: Harper, 1919.

Schilder, Klaas. *Heidelbergsche Catechismus*. 4 vols. Goes: Oosterbaan & Le Cointre, 1947–1951.

Schoonenberg, Piet J. A. M. *The Christ: A Study of the God-Man Relationship in the Whole of Creation and in Jesus Christ*. Translated by Della Couling. New York: Herder & Herder, 1971.

———. "Trinity—The Consummated Covenant: Theses on the Doctrine of the Trinitarian God." *Studies in Religion/Sciences Religieuses* 5.2 (1975/76) 111–16.

Schweitzer, Don. "Aspects of God's Relation to the World in the Theologies of Jürgen Moltmann, Bonaventure, and Jonathan Edwards." *Religious Studies and Theology* 26.1 (2007) 5–24.

———, ed. *Jonathan Edwards as Contemporary: Essays in Honor of Sang Hyun Lee*. New York: Peter Lang, 2010.

Schweitzer, William M. *God Is a Communicative Being: Divine Communicativeness and Harmony in the Theology of Jonathan Edwards*. Edited by John Webster, et al. T. & T. Clark Studies in Systematic Theology 14. London: T. & T. Clark, 2012.

———. "Rage Against the Machine: Jonathan Edwards Versus the God of Deism." *Scottish Bulletin of Evangelical Theology* 25.1 (2007) 61–79.

Sibbes, Richard. *Evangelicall Sacrifices*. London: T. B., 1640.

Simonson, Harold P. *Jonathan Edwards: Theologian of the Heart*. Grand Rapids: Eerdmans, 1974.

Smith, David. "Millenarian Scholarship in America." *American Quarterly* 17 (1965) 535–49.

Smith, Shelton. *Changing Conceptions of Original Sin: A Study in American Theology Since 1750*. New York: Scribner's Sons, 1955.

Stahle, Rachel S. *The Great Work of Providence: Jonathan Edwards for Life Today*. Eugene, OR: Cascade, 2010.

Stein, Stephen J. "Editor's Introduction." In *The "Blank Bible,"* edited by Stephen J. Stein, 1–4. Vol. 24 of *The Works of Jonathan Edwards*. New Haven: Yale University Press, 2006.

———. *Jonathan Edwards's Writings: Text, Context, Interpretation*. Bloomington, IN: Indiana University Press, 1996.

Stephens, Bruce M. *God's Last Metaphor: The Doctrine of the Trinity in New England Theology*. AAR Studies in Religion 24. Chico, CA: Scholar's, 1981.

Stewart, Carole Lynn. *Strange Jeremiahs: Civil Religion and the Literary Imagination of Jonathan Edwards, Herman Melville, and W. E. B. DuBois*. Edited by David Carrasco and Charles H. Long. Religions of the Americas Series. Albuquerque University of New Mexico Press, 2010.

Stirling, Andrew, ed. *The Trinity: An Essential for Faith in Our Time*. With a forewordby Wolfhart Pannenberg. Nappanee, IN: Evangel, 2002.

Stoever, William K. B. *'A Faire and Easie Way to Heaven': Covenant Theology and Antinomianism in Early Massachusetts*. Middletown, CT: Wesleyan University Press, 1978.

Stoughton, John Alden. *"Windsor Farmes": A Glimpse of an Old Parish*. Hartford: Clark & Smith, 1883.

Stout, Harry S. *The New England Soul: Preaching and Religious Culture in Colonial New England*. New York: Oxford University Press, 1986.

———. "The Puritan and Edwards." In *Jonathan Edwards and the American Experience*, edited by Nathan O. Hatch and Harry S. Stout, 142–59. New York: Oxford University Press, 1988.

Stout, Harry S., et al., eds. *Jonathan Edwards at 300: Essays on the Tercentenary of His Birth*. Lanham, ML: University Press of America, 2005.

Strange, Alan D. "Jonathan Edwards on Visible Sainthood: The Communion Controversy in Northampton." *Mid-America Journal of Theology* 14 (2003) 97–138.

Strobel, Kyle. "By Word and Spirit: Jonathan Edwards on Redemption, Justification, and Regeneration." In *Jonathan Edwards and Justification*, edited by Josh Moody, 45–69. Wheaton, IL: Crossway, 2012.

Stuart, Robert Lee. "'Mr. Stoddard's Way': Church and Sacraments in Northampton." *American Quarterly* 24.2 (1972) 243–53.

Studebaker, Steven M. *From Pentecost to the Fellowship of the Triune God: A Pentecostal Trinitarian Theology*. Grand Rapids: Eerdmans, 2012.

———. "Jonathan Edwards's Pneumatological Concept of Grace and Dispositional Soteriology: Resources for an Evangelical Inclusivism." *Pro Ecclesia* 14.3 (2005) 324–39.

———. "Jonathan Edwards's Social Augustinian Trinitarianism: An Alternative to a Recent Trend." *Scottish Journal of Theology* 56.3 (2003) 268–85.

———. *Jonathan Edwards's Social Augustinian Trinitarianism in Historical and Contemporary Perspectives*. Gorgias Studies in Philosophy and Theology 2. Piscataway, NJ: Gorgias, 2008.

———. "Supreme Harmony or Supreme Disharmony? An Analysis of Amy Plantinga Pauw's 'The Supreme Harmony of All': The Trinitarian Theology of Jonathan Edwards." *Scottish Journal of Theology* 57.4 (2004) 479–85.

———. *The Trinitarian Vision of Jonathan Edwards and David Coffey*. Amherst, NY: Cambria, 2011.

Studebaker, Steven M., and Robert W. Caldwell. *The Trinitarian Theology of Jonathan Edwards: Text, Context, and Application*. Surrey, UK: Ashgate, 2012.

Suchocki, Marjorie Hewitt. *Divinity and Diversity: A Christian Affirmation of Religious Pluralism*. Nashville: Abingdon, 2003.

———. *God-Christ-Church: A Practical Guide to Process Theology*. New York: Crossroad, 1982.

———. "God, Trinity, Process." *Dialog* 40.3 (2001) 169–74.

Summers, Joseph H., ed. *The Lyric and Dramatic Milton: Selected Papers from the English Institute*. With a foreword by Joseph H. Summers. New York: Columbia University Press, 1965.

Sweeney, Douglas. "The Church." In *The Princeton Companion to Jonathan Edwards*, edited by Sang Hyun Lee, 167–89. Princeton: Princeton University Press, 2005.

———. "Justification by Faith Alone?: A Fuller Picture of Edwards's Doctrine." In *Jonathan Edwards and Justification*, edited by Josh Moody, 129–54. Wheaton, IL: Crossway, 2012.

Toon, Peter, ed. *Puritans, the Millenium, and the Future of Israel: Puritan Eschatology 1600 to 1660*. London: Clarke and Co., 1970.

Torrance, Thomas F. *The Christian Doctrine of God: One Being Three Persons*. Edinburgh: T. & T. Clark, 1996.

Tracy, Patricia J. *Jonathan Edwards, Pastor: Religion and Society in Eighteenth-Century Northampton*. Jonathan Edwards Classic Studies Series 2. 1980. Reprint, Eugene, OR: Wipf and Stock, 2006.

Turretin, Francis. *Institutes of Elenctic Theology*. Translated by George Musgrave Giger. Edited by James T. Denison, Jr. 3 vols. Phillipsburg, NJ: Presbyterian and Reformed, 1992–1997.

———. *Institutio theologiae elencticae*. 3 vols. Geneva: Samuel de Tournes, 1679–1685.

Van Buren, Paul Matthews. "Theological Education for the Church's Relationship to the Jewish People." *Journal of Ecumenical Studies* 21.3 (1984) 489–505.

———. "Toward an Ecumenical Consensus on the Trinity." *Theologische Zeitschrift* 31.6 (1975) 337–50.
Van Dusen, Henry P. "The Trinity in Experience and Theology." *Theology Today* 15.3 (1958) 377–86.
Vickers, Jason E. *Invocation and Assent: The Making and Remaking of Trinitarian Theology*. Grand Rapids: Eerdmans, 2008.
Volf, Miroslav. *After Our Likeness: The Church as the Image of the Trinity*. Grand Rapids: Eerdmans, 1998.
———. *Exclusion and Embrace: A Theological Exploration of Identity, Otherness, and Reconciliation*. Nashville, TN: Abingdon, 1996.
———. "'Trinity Is Our Social Program': The Doctrine of the Trinity and the Shape of Social Engagement." *Modern Theology* 13.3 (1998) 403–23.
Volf, Miroslav, and Michael Welker, eds. *God's Life in Trinity*. Minneapolis, MN: Fortress, 2006.
Von Rohr, John. "Covenant and Assurance in Early English Puritanism." *Church History* 34.2 (1965) 195–203.
———. *The Covenant of Grace in Puritan Thought*. Edited by Charley Hardwick and James O. Duke. American Academy of Religion Studies in Religion 45. Atlanta, GA: Scholars, 1986.
Waddington, Jeffrey C. "Jonathan Edwards's 'Ambiguous and Somewhat Precarious' Doctrine of Justification?" *Westminster Theological Journal* 66 (2004) 357–72.
Wainwright, William J. "Jonathan Edwards, William Rowe, and the Necessity of Creation." In *Faith, Freedom, and Rationality: Philosophy of Religion Today*, edited by Jeff Jordan and Daniel Howard-Snyder, 119–33. Lanham, MD: Rowman and Littlefield, 1996.
Walker, George L. "Jonathan Edwards and the Half-Way Covenant." *The New Englander* 43 (1884) 601–14.
Walker, Williston. *The Creeds and Platforms of Congregationalism*. New York: Scribner's Sons, 1893.
Watts, Emily Stipes. "Jonathan Edwards and the Cambridge Platonists." PhD diss., University of Illinois, 1963.
Webber, Richard M. "The Trinitarian Theology of Jonathan Edwards: An Investigation of Charges Against Its Orthodoxy." *Journal of the Evangelical Theological Society* 44.2 (2001) 297–318.
Weddle, David L. "Jonathan Edwards on Men and Trees, and the Problem of Solidarity." *Harvard Theological Review* 67.2 (1974) 155–75.
Weir, David A. *The Origins of the Federal Theology in Sixteenth-Century Reformation Thought*. Oxford: Clarendon, 1990.
Whittemore, Robert C. "Jonathan Edwards and the Theology of the Sixth Way." *Church History* 35.1 (1966) 60–75.
Wiles, Maurice F. "Some Reflections on the Origins of the Doctrine of the Trinity." *Journal of Theological Studies* 8 (1957) 92–106.
Willard, Samuel. *Compleat Body of Divinity*. Boston: B. Green and S. Kneeland, 1726.
———. *The Doctrine of the Covenant of Redemption: Wherein is laid the foundation of all our hopes and happiness. Briefly opened and Improved*. Boston, 1693.
Williams, Carol A. "The Decree of Redemption Is in Effect a Covenant: David Dickson and the Covenant of Redemption." PhD diss., Calvin Theological Seminary, 2005.

Wilson, John F. "Editor's Introduction." In *A History of the Work of Redemption*. Vol. 9 of *The Works of Jonathan Edwards*. Edited by John E. Smith. New Haven: Yale University Press, 1989.

———. "Jonathan Edwards as Historian." *Church History* 46.1 (1977) 5–18.

———. *Pulpit in Parliament: Puritanism during the English Civil Wars, 1640–1648*. Princeton: Princeton University Press, 1969.

Wilson-Kastner, Patricia. *Faith, Feminism and the Christ*. Philadelphia: Fortress, 1983.

Winthrop, John. "A Model of Christian Charity." In *The Puritans in America: A Narrative Anthology*, edited by Alan Heimart and Andrew Delbanco, 81–92. Cambridge, MA: Harvard University Press, 1985.

Withrow, Brandon G. *Becoming Divine: Jonathan Edwards's Incarnational Spirituality Within the Christian Tradition*. Eugene, OR: Pickwick, 2011.

———. "Jonathan Edwards and Justification by faith (Part 1)." *Reformation & Revival* 11 (2002) 93–109.

———. "Jonathan Edwards and Justification by faith (Part 2)." *Reformation & Revival* 12 (2002) 98–111.

Witsius, Herman. *The Oeconomy of the Covenants between God and Man: Comprehending a Complete Body of Divinity*. 3 Vols. Edinburgh, 1771–1772.

Wollebius, Johannes. *Compendium theologiae christianae*. Basel: Ex officina R. Danielis, 1642.

Woodbridge, Frederick J. E. "Jonathan Edwards." *The Philosophical Review* 13.4 (1904) 393–408.

Woolsey, Andrew A. *Unity and Continuity in Covenantal Thought: A Study in the Reformed Tradition to the Westminster Assembly*. With a foreword by Richard A. Muller. Edited by Joel R. Beeke and Jay T. Collier. Reformed Historical-Theological Studies. Grand Rapids: Reformation Heritage, 2012.

Wyrtzen, David B. "The Theological Center of the Book of Hosea." *Bibliotheca Sacra* 141.564 (1984) 315–29.

Youngs, Frederick W. "The Place of Spiritual Union in Jonathan Edwards's Conception of the Church." *Fides et Historia* 28.1 (1996) 27–47.

Zahniser, H. Mathias. "The Trinity: Paradigm for Mission in the Spirit." *Missiology: An International Review* 17.1 (1989) 69–82.

Zakai, Avihu. *Exile and Kingdom: History and Apocalypse in the Puritan Migration to America*. Cambridge, MA: Cambridge University Press, 1992.

———. "Jonathan Edwards and the Language of Nature: The Re-Enchantment of the World in the Age of Scientific Reasoning." *The Journal of Religious History* 26.1 (2002) 15–41.

———. *Jonathan Edwards's Philosophy of History*. Princeton: Princeton University Press, 2003.

———. *Jonathan Edwards's Philosophy of Nature: The Re-Enchantment of the World in the Age of Scientific Reasoning*. London: T. & T. Clark, 2010.

———. "The Theological Origins of Jonathan Edwards's Philosophy of Nature." *Journal of Ecclesiastical History* 60.4 (2009) 708–24.

Zizioulas, John. *Being as Communion: Studies in Personhood and the Church*. With a foreword by John Meyendorff. Crestwood, NY: St. Vladimir's Seminary Press, 1985.

———. *Communion and Otherness: Further Studies in Personhood and the Church*. Edited by Paul McPartland. New York: T. & T. Clark, 2006.

Name and Subject Index

Ad intra, ad extra, 30, 41, 42, 43, 51, 54, 57, 76, 77, 84, 109, 111, 137, 161, 169, 170, 183, 189
Archetype, ectype, 41, 110, 117, 129, 142, 184
Arendt, Hannah, 14
Arminianism, 114, 121, 123, 125
attributes, divine, 66, 85, 90, 119
Augustine, 112

Babcock, William S., 200,
Baik, Chung-Hyun, 204
Ball, John, 27
Barth, Karl, 17, 19
beatific vision, 188, 194
beauty, 85, 90, 92, 104, 109, 111, 116, 119, 120, 130, 133, 168, 186, 188
Beckwith, Roger T., 34, 71
Bercovitch, Sacvan, 150, 158
Biehl, Craig, 187
Bierma, Lyle D., 10
Bogue, Carl W., 9, 12
Bombaro, John J., 82, 97, 98, 103, 104, 110, 184
Bozeman, Theodore Dwight, 10, 149
Bracken, Joseph A., 202
Brueggemann, Walter, 11
Bucanus, Gulielmus, 68
Buckley, Michael J., 201
Bulkeley, Peter, 68, 170
Burgess, 68

Caldwell, Robert, 9, 64, 67, 76, 85, 99, 103, 133, 183
Charnock, Stephen, 205

Cherry, Conrad, 9, 152
Coccejus, Johannes, 68
Cohen, Charles Lloyd, 29
Communication, 4, 57, 77, 78, 81, 82, 83, 81-86, 90, 92, 93, 99, 101, 104, 105, 109–12, 122, 133, 138, 145, 167–71, 173, 185,187, 190
Cotton, John, 170
Covenant
    in general, 26, 140, 141, 158, 160, 173, 174
    of redemption (*pactum salutis*), 9, 10, 13, 30, 31, 32, 33, 34, 36, 37, 38, 39, 41, 42, 43, 47, 50, 51, 58, 59, 60, 62, 64, 67, 68,69,71, 72, 73, 74, 75, 76, 104, 105, 108, 112, 117, 122, 124, 126, 129, 132, 134, 135, 136, 142, 144, 147, 158, 159, 162, 164, 165, 166, 169, 177, 183, 184, 187, 188, 191, 195, 199, 204, 207
    of grace, 28, 29, 32, 43, 50, 71, 72, 73, 74, 117, 129, 135, 140, 141, 142, 144, 145, 147, 152, 158, 159, 160, 161, 171, 174, 175, 176, 177, 191, 192
    of works, 28, 29, 43, 44, 71, 74, 116, 117, 158, 173, 174, 175, 176
covenant, church, 136, 143, 144, 161
covenant, external and internal, 141, 142
covenant, half-way, 141
covenant, national, 147, 148, 157, 158, 159, 160, 161

Name and Subject Index

Communion controversy, 139, 140, 144
Coyle, Suzanne Murphy, 11
Creation, 83, 84, 161, 168, 171, 183, 184, 186, 195
Creggan, Nicola Hoggard, 90
Crisp, Oliver, 95, 96, 98, 100

Danaher Jr., William D., 129
Davenport, John, 170
decree (election), 124, 137, 145, 169, 179, 181, 184, 185, 186
Delattre, Roland A., 56
De Regnon, Theodore, 14
Dickson, David, 31, 32, 33, 34, 36, 48, 63, 68, 205
disposition, 90, 91, 93, 95, 96, 100, 113
Donovan, Mary Ann, 2
Durham, James, 31

Edwards, Jonathan, 7, 51, 57, 59, 63, 66–68, 71–78, 82–87, 90–130, 136–38, 141, 142, 147, 148, 155–60, 163, 165–68, 171–73, 177, 179, 181, 182, 184, 189–92, 195, 199, 204
Edwards, timothy, 151
Elwood, Douglas J., 93
emanation, 59, 90, 91, 92, 98, 170
eschatology, 184, 186, 188, 190–92, 194
Evans, William B., 10
excellency, 64, 65, 89, 92, 111, 116, 119, 168, 186

federal theology, 116, 117, 118
Forrer, Richard, 10

Gay, Peter, 18, 206
Gill, John, 205
glory, 84, 89, 90, 96, 110, 111, 112, 129, 145, 168, 169, 177, 179, 183, 184–88, 189, 191, 194
Goodwin, Thomas, 32, 35, 47, 136, 205
Grenz, Stanley, 202

Haight, Roger, 203
happiness (felicity), 178, 179, 180, 187, 188, 192, 193, 194, 195
harmony, 89, 164
Hartshorne, Charles, 100
heart, 111, 130, 142, 143, 182
Heidegger, 27
history, 162, 164, 165, 166, 168–74, 177, 180–86, 194, 199
Holmes, Stephen L., 95
Hooker, Richard, 170
Hooker, Thomas, 170

Idealism (immaterialism), 81, 82, 88, 90, 98
imputation, 116, 121, 165
infusion, 113, 130
Intellectual Fathers, 170

Jang, Kyoung-Chul, 166
Jenson, Robert, 19
jeremiad, 148, 149, 150–53, 158, 160
Junius, 27
justification, 107, 109, 112, 113–22, 126, 129, 130, 161, 181, 195

Kaiser Jr., Walter C., 11
Kang, Kevin Woongsan, 71, 72, 73, 75
Karkkainen, Veli-Matti, 6
Kaufman, Gordon D., 7
kingdom, 180, 187, 193
Kirkpatrick, Wm. David, 5
Knight, Janice, 101, 169, 172, 173, 184, 190
Krause, Karl, 91, 170

LaCugna, Catherine Mowry, 6, 203
Lee, Sang Hyun, 8, 18, 57, 58, 59, 61, 93, 94, 98–100, 101, 108
Loonstra, Bert, 70

Marsden, George M., 17, 103, 139, 159, 160, 207
Mastricht, Petrus, 27, 63, 69, 105, 205
McClymond, Michael J., 97, 107, 157
McDermott, Gerald R., 14, 15, 97, 107, 114, 147, 152, 156, 157
McGiffert, Michael, 10, 27,

McKee, William Wakefield, 26,
Migliore, Daniel, 4
Miller, Perry, 18, 19, 71, 101, 114, 149, 150, 152, 206
Moltmann, Jurgen, 4
Morimoto, Anri, 14, 15, 97, 107, 113, 114, 115, 117
Mount Jr., Eric, 11
Muller, Richard, 41

Niebuhr, H. Richard, 1

Olevianus, Casper, 10, 27

panentheism, 91, 93, 98, 100, 101, 102, 103,
participation (communion), 2, 6, 13, 30, 32, 33, 38, 42, 44, 47, 49, 51, 54, 55, 77, 88, 92, 93, 104, 106, 114, 117, 121, 122, 126, 128, 129, 132-136, 139–44, 160, 161, 165, 167, 169, 178, 180, 181, 183-87, 190, 192-95, 206
Perkins, William, 68, 69
perseverance, 118, 126, 127, 129, 145, 146, 174
Peters, Ted, 204
Placher, William C., 199, 200
Plantinga Pauw, Amy, 8, 12, 13, 14, 63, 64, 65, 66, 194
Practice (Christian life, piety), 2–5, 6, 8, 10, 11, 20, 21, 28, 46, 47, 49, 50, 63, 68, 71, 90, 105, 106, 129-33, 136, 139, 140, 142, 144, 146, 150, 194, 200, 201, 204, 205, 206, 207
Rahner, Karl, 1, 2, 202
Ramsey, Paul, 129, 188, 189, 190
Rast Jr., Lawrence R., 121
Reese, William L., 100
Reformed scholastics (Protestant orthodoxy), 25, 27, 30, 38, 40, 41, 47, 50, 63, 67, 68, 69, 71, 75, 106, 114, 115, 205
regeneration, 119, 120, 140, 142, 146, 159, 161, 192
Richardson, Cyril C., 7
Robertson, O. Palmer, 34

sanctification, 129, 130, 161, 168, 181, 195
Savoy Declaration of Faith, 31
Schafer, Thomas, 114, 117, 138
Schepard, Thomas, 170
Schoonenberg, Piet J. A., 203
Schweitzer, William M., 167, 183
Sibbes, Richard, 50, 101, 170, 171
Simplicity, divine, 64, 65, 67
Smith, Shelton, 114, 117
soul, 72, 78, 83, 85, 92, 102, 107, 111, 113, 115, 117, 119, 120, 123, 127, 131, 132, 133, 134, 158, 168, 181
Spiritual Brethren, 170, 171
spouse, 186, 187
Stein, Stephen J., 105
Stephens, Bruce M., 27, 71
Stewart, Carole Lynn, 14
Stoddard, Solomon, 141, 160,
Stoever, William K. B., 28, 29, 75
Stout, Harry S., 147, 152, 157
Strobel, Kyle, 112
Studebaker, Steven M, 9, 13, 14, 64, 65, 67, 76, 77, 85, 96, 98, 99, 103
Suchocki, Marjorie Hewitt, 203
Surety (*Sponsor*), 45, 75, 175
Sweeney, Douglas, 107, 136, 144

Torrance, Thomas F., 4,
Trinity, 11, 43, 46, 88, 96, 97, 105, 165, 166, 169, 171, 194, 200, 202
  Immanent (ontological) Trinity, 3, 6, 13, 41, 46, 51, 57, 75, 77, 78, 90, 94, 105, 132, 167, 168, 183, 195, 199, 202, 203, 204
  Criticism of, 7, 46, 51, 199, 202, 205, 207
  Economic Trinity, 3, 41, 46, 57, 75, 77, 78, 195, 202, 203, 204
  Father, 59, 60, 61, 62, 64, 65, 67, 73, 75, 76, 108, 110, 117, 120, 121, 124, 126,132, 133, 135, 144, 162, 165, 168, 174, 177, 183, 192, 193
  Son, 60, 61, 62, 64, 65, 73, 75, 76, 77, 84, 85, 108, 117,120, 121, 124, 132, 133, 135, 137, 138, 162, 166, 174, 178, 183, 191, 194

Trinity *(continued)*
    Spirit, 30, 31, 54, 55, 56, 57, 59, 65, 66, 67, 77, 84, 85, 93, 108, 111, 118, 119, 130, 132, 133, 134, 146, 165, 181, 182, 183, 184, 200, 201, 203
Tritheism, 39, 40
Turretin, Francis, 27, 40, 63, 69
Typology, 86, 87, 88, 89, 143, 148, 149, 169, 171, 172, 173, 174, 175, 176, 177

union with Christ, 113, 120, 121, 126, 132, 134, 138, 142, 143, 187, 188, 190, 194
Ursinus, 27

Van Asselt, William J., 29
Van Dusen, Henry P., 4

Vane, Henry, 170
Volf, Miroslav, 2
Von Rohr, John R., 10, 33, 49, 50

Westminster Confession of Faith, 31
Wiles, Maurice F., 7
Willard, Samuel, 33, 35, 37, 38, 69, 205
Wilson, John F., 173, 179
Wilson-Kastner, Patricia, 201
Winthrop, John, 150, 170
Withrow, Brandon, 160
Witsius, Herman, 27, 45, 63, 68, 69, 205

Yongs, Frederick W., 142

Zahniser, A. H. Mathias, 2
Zakai, Avihu, 89, 104, 181

www.ingramcontent.com/pod-product-compliance
Lightning Source LLC
Chambersburg PA
CBHW051054230426
43667CB00013B/2288